THE
CANADIAN
ROCKIES

EARLY TRAVELS AND
EXPLORATIONS

MW00982026

THE
CANADIAN
ROCKIES

EARLY TRAVELS AND
EXPLORATIONS

ESTHER FRASER

FIFTH
HOUSE

Dedicated to the memory of the pioneers of the Canadian Rockies

Copyright © 2002 Esther Fraser

Design by John Luckhurst / GDL
Front cover photographs by Darwin Wiggett and Glenbow Archives (NA-445-12)
All scans by St. Solo Computer Graphics Inc.

All rights reserved. No part of this publication may be reproduced, stored in a retrieval system,
or transmitted, in any form or by any means, electronic, mechanical, recording, or otherwise, without
the prior written permission of the publisher, except in the case of a reviewer, who may quote brief
passages in a review to print in a magazine or newspaper, or broadcast on radio or television. In the
case of photocopying or other reprographic copying, users must obtain a licence from the Canadian
Copyright Licencing Agency.

The publisher gratefully acknowledges the support of The Canada Council for the Arts and the
Department of Canadian Heritage. We acknowledge the financial support of the Government of
Canada through the Book Publishing Industry Development Program for our publishing activities.

Printed in Canada by Transcontinental

02 03 04 05 06 / 5 4 3 2 1

National Library of Canada Cataloguing in Publication Data

Fraser, Esther, 1919-1978.
    The Canadian Rockies

    Includes bibliographical references and index.
    ISBN 1-894004-85-X

    1. Rocky Mountains, Canadian (B.C. and Alta.)—Discovery and exploration.
* I. Title.
FC219.F72 2002   917.11   C2002-910198-0
F1090.F72 2002

Fifth House Ltd.
A Fitzhenry & Whiteside Company
1511-1800 4 St. SW
Calgary, Alberta, Canada
T2S 2S5

1-800-387-9776
www.fitzhenry.ca

Contents

Foreword

In the autumn of 1787, seventeen-year-old David Thompson crossed the western plains to the foothills of the Rocky Mountains with a party of Hudson's Bay Company fur traders.

> At length the Rocky Mountains came in sight like shining white clouds in the horizon but we doubted what our guide said, but as we proceeded they rose in height, their immense masses of snow appeared above the clouds and formed an impassible barrier, even to the Eagle.

Thompson's "impassible barrier" is the most remarkable and rugged mountain range in North America—a nearly unbroken wall of rock and glacial ice that rises to elevations of more than 3600 metres. And while not impassable, its 1200-kilometre length is breached by fewer than a dozen passes that can be considered reasonable routes for travel.

David Thompson would return in 1800 as a trader and mapmaker for the North West Company to begin the search for a passage through the range. He would eventually establish the first trade route across the Rockies via Howse Pass in 1807 and, following his discovery of Athabasca Pass in 1811, the first transcontinental trade route to the Pacific.

For the next three decades, fur traders would follow Thompson's route between the Athabasca and Columbia Rivers, enduring the most excruciating portage imaginable over Athabasca Pass. Guarded by towering, glaciated peaks and swept by avalanches, this gap would be the bane of everyone who hiked for days to cross its summit. One early voyager was moved to exclaim, "I'll take my oath, my dear friends, that God Almighty never made such a place!"

George Simpson, governor of the Hudson's Bay Company, would hold dominion over most of the Canadian West, including the Rocky Mountains, from 1821 until his death in 1860. In addition to supporting the annual movement of traders back and forth through the range, his forts and employees often provided assistance to independent travellers bound to and from the Columbia River. These adventurous souls included botanists, settlers, missionaries, artists, and sportsmen.

Most of these early travellers were intent on crossing the range as directly and quickly as possible, but all would linger long enough to gaze in amazement at this remarkable landscape. Several, like Lieutenant Henry James Warre, would publish accounts of their journey, providing the world with the earliest graphic images of the range in all its terrible beauty:

> The scenery through which we passed onwards was grand beyond description, but oh how desolate! Mountains upon mountains raised their naked heads high above the mists which rolled upwards from the valleys below.

In 1858 and 1859, Captain John Palliser, Dr. James Hector, and other members of the British North American Exploring Expedition would view the Rocky Mountains in a less romantic fashion. Dispatched by the British government, they explored the range between the international boundary and the Athabasca River, mapping its valleys and passes for a railway that might someday connect the eastern provinces of British North America with the Pacific. Dr. Hector, the expedition's physician and geologist, surveyed much of the territory contained within today's mountain national parks and, after being kicked senseless by his horse, discovered the appropriately named Kicking Horse Pass.

The discovery of gold in British Columbia's interior in 1862 unleashed yet another wave of travel. Inexperienced and lacking the guidance of fur trade brigades, these independent travellers stumbled blindly into the mountain wilds. The journey for some, like Viscount Milton, Dr. W. B. Cheadle, and their improbable hitchhiker Mr. O'Byrne, bordered on comedy. But for many in the scattered parties of gold-seekers, known as Overlanders, the trail often ended in tragedy far from their El Dorado.

The dream of a railway across the Rockies became reality with the completion of the Canadian Pacific Railway in 1885, but not before the young Dominion of Canada dispatched a score of surveyors to bushwhack their way through every conceivable pass in the range. In the end, their chosen routes were all abandoned in favour of Hector's Kicking Horse Pass.

With all the activity of the previous century, the Rockies should have been well-explored by the time the first passenger train crossed to the Pacific. But the range still held many secrets. The last uncharted gaps along the Great Divide, that included its greatest scenic wonders, were discovered by a new and unlikely generation of explorers—the first tourists. Together with trailblazing outfitters and guides, these adventurous mountaineers and travellers, both men and women, journeyed by pack train to the final prizes—the Columbia Icefield, Maligne Lake, and the highest mountain summits.

The exploration of the Rockies ranks as one of the most dramatic and colourful episodes in the history of Canada and its first national parks. Yet the story was retold in a piecemeal manner until the publication of Esther Fraser's *The Canadian Rockies: Early Travels and Explorations* in 1969.

Esther Fraser's discovery of the Rockies was nearly as serendipitous as that of the early fur traders. Born in Hanna, Alberta in 1919, she moved to Edmonton at age 15. In 1939, after working for the *Edmonton Journal,* she married and began raising a family. Amazingly, it wasn't until the summer of 1956, on a driving holiday west from Edmonton with her family, that she saw the Rockies for the first time.

"As we rounded a corner near a high point on the highway," recalls her daughter Lia, "my mother gasped, overwhelmed by the sudden appearance of snow-capped peaks that stretched like an endless ribbon before her. At that moment, her life changed."

For the rest of their holiday, Esther wondered about the first non-Native people who saw the Rockies, explored its valleys and passes, and climbed to the summits of its highest peaks. Upon returning to Edmonton, she immediately began searching for books that would reveal this past, but discovered that no comprehensive history had ever been written.

Over the next ten years, she devoted much of her spare time to researching the history of the Canadian Rockies. After hundreds of hours in libraries and archives, and dozens of trips to the mountain parks armed with topographic maps, she finally tied the story together.

Esther eventually wrote a series of educational radio scripts entitled "Trailblazers of the Canadian Rockies," which was produced by CKUA radio in Edmonton. Following these successful broadcasts, a book-length manuscript was produced and accepted for publication by Hurtig Publishers in

1969. The book was an immediate best-seller, remaining in print for nearly 20 years and selling over 20,000 copies.

The Canadian Rockies: Early Travels and Explorations spans a period of more than 120 years, from first contact by fur traders to the conquest of the highest peak by mountaineers in 1913. It does not pretend to be a comprehensive, academic history of the Canadian Rockies, but rather a lively and entertaining account of the most influential and interesting characters who travelled through the heart of the range when it was still an unmapped and little-known wilderness.

Esther's second and final book *Wheeler*, a biography of the pioneer mountain surveyor A. O. Wheeler, was published in 1979, a few months after her death. Her passionate love of the Rockies and its early pioneers lives on in both of these books, but most particularly in *The Canadian Rockies*, which remains a wonderful introduction to a grand chapter of western Canadian history.

— BRIAN PATTON

PREFACE

When the young English poet, Rupert Brooke, visited the Canadian Rockies he thought them "windswept and empty"—no ghosts of the past "ennobled these unmemoried heights . . . No recorded Hannibal has struggled across them . . ."

True, no conquering armies marched here. But men of buoyant courage struggled relentlessly to surmount this massive continental barrier. They waged ruthless competition for the wealth that lay beyond it, risked their lives for the gold that sparkled in its rushing streams; they came in search of adventure, pursued a vision of a nation reaching from sea to sea and finally, fascinated by a land unknown and alluring, sought out its hidden peaks and valleys.

The record of their achievements makes an exciting chapter in Canadian history. Fortunately some of the participants left written records and it is their story this book attempts to tell. Because much of this material is no longer readily available, the original writers are quoted extensively to add the colour and vitality of firsthand experience.

A comprehensive history of the whole of the Canadian Rockies is beyond the scope of this work. I have written for the general reader an account of the white man's discovery and exploration of the chief passes through the main chain of the Rockies and the Selkirks, and focussed on that portion of the mountains lying within the boundaries of the Banff, Kootenay, Yoho, Glacier, Jasper and Mount Robson parks, with emphasis on events leading to the development of Jasper and Banff national parks. The book was written with the hope that it would enhance the enjoyment of our mountain heritage.

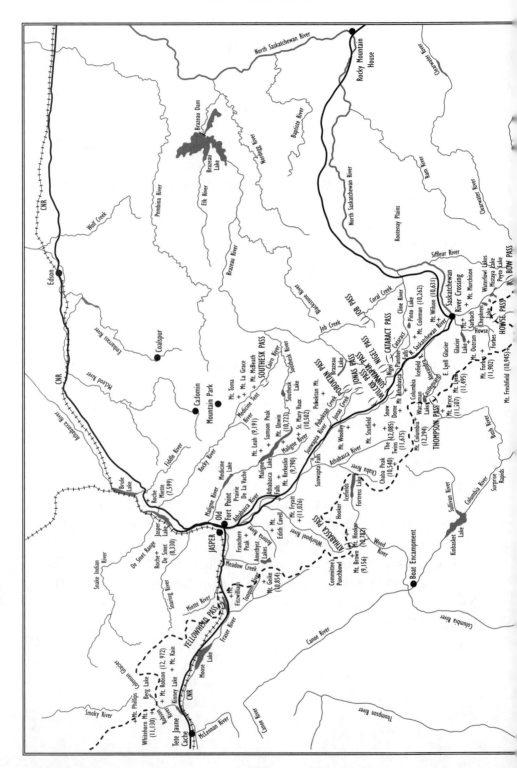

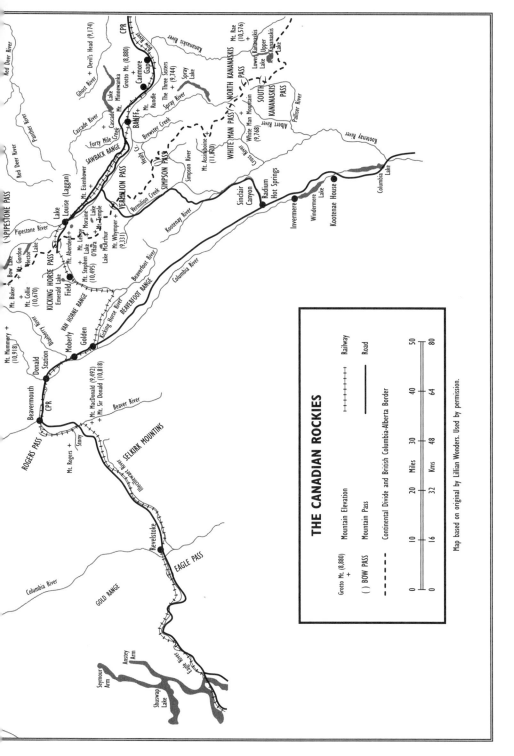

THE CANADIAN ROCKIES

		Railway
Grotto Mt. (8,880) +	Mountain Elevation	Road
( ) BOW PASS	Mountain Pass	Continental Divide and British Columbia-Alberta Border

| Miles | 0 | 10 | 20 | 30 | 40 | 50 |
| Kms | 0 | 16 | 32 | 48 | 64 | 80 |

Map based on original by Lillian Wonders. Used by permission.

Author's Note

As this book was written for the general reader it is unencumbered with footnotes. For the convenience of those with a more professional interest in history the bibliography shows the major sources consulted for each chapter. Similarly, the few notes considered necessary appear at the end of each chapter's bibliography; the longer quotes are acknowledged there as well.

ACKNOWLEDGEMENTS

I enjoyed the cooperation of many people during the preparation of this book; it is a pleasure to acknowledge my indebtedness to them.

I wish especially to thank Mr. Hugh Dempsey, Miss Sheilagh Jameson, Mr. T. R. McCloy and their staff at the Glenbow Historical Library and Archives, Calgary for their unfailing courtesy, interest and assistance; the staff of the reference and information department of the Centennial Library, Edmonton; Miss Dorothy I. Hamilton, rare book and archives department, the Cameron Library, University of Alberta, Edmonton; Mr. Eric Holmgren and the staff of the Provincial Library, Legislative Building, Edmonton; Maryalice H. Stewart, director, Archives of the Canadian Rockies, Banff; Mr. W. E. Ireland, Provincial Archives, Victoria, B.C., Miss S. A. Guillaume, Department of Public Records and Archives, Toronto and Mrs. M. I. Peterson and the late Major Fred Brewster of the Jasper-Yellowhead Historical Society.

I am grateful to Mrs. Pearl Brewster Moore, Mr. Sidney Vallance, Mr. Don Harmon, Miss E. Harmon of Banff and Mr. T. E. Wilson of Calgary who were most helpful in obtaining photographs for the book. Special thanks are due to Sir Charles Alexander Carnegie, eleventh Earl of Southesk for supplying a specially prepared photograph of his grandfather.

It is a real pleasure to acknowledge my sincere gratitude to Jim Simpson and the late Mrs. Simpson of Banff—they gave most generously of their time patiently to answer my many questions.

I wish to thank Doctor Lewis H. Thomas, Department of History, University of Alberta for reading the manuscript and offering valuable suggestions for corrections and revision. Tony Cashman and Mrs. Maryalice Stewart also read the manuscript and gave helpful advice. Any errors in the book, however, are the author's responsibility.

I acknowledge with gratitude the work of Mrs. Lillian Wonders who brought to the mapmaking an interest that went beyond that required by technical competence; the editorial assistance of Miss Susan Kent and the encouragement extended by my publisher.

Miss Sheilagh Jameson, archivist of the Glenbow Foundation, gave kind permission to quote from the Tom Wilson correspondence and the Alpine Club of Canada graciously agreed to the use of extensive quotations from the *Canadian Alpine Journal.*

Lastly, I am grateful to the kind friends who loaned valuable books and journals for months at a time and to my family, who were not only patient with the absorption entailed in the writing of the book, but warmly encouraging.

BANFF'S FIRST TOURIST

Emperors, kings and princes have not been uncommon visitors to Banff since the August day in 1841 when the Little Emperor passed that way. But Sir George Simpson, governor of the Hudson's Bay Company's vast fur empire, was the first.

Unlike present-day potentates who enjoy the baronial luxury of the Banff Springs Hotel, he camped at Lake Minnewanka with nothing more to eat than a bit of pemmican and two partridges made into "a sort of burgoo, which served as breakfast and supper for eight hungry travellers."

Not that the most powerful man in all British North America was unaccustomed to travelling in grand style. Usually he dashed across the continent on his frequent inspection tours in a beautifully painted canoe, impeccably dressed in dark suit, white shirt, velvet stock, frock coat, long Stuart tartan cloak lined with scarlet, and topped with a fine beaver hat. Skilled Iroquois canoemen, vermilion paddles flashing, sped him across Canada's great river highways at the rate of a hundred miles a day, pausing only long enough to gulp a mouthful of pemmican after they had carried the little dynamo ashore and laid out his cold cut and glass of fine wine. In a few minutes his imperious "Take away!" sent the voyageurs scurrying; he was gently lowered into his state canoe and hurried toward the next trading post where he swept up with proper pomp and ceremony, preceded by his kilted Highland piper, as flags unfurled and guns boomed in royal salute.

But this time he was travelling light, slashing his way through the

wilderness on horseback, combining business with the adventure of exploration. He was in fact on a phenomenal trip around the world, the first from
east to west overland (as distinguished from a sea voyage). Queen Victoria
had just honoured him with a knighthood; in March he had left London,
crossed the Atlantic by fast packet and rushed with breathtaking speed to
Fort Garry, the site of modern Winnipeg, arriving in early June.

On the nine hundred-mile journey from there to Fort Edmonton he
overtook a dusty cavalcade of emigrants in Red River carts, led by James
Sinclair. This perilous expedition, undertaken by twenty-three Métis families
of one hundred and twenty-one people including a seventy-five-year-old
woman and babies born en route, was instigated by Sir George who hoped
to reinforce British claims in the disputed Oregon Territory by bringing in
settlers. He tarried long enough with them to enjoy a brisk buffalo hunt and
treat them "with a dram" before hurrying on to Edmonton. There, as promised, he made arrangements for the cavalcade to travel over the Rockies by
Athabasca Pass (in what is now Jasper Park), the usual route at that time.
Little did he imagine that Sinclair, in flagrant disregard of his express
instructions, would follow hard on his heels in order to share the glory of
discovering yet another southern mountain pass.

Sir George may have been looking for a new pass to add lustre to his reputation—he was after all a vain and ambitious man. But he was also an
extraordinarily competent administrator who in twenty years had reorgan-
ised the Canadian fur trade to make it pay as it had never paid before. At
fifty-one his was already a complete success story: an illegitimate Scottish lad
moving from his grandfather's manse to a clerk's stool in an uncle's ware-
house, becoming a fur trader with the Hudson's Bay Company at one of its
isolated posts, leapfrogging within a few short years to the position of governor and, with astonishing energy and audacity, raising his own and the
company's fortunes to their present glory. No, it is much more likely that his
motive was a practical one. A shorter route meant economy.

On the three previous occasions that the white man had pierced the
ramparts of the Rockies, Indians had taken him through, so at Fort
Edmonton Sir George met the guide Chief Factor Rowand had been
instructed to hire. He was a "half-breed Chief of the mountain Crees" named
Peechee. Here too the governor, with appropriate ceremony, received nine

"*The Little Emperor,*" *Sir George Simpson.*
COURTESY HUDSON'S BAY COMPANY ARCHIVES, WINNIPEG (N1987/335/A2)

chiefs of the Blackfoot, Piegan, Blood and Sarcee tribes dressed in full regalia complete with scalp locks. They thanked him for his gifts of tobacco and begged him as a great magician to ensure that the buffalo would always abound, that their horses would always be swift and their wives stay young forever!

At 5 A.M. on the 28th of July the journey was resumed. Simpson, Peechee, Mr. Rowand, twenty men and forty-five crack horses headed southwest over much less travelled country, in stifling heat with mosquitoes "annoying us to an almost insupportable degree." A band of menacing Indians made them "march more briskly than usual away from our doubtful friends"; after four days they were struggling through burnt and fallen timber in the foothills, where they camped amid dark forests resembling "venerable cathedrals."

They had been straining their eyes to catch the first glimpse of "the perpetual snows of the mighty barrier that lay in our path." Soon they saw them, "white peaks, looking like clouds on the verge of the horizon." As the horses floundered through muskeg up to their girths or went "diving into pathless forests" where they got lost and dislodged their packs, the party forged ahead, their cries and imprecations "ringing through the usual solitary glades for miles." At last they "emerged from the woods in a long open valley terminating in a high ridge . . . As far as eye could reach, mountain rose above mountain." It was August 1st and they were about to enter what is now Banff National Park.

Next morning they marched for nine hours and at breakfast time discovered that six horses were missing. (This pre-breakfast stint was the usual practice of His Excellency.) The men were "instantly despatched" to hunt for them. The little demon for speed had to cool his heels all day on the shores of today's Lake Minnewanka and as the missing horses unfortunately "carried the best provisions," had to make do with burgoo while mountain sheep and goats—sources of longed-for steaks—clambered "in playful security" on the inaccessible crags above. However, "the beauty of the scenery formed some compensation for the loss of time."

The men hunted all day and all night for the horses. When they returned at six the next morning, a start was made at once and by two o'clock they had reached the spot (probably near the present townsite of Banff) where the

Bow River, 150 feet wide, had to be crossed. The men constructed a raft for horses and baggage while Sir George had porcupine for lunch and then enjoyed a cool bathe in the Bow; the men, however, had "had quite enough of this luxury" in the three or four hours it had taken to raft the supplies across the swiftly flowing current.

Next day, following today's Healy Creek, they toiled for seven hours to the summit of the Continental Divide at what is now Simpson Pass— in time for breakfast! "Filling our kettles for this our lonely meal, at once from the crystal sources of the Columbia and the Saskatchewan, while these two feeders of two opposite oceans . . . bid each other a long farewell," Sir George could not help but be impressed by "the sublimity of the scene." To his further delight he found "an unexpected reminiscence of my own native hills," a spray of heather. Not in twenty years of wandering on the North American continent had he come across anything like it. He carried it away with him.

Their descent westward from the height of land was maddeningly slow as "our bad roads surpassed themselves," and the horses leapt, scrambled and crouched in desperate attempts to make their way through the labyrinth of forest and windfalls. They covered only twenty miles the first day. Sir George chafed at such unwonted delay and had the men roused at midnight to round up the horses for an even earlier start (it was impossible to tie the horses as they needed to wander in order to find enough grass); even so they weren't underway until five o'clock. That was certainly not soon enough for the Little Emperor, but as they proceeded he reflected: "the mere fact that the animals could be caught at all amid the thick forests in the dark spoke volumes for the patience, steadiness, the carefulness and sagacity, the skill and tact, of our halfbreed attendants. Perhaps all the grooms in an English county could not have done this morning's work."

Following the Simpson River to its junction with the Vermilion, they continued along the route of today's Banff-Windermere highway to Radium. "At one remarkable spot, known as the Red Rock . . . the narrow ravine was literally darkened by almost perpendicular walls of a thousand or fifteen hundred feet in height . . . and to render the chasm still more gloomy, the opposite crags threw forward each its own forest of sombre pines into the intervening space . . . The rays of the sun could barely find their way to

5

the depths of this dreary vale . . . and the hoarse murmur of the angry stream, as it bounded to escape from the dismal jaws of its prison, only served to make the place appear more lonely and desolate. We were glad to emerge from this horrid Gorge . . ."

Modern visitors may not find Sir George's horrid gorge at Sinclair Canyon quite so depressing. But he was hungry. In his impatience he had driven his men at such a pace that the pack horses carrying provisions were way behind; as "the noise of our cavalcade" had scared away the game they "fasted for twenty-four hours."

Then too, His Excellency was put out because the guide who had been ordered to meet them with fresh horses from Fort Colville (in modern Washington) hadn't arrived. Soon, however, they found "a welcome letter" sketched on a tree with a piece of burnt wood. This "hieroglyphic epistle" was speedily interpreted: Edward Berland, the guide, "was waiting with twenty-seven horses at the point where our river received a tributary before expanding into two consecutive lakes." He had selected this place (near present-day Invermere) as his "post office" because here "the only two routes by which one could have crossed the height of land in this part of the country, happened to connect." Peechee was "despatched to secure our phantom guide."

Hurrying south over country familiar to Simpson from previous journeys, they camped one night in "a fearful nest of mosquitoes." While men and beasts nearly suffocated from "the smoke that had been raised to drive them away," the "formidable" insects "kept coolly and steadily sucking our blood." Eating, reading or writing was impossible ("our hands being constantly employed in repelling or slaughtering our small but powerful enemies"), and the irrepressible voyageurs soundly cursed "the old maid" who, according to legend, had loosed "this scourge upon earth." With boisterous good humour they "prayed for something to fill up the hopeless leisure of her single blessedness." No doubt they conjured up some highly imaginative ways of enlivening her celibate existence! At last they agreed that it would be much more fitting and just if the tiny tormentors "would but confine" their tortures to "nunneries and monasteries"!

At one camp Indians solemnly watched the governor having dinner and looked wistfully at the wine flagon containing "Great Chief's Rum"; he treated them to a drink which they accepted "with all becoming gravity" but "they were evidently disappointed by the want of pungency in the draught."

While they were galloping the last fifty miles to the company post at Fort Colville a delegation from the fort dashed out to meet them, bringing "materials for a feast." At "the base of the Rocky Mountains" a picnic was spread: "a roast turkey, a suckling pig, new bread, fresh butter, eggs, ale &c." But this time the usually elegant Sir George sat down to the regal fare in "tattered garments and crownless hat" such as many of the men from the fort would "not have deigned to pick up at their feet."

Always meticulous about keeping records, he was pleased that on this long and labourious part of the two thousand-mile journey across the continent they had, in six weeks of constant travel, five days a week, averaged about eleven and a half hours a day in the saddle; between Fort Garry and Fort Edmonton they had made fifty miles a day. But he was chagrined to note that since leaving Fort Edmonton they "had fallen short of forty miles a day."

Following a brisk but thorough inspection of posts in the Columbia River District, Sir George sailed to Sitka in the company steamer, *The Beaver*, was royally received by officials of the Russian American Fur Company there and came back down the coast to visit the Hudson's Bay Company establishment at San Francisco. Enjoying the hospitality of Spanish American colonial governors at Santa Barbara, he admired the women: "It is difficult to exaggerate their physical charms, their sparkling eyes and glossy hair, sylph-like forms, neatly-turned feet and ankles"; they were enchanting in the "beautiful and mysterious mantilla." (The governor was notorious for succumbing to feminine charms, acknowledging seven children born out of wedlock and many more "bits of brown" scattered across North America as witness to amours with dusky maidens.)

Business and social obligations completed there, he sailed to Hawaii where the company had another outpost, then back up to Siberia where he flung himself on horseback and ran the legs off his Cossack escorts as he continued the business of his far-flung empire with the Czar's representatives. By stagecoach, riverboat, carriage and steamer he crossed Russia and Europe, ending his journey of nineteen months and twenty-six days in England.

The first Banff tourist had come and gone. Lake Minnewanka lay placid; to the east, dark and menacing, Devil's Head Mountain and Phantom Crags towered above Devil's Gap. For the second time in a year white men approached the portal they guarded.

At Fort Edmonton James Sinclair had persuaded his emigrants to abandon the relative comfort of their carts and travel on horseback, carrying only the barest necessities. Maskepetoon, the great chief of the Wetaskiwin Crees, readily agreed to take them across another mountain pass unvisited by the white man. Following Sir George's route into the mountains, they rested at Lake Minnewanka a few weeks after his visit and in the days that followed, the silent forests echoed again with the ring of the axe. This time the cries of children broke the hush of night. Working their way labouriously toward present-day Canmore, they forded the Bow and, ascending the range near today's Three Sisters, entered the valley of the Spray River. Following a tributary to the height of land, Maskepetoon led them triumphantly across the Divide, probably at what is now White Man Pass.

After descending to the Cross River and the Kootenay, they travelled in Sir George's footsteps, arriving at Fort Colville in late autumn. They had endured fearful hardships to reach their destination; frustration and disappointed hopes awaited them. There were rumours that neither the Hudson's Bay Company nor the British government had the right to grant land for settlement and when some of the emigrants finally were settled, they found conditions so disheartening that most of them eventually went south and became American citizens.

Sir George considered White Man Pass infinitely superior to Simpson Pass but neither was ever developed into a well-travelled route. In the Banff area, the awesome solitude of uninhabited wilderness remained virtually unbroken for another seventeen years.

For eons these valleys had known no human intrusion; when scattered bands of native people began to come they barely rippled the tranquillity of the centuries. An event foreshadowing a momentous change in this ancient pattern took place eighty-seven years before Sir George's journey through Simpson Pass. Fur trader Anthony Henday climbed a hill near today's Innisfail, Alberta, and saw the majestic procession of snowy peaks reaching into the dim distance of the northern horizon. The white man had at last seen the Shining Mountains. Henday's Cree Indian companions knew nothing of what lay beyond those mighty ramparts and he returned east.

He was the advance scout of a company of rugged and dauntless men who penetrated ever deeper into the unexplored recesses of the Rockies, establishing the routes which would incorporate the great barrier into the fabric of the nation.

2

GATEWAY TO WEALTH AND POWER

Sir George Simpson never saw a beaver until he was thirty-five, but when he died almost forty years later he was governor of the greatest fur empire in the world. David Thompson, a Welsh student in a London charitable school, was apprenticed to that same Hudson's Bay Company as a boy of fourteen; he died seventy-three years later in abject poverty. Sir George, in a final blaze of glory ten days before his death, stood beside the Prince of Wales proudly surveying the pomp and ceremony he had arranged for his royal guest. David Thompson was a forgotten man for years before his death. Today he is esteemed as one of the world's greatest geographers.

When Thompson began his apprenticeship in 1784, a threat to the venerable Company of Adventurers of England Trading into Hudson's Bay was taking shape. Acquisitive, intrepid Scots were organizing; three years later these Nor'westers, employing the gay, strong-backed French Canadian voyageurs, were fighting for supremacy in the fur trade. The vicious rivalry of wilderness entrepreneurs was underway, sending them probing into the unknown hinterland in a race for the untapped wealth of fur in the Northwest.

In 1787 dark, stocky seventeen-year-old David Thompson, with five men, was sent far west where only a handful of white men had ventured, right into the heart of hostile Indian territory. The tiny expedition had orders to make friendly contact with the Indians of the plains, learn their language and persuade them to bring furs to the Hudson's Bay posts.

Crossing what is now Alberta, they left the treed parklands and rode southwest over the empty prairie toward One Pine, a former landmark near today's Olds. Massive and forbidding, the snow-covered wall of the Rockies glistened in the sunlight. At the foot of the mountains Piegan Indians were camped. David Thompson had encountered the two forces destined to play such a dramatic role in his life: the Piegans with whom he wintered became his friends, but in years to come his pressing need to cross the Rockies would make these Indians his fierce and implacable foes.

What lay beyond the mountain barrier? Even as he reluctantly turned away from it, the hard-driving Nor'westers were nurturing a dream which in twelve years would bring him back.

The audacious Nor'westers intended to extend their domain right to the Pacific. There gleamed the prospect of fantastic wealth—the sea-otter, royal fur of Chinese Mandarins, and the lustrous beaver. To reap this harvest they had to find the legendary Great River of the West. Only by discovering a waterway emptying into the Pacific could they hope to tap economically the enormous resources that lay on the Pacific watershed and compete with their arch rivals, who enjoyed the exclusive advantage of ready access to their inland posts via Hudson's Bay.

Through frigid, barren lands Nor'wester Alexander Mackenzie pursued the quest. His search ended in shattering disappointment when he stood on the bleak shores of the Arctic Ocean. Four years later, in 1793, he tried again—up the mighty Peace, across the mountains and on, at last, to the shore of the western sea. An epic achievement: the first crossing of the continent north of Mexico, but a hollow victory for the profit-hungry Nor'westers. On that momentous expedition Mackenzie had found no navigable stream flowing into the Pacific.

In spite of these tremendous setbacks, Mackenzie remained a most forceful advocate of the need for westward expansion. Returning east, he fired the imagination of another youthful Nor'wester. Tall, husky, swash-buckling Duncan McGillivray, ambitious to make his mark as a junior member of the firm, was captivated by the returning explorer's dream of a continent-spanning fur empire. Stationed at a bleak outpost far out on the Saskatchewan as the competing companies flung their posts along that great river highway, Duncan was already taking part in the expansion westward.

But where was the Great River of the West the Nor'westers sought?

In the spring of 1792 when Mackenzie was setting out from Montreal on his expedition to the Pacific, an American, Captain Robert Gray, was sailing the foggy Oregon coast where he found the mouth of the great river which he named for his ship, the *Columbia*. Soon after, one of the men from an English ship commanded by Captain Vancouver explored the river a hundred miles upstream. Where was its source?

By 1799 the Hudson's Bay Company and the Nor'westers had pushed up the North Saskatchewan to Rocky Mountain House where they were poised cheek by jowl at the foot of the Rockies. The Nor'westers were ready to resume their search for the Great River of the West, which they now knew from Captain Vancouver's book was the Columbia. There was a good chance that the long-sought waterway had its source somewhere in that maze of high peaks which closed the western horizon at Rocky Mountain House.

In 1800 Duncan McGillivray was sent to find out. With the Nor'westers at Rocky Mountain House, ready to assist him, was David Thompson.

Since his winter in the foothills with the Piegans Thompson had been trained and equipped by the Hudson's Bay Company and had proven himself an excellent surveyor and diligent trader. When, in 1797 (feeling that his zest for exploration would be given greater scope by the younger company), he left the Hudson's Bay Company, the Nor'westers welcomed him with open arms. Now he was to use his skill to chart the transmountain route McGillivray would make every effort to find.

Even if no pass could be found across these high mountains the Nor'westers had an opportunity to crack the trade of the Pacific watershed: word had been received that Kootenay Indians were slipping across the mountains and David Thompson was sent to meet them.

Again he rode over the foothills beside the mountains, and once again he met his friends the Piegans. This time they trailed him suspiciously. Why was their old friend riding along the mountains with pack horses laden with trading goods? Was he meeting their enemies the Kootenays? They themselves had driven the Kootenays across the Rockies as soon as the white man's guns gave them power to do so, and they intended them to stay there, unarmed. They warned him: he would never be able to find the Kootenays;

he and his horses would die of hunger and exhaustion. But Thompson refused to be turned back.

Somewhere west of present-day Sundre, Alberta, he met the poor straggling little group of Kootenays with their half-starved horses—an old chief with twenty-six men and seven women. They had brought a few furs to trade. But the Piegans were spoiling for trouble and as they outnumbered the Kootenays about twenty to one, Thompson escorted the beleaguered visitors to the safety of Rocky Mountain House. It took a nice combination of firmness and diplomacy to prevent bloodshed and at the same time avoid any action which might further alienate the truculent Piegans.

When the bartering was done Thompson loaned the little band some horses to replace those stolen by the Piegans and saw them safely off on their return journey. With them he sent voyageurs La Gassi and Le Blanc to winter in their country and report on the prospects beyond the watershed; they travelled by an unidentified route and were probably the first men—apart from the Indians—to cross the Rockies south of Mackenzie's route. The transmountain trade had been initiated.

Shortly after their departure McGillivray arrived to start his ambitious quest for the mountain pass. With four men, a Piegan guide and David Thompson along to smooth the way with the Piegans, he rode south along the mountains, "everywhere covered with Snow" and seeming to "present an impenetrable Bank." Late on a November afternoon they looked down on the valley where modern Calgary nestles; the Bow River flowed gently there and on the horizon the icy splendour of the Rockies was sharply etched against a clear blue sky. Somewhere in that tangle of ranges was there a gap, a valley that would thread a way through? Would the Piegans know the answer?

They camped beside the Bow and then rode toward today's High River, Alberta, where the Piegans' teepees dotted the plain. Their welcome was cordial, but reserved. The white man's gifts of tobacco and the leisurely talk-filled hours spent in its enjoyment yielded no happy solution; when the visitors said they hoped to go into the mountains and if possible, cross them, no one volunteered to point the way. Instead, dark warnings were issued about treacherous tribes from the west who lurked ever ready to ambush small parties such as theirs.

McGillivray and Thompson rode back to the Bow and turned west. Right up to the first mountain ridge they rode, left their horses and climbed an "inaccessible steep." Up to the seven thousand-foot level of the mountain behind today's lime plant at Kananaskis they ascended, and for four hours looked out upon a scene of wild and awe-inspiring grandeur, hoping for some clue to the mystery they longed to solve. Only a few miles away lay the passes they sought, but the two young men might just as well have been adrift on a trackless ocean lashed by a winter storm. No obvious route was in sight, and so late in the season, without a knowledgeable guide, a search was out of the question.

Northwest from Rocky Mountain House McGillivray pressed his reconnaissance, far along the mountains toward the Pembina River, looking up valley after valley and gathering information from Indians about a pass away to the northwest. Probably following for a time the departed Kootenays' route along the Saskatchewan, he struck across country to the Brazeau River and on past Brazeau Lake, where he crossed the "chain of mountains" forming the watershed between the Brazeau and Athabasca and saw a stream flowing west, uniting with another and "disappearing among high mountains." He was probably the first white man to see a tributary of the Sunwapta of today, but there was no way through that tremendous aggregate of peaks to the west.

Duncan McGillivray returned to Rocky Mountain House, exhausted and ill. During the long winter he and Thompson read and reread Captain Vancouver's book, speculating about the source of the Columbia; surely the Saskatchewan must be the best approach to the great river. But when the spring of 1801 came, McGillivray was too sick to resume the search. He left for the East on crutches; the rheumatism that had plagued him all winter may well have been rheumatic fever for he never fully recovered his health. But he departed from the West with his dream of the Nor'westers' Columbian Enterprise more compelling than ever and left instructions for James Hughes, the man in charge at Rocky Mountain House, to try again for a pass on the Saskatchewan.

As soon as weather permitted, Hughes and Thompson went with an Indian guide who said he knew a pass by way of the Ram River; it proved impassable for horses. They tried ascending the Saskatchewan in canoes, but the river was in spring flood; snags at the shore threatened to tear their frail craft to smithereens and it was impossible to drag it with lines from shore. They were forced to abandon their search for the Columbia.

For the next few years the mounting rivalry of the fur trade demanded the full attention of the Nor'westers. They had now to deal as well with Alexander Mackenzie, who had left in 1798 to form his own company. But in 1804 he was back in the fold and the reinvigourated Nor'westers began a determined assault to establish transmountain trade. McGillivray went to London to negotiate for transit rights through Hudson's Bay (which would make their leap to the Pacific economically sound); Mackenzie pressed their claim for a continent-spanning monopoly; the bull-necked, tenacious Scot, Simon Fraser, was ordered to establish forts west of the mountains along Mackenzie's route to the Pacific—and to have another look for the Columbia. In the fall of 1806 David Thompson, promoted to partnership, was sent again to Rocky Mountain House to develop the trade on the Pacific slope.

To assist Thompson, Nor'wester Jaco Finlay and three men were cutting trail west of the fort when they saw signs of an encampment at a spot since known as Kootenay Plains; Finlay waited there until the friendly Kootenays once again slipped across the mountains. They took him to the Divide where he saw a westward-running stream. Back at the fort, under the watchful eye of the Hudson's Bay Company men, Thompson unobtrusively prepared for his spring expedition.

In May of 1807 all was ready. The sullen Piegans watched. Under cover of darkness, the men slipped their laden canoes silently on their way up the Saskatchewan and Thompson waited impatiently for the Piegans to disperse. At the last minute, dramatically, they disappeared. An Indian courier had just brought word that the year before two of their confederates had been killed by a member of the American Lewis and Clark expedition. The warriors headed south for revenge.

On May 10th, accompanied by his twenty-one-year-old Métis wife, Charlotte, carrying thirteen-month-old Emma and with Fanny, almost six, firmly holding three-year-old Samuel, David Thompson and a small party of men rode into the mountains. On the sixth of June they entered what is today Banff National Park.

Looking into Howse Pass, traversed by David Thompson in 1807. From its summit a little stream flows to join the Columbia, the Nor'westers' Great River of the West.
COURTESY WHYTE MUSEUM OF THE CANADIAN ROCKIES, BANFF (M517/42)

16

Present-day travellers driving between Lake Louise and the Columbia Icefields on the Banff-Jasper highway can stop at the bridge crossing the Saskatchewan and, from a bluff overlooking the historic valley, enjoy a superb view of the route Thompson took to the long-sought pass. Coming from the east, the party passed through the gateway formed by the castellated crags of Mount Wilson and massive Mount Murchison; they passed the green Mistaya River rushing in from Bow Pass to the south. Ahead, in the west, the Lyell Icefields merged with the skyline and the sharp black pyramid of Mount Forbes towered above its entourage of peaks.

At noon they turned southwest, following the branch of the river which winds round the flanks of Mount Sarbach, and four miles up the valley where the river became impassable for canoes, they camped. "Here among the stupendous and solitary Wilds covered with eternal Snow, and Mountain connected to Mountain by immense Glaciers ... I staid 14 Days more, impatiently waiting the melting of Snows on the Height of Land ..."

The men brought up the laden canoes and repacked supplies and trade goods in "boxes of thin Boards sewed together," in preparation for loading pack horses for the mountain portage.

On June 25th they started out again and camped in the evening "where the Springs send their Rills to the Pacific Ocean ..." They were at the summit of the white man's first pass through the Rockies south of Mackenzie's crossing—Howse Pass, named, ironically, for a Hudson's Bay man who used the route two years later.

Down the precipitous timber-choked banks of the little stream they struggled for five days until it joined a large river—flowing north! The Columbia, as Thompson knew from Vancouver's book, flowed south and west. It would be several years before he realized that he had indeed found the Great River of the West on that June day. On its shores they built birchbark canoes, again repacked goods and paddled against the stiff current until, on July 18th, the river widened into a beautiful placid lake encircled by soft blue mountains. They camped at Lake Windermere and, just northwest of modern Athalmer, B.C., Thompson built Kootenae House, the first post on the Columbia River. There he spent the winter trading; in early spring he left his family and started his search for new sources of fur.

Portaging from the Columbia to the Kootenay River, he proceeded down to what are now northern Idaho and Montana patiently making the indispensable overtures to the Indians, most of whom had never seen a white man. Promising them that he would return with trade goods, he made a difficult journey back (the countryside was often inundated by floods) to Kootenae House where he rejoined his family. Almost a year to the day they again crossed Howse Pass. As Charlotte was due to have another child in a month or so, the family was left at a little post downriver from Rocky Mountain House while Thompson hurried along the river highways to eastern headquarters with the first furs from the Columbia Department.

Duncan McGillivray, who had hoped so fervently to cap his career with explorations ranking with those of Mackenzie, never knew that Thompson had succeeded in initiating the Nor'westers' Columbian Enterprise. He died before Thompson reached the source of the Columbia in the spring of 1808. Nor did he hear of Simon Fraser's incredibly dangerous voyage down the river now bearing his name. That waterway had taken the bold explorer to the Pacific, but since its mouth was above the forty-ninth parallel it couldn't be the Columbia. And certainly the tearing cauldron of the Fraser, treacherously convulsed between naked cliffs, was not the desperately needed canoe route!

Thompson had no news of Fraser's disappointment either when he returned west of the mountains to develop the trade. In charge of the Columbia Department, he proceeded to build the first fur trade posts west of the Rockies in the northern United States: Kullyspell on Pend Oreille Lake and Saleesh House in Montana. With Fraser's posts to the north, the Nor'westers were now established on the major rivers west of the Divide; they had every confidence that this, along with their daring explorations, would give sufficient weight to Mackenzie's appeal for an exclusive charter to carry their posts across the continent and into the basin of the Columbia. Supremacy was within reach for the Lords of Northern Rivers, Lakes and Forests.

But American President Jefferson had read of Mackenzie's ambitious plans for control of the fur trade. He sent Lewis and Clark on a transcontinental expedition and in 1805 they reached the mouth of the Columbia. A rags-to-riches American tycoon grasped the significance of that crossing.

Sixteen-year-old John Jacob Astor had left his father's butcher shop in

Waldorf, Germany and arrived in America in 1784. Penniless, he eked out a living by tramping the backwoods with a pedlar's bag of trinkets to trade for furs. Within four years he was buying furs in Montreal; a few more years and he had ships trading with China and was welcomed at Montreal's exclusive Beaver Club, where the elegant barons of the fur trade dispensed lavish hospitality. Like them, he would string his posts to the Pacific, now that Lewis and Clark had demonstrated the feasibility of crossing the continent. He began to manoeuvre for big stakes—a monopoly of the American fur trade.

Would his Nor'wester friends bargain? He could be useful if they would allow him a clear field south of the border, including the Columbia. In 1808 the Nor'westers were in no mood to surrender their dearly won advantage on the Columbia; instead they appealed to the British government to forestall Astor's Columbia ambitions. So Astor prepared to challenge them, but characteristically, still played it both ways: he offered them a third interest in his Pacific enterprise, which the Nor'westers didn't take very seriously. In 1810, however, Astor was actually ready for his westward leap and by then the Nor'westers had discovered that the Fraser River was unsuitable. They had to have access to the Columbia. Belatedly, tentatively, shrewdly, they accepted the one-third interest he had offered. However, they still intended to safeguard and extend their interest in the trade already established on the upper Columbia. David Thompson's eastward-bound canoe was intercepted in the spring of 1810 and turned back; he was ordered to establish, unassailably, the Nor'westers' rights on the upper Columbia. And at last, he was to make his way to the mouth of the great river.

But at Rocky Mountain House the Piegans were waiting. For the first time they had been defeated in battle by their enemies beyond the mountains—with the white man's arms. No longer would they be defied. With four tents of warriors Chief Black Bear was camped upriver, barring the way to the Columbia. Thompson felt his life to be in peril and retreated.

Howse Pass, the long-sought gateway to wealth and power, was left to heal the wounds of the white man's passing. The sombre peaks stood guard over the quiet valley. When white men, probing again for breaches in the continental barrier, returned nearly half a century later, even the scars were erased. Howse Pass was dense, matted with new growth, rank.

To hold all that the Nor'westers' vision and daring had won beyond the mountains David Thompson had to find a new pass, one where the Piegans would no longer be a menace. There was a rumour that some years before a small party of Nipissing Indians and trappers had crossed a pass at the head of a river flowing into the Athabasca. Thompson turned north.

3

Gateway for Thousands

Flanked by glaciers and icefields, Athabasca Pass breaks through the Continental Divide in a remote corner on the western boundary of Jasper Park. It always remained a mystery to Sir George Simpson "how any human being should have stumbled on a pass through such a formidable barrier . . ."

Whether he would find the pass must have been a burning question in Thompson's mind; he could only hope that Thomas, his Iroquois guide, would get him to it. But even if he did, could they cross it so late in the season? Thompson hadn't arrived at Rocky Mountain House until the autumn of 1810; after the setback on the Saskatchewan, men, horses and provisions had to be assembled and it was October 28th before the expedition could start on its quest. It became a trek of desperation.

For weeks Thompson and his men fought through one hundred and seventy-five miles of burnt forest tangled with windfall; starvation threatened them when the ravaged forest was found to be devoid of game; the temperature dropped to thirty-two below zero. Eventually word reached Alexander Henry at Rocky Mountain House that "their situation is pitiful."

After thirty-eight days they approached what is now Jasper Park; near Brûlé Lake a halt was imperative. Deep snow made it impossible to continue with horses, so sleds and snowshoes were constructed. Game and food were scarce and most of the men had to be sent back to Rocky Mountain House, some of them to return with provisions; the remaining men needed shelter from the bitter subzero weather. Thompson and his tiny party built a hut in the lonely valley and prepared for the next stage of their journey.

On a wintery day ten years before, David Thompson and Duncan McGillivray had ridden to the approaches of Banff National Park—probably the first white men to do so. Now Thompson had become the first white traveller to record a visit to Jasper.

Late in December his expedition started up the Athabasca. At the Miette River, just upstream from the present Jasper townsite, they had to lighten the loads and William Henry, Alexander's nephew, was left there to establish a camp. Early in January of 1811, leaving the last of the horses at Prairie de la Vache on the east side of the Athabasca, they approached "a bold defile"— the way to the pass.

Thirteen snowshoed men and eight dogsleds crossed the main Athabasca and turned west and south up the Whirlpool River. At last they felt the first breath of warm air from the Pacific, breaking a month of frigid temperatures, but soon they found themselves trudging through seven feet of heavy wet snow as gales raged around the hidden peaks. The dogs could scarcely drag the sleds; the weary men shouldered heavier loads and trekked slowly upward, for thirty-six miles. At night they huddled beside a few stunted trees.

Five days after they had struck the Whirlpool River, in the afternoon, the snow and wind abated. "The view now before us was an ascent of deep snow, in all appearance to the Height of Land between the Atlantic and the Pacific Oceans; it was to me an exhilarating sight, but to my uneducated men . . . the scene of desolation before us was dreadful . . . a heavy gale of wind much more a mountain storm would have buried us beneath it, but thank God the weather was fine."

Between a glacier and an avalanche-swept ridge, on snow more than twenty feet deep, the men made a platform of poles they had cut and dragged along, and on it they kindled their meagre fire. Thompson walked ahead to examine the country "and found we had now to descend the west side of the mountains . . ." They had found Athabasca Pass.

"My men were not at their ease, yet when night came they admired the brilliancy of the Stars, and as one of them said, he thought he could almost touch them with his hand . . ." As Thompson joined them on their bed of snow: "Many reflections came on my mind; a new world was in a manner before me, and my object was to be at the Pacific Ocean before the month of August, how were we to find Provisions, and how many Men would remain with me . . . ?"

Leaving the Whirlpool, they began the descent of the steep Pacific slope, where the dogs seemed "to swim" in the path the men made for them with snowshoes or careened into trees on the densely wooded ridge, hopelessly entangling sleds and loads. They rested for a day. Thompson wrote an urgent message for more supplies and some of the men left to take it to Rocky Mountain House; others brought over goods that had been left just east of the summit. Following the Wood River, on the 18th of January they reached the place where the Columbia makes its hairpin bend around the Selkirk Mountains. For four days they slogged along the Columbia in wet snow, often hip-deep—they made only twelve miles. The dogs were exhausted and the men refused to go on. Thompson returned to the Columbia-Canoe River junction, to the spot ever since known as Boat Encampment.

One man was ill and three deserted what seemed a hopeless undertaking. "We were pygmies, in such forest what could we do with Axes of two pounds weight?" They hacked down trees and built a hut with boards cut from the giant cedars. On February 17th three men arrived from Rocky Mountain House with dried provisions and more trade goods; on the first of March Thompson and his men began to build a boat. There were no birch trees available, so with great ingenuity and dogged persistence they split the great cedars, bent the boards to fit a canoe frame and sewed them together with pine roots.

By April 18th there was enough open water to start out on the Columbia. For three weeks they toiled past its rapids, waded in icy water towing the unwieldy boat with lines, dragged it over the frozen expanse of Kinbasket Lake and paddled against the stiff current. On May 8th they passed the stream coming from forbidden Howse Pass and, along familiar territory now, they at last met and enlisted the help of a few Indians. Labouriously they worked their way south and west.

For five more weeks they navigated swollen rivers, portaged and, on horses obtained from the Indians, rode across swamps and flooded streams.

Having abandoned their battered boat, they built a canoe to descend Clark Fork River to Pend Oreille Lake in Idaho. Two months after leaving Boat Encampment David Thompson rode to Spokane House (nine miles from today's Spokane), a post his men had established during the winter.

At last he was able to take up the work he had been sent to do: strengthen the Nor'westers' position on the upper Columbia. Riding to Kettle Falls where the Indians were gathered in large numbers at a fishing village, he made his usual friendly overtures—the loyalty of the natives was indispensable to his mission. A voyage on the Columbia was just as vital.

To build the canoe required, men scoured the burned forest for suitable logs; on July 3rd the craft was ready and Thompson embarked. Following the Columbia to the Pacific was a long-cherished dream, but all along the way he delayed his journey to stop wherever Indians congregated. Patiently he explained that he would be back to trade; these diplomatic efforts to win the natives' allegiance were not without danger for many of them had never seen a white man.

On July 9th, at the junction of the Snake and the Columbia he made an official proclamation of the Nor'westers' intention. On a wooden stake he put up his famous notice: "Know hereby that this country is claimed by Great Britain . . . and that the North West Company of Merchants from Canada . . . do hereby intend to erect a factory in this place for the commerce of the country around." Whatever might result from future manoeuvring, the upper Columbia was staked for the Nor'westers. Thompson then continued toward the estuary of the Columbia.

On the last day of the voyage he dressed in his best European clothes; his voyageurs put on their brightest caps and sashes and launched the large cedar canoe. It was July 15th, 1811, and on that day Thompson looked out onto the Pacific. For nearly a quarter of a century the Nor'westers had sought the Great River of the West. The search was over—the Columbia had at last been run from its source to the sea.

When David Thompson stepped briskly ashore at Fort Astoria he was warmly greeted by the former Nor'westers who had superintended the building of Astor's post at the mouth of the Columbia. A rumour had reached them that the deal between Astor and the Nor'westers had in fact fallen through and they discussed the matter with Thompson. Agreeing that they had no definite knowledge of what had transpired, Thompson and the Astorians exchanged formal notes, acknowledging that the Nor'westers had a third interest in Astor's Pacific Fur Company and hoping "that the respective parties at Montreal may finally settle the arrangement between the two Companies . . . to the mutual satisfaction of both parties . . ." Thompson then left to recross the Rockies.

Proceeding to the mouth of the Kootenay River, he started up the unexplored leg of the Columbia, going by way of the Arrow Lakes. Once again he and his men poled and hauled canoes through rapids; when Thompson stepped ashore beside his old hut at Boat Encampment he had surveyed the entire 1210-mile course of the river.

He crossed Athabasca Pass, picked up trade goods at the little depot William Henry had built in the Jasper valley and returned to consolidate the Nor'westers' trade in the Columbia basin.

On May 12th, 1812, he ascended Athabasca Pass again—for the last time. Ahead, the voyageurs plodded, carrying eleven thousand pounds of fur. Did Thompson stand for a moment thinking of the vast exhilarating sweep of country he had seen in his twenty-five years in the Northwest—the beckoning turns of great rivers, the vast plains, the forested foothills beneath the Shining Mountains?

He never returned west, but the memory of it remained sharp and clear for the rest of his long life. In his seventies, half-blind, he pored over his field journals and wrote his *Narrative*. As Doctor J. J. Bigsby remarked, he had "a singular faculty of picture-making. He can create a wilderness and people it with warring savages or climb the Rocky Mountains with you in a snowstorm, so clearly and so palpably that only shut your eyes and you hear the crack of the rifle or feel the snowflakes on your cheeks." Thompson's book, among the most detailed and comprehensive of any accounts left by the fur traders, is a vivid representation of a bygone era. He left also the legacy of his map.

Leaving active service in the fur trade, he was retained by the Nor'westers as a partner until he finished his map. In two years it was completed and many of the blank spaces on existing maps of North America had been filled in. With his own exploration of the Columbia River, his "survey of the Oregon Territory to the Pacific Ocean," with Mackenzie's voyage to the

Arctic and the Pacific and the survey of the Fraser River, the Nor'westers had indeed extended the boundaries of their empire. Proudly they hung the great map, with its seventy-eight posts pinpointed, on the walls of their council chambers at Fort William. But the information it embodied was their secret. Thompson received little public recognition for his work.

He retired from the fur trade and for ten years served as a member of the International Boundary Commission, where he met Dr. Bigsby who recorded this impression of him: "Plainly dressed, quiet and observant. His figure was short and compact, and his black hair was worn long all round, and cut square, as if by one stroke of the shears, just above the eyebrows. His complexion was of the gardener's ruddy brown, while the expression of deeply furrowed features was friendly and intelligent . . ."

Thompson ended his days in obscurity and humiliating poverty. At his home near Montreal, in 1857, he died; three months later his wife Charlotte was buried beside him in Mount Royal Cemetery.

Seventy years later a monument was raised over his forgotten grave in tribute to "the greatest of Canadian geographers who for thirty-four years explored and mapped the main travel routes between the St. Lawrence and the Pacific."

In the 1880s surveyor J. B. Tyrrell, retracing the steps of his great predecessor in the West, was impressed by "the accuracy of the main features of the maps then in use" and sought out the source of the geographic information. He found it when he unearthed Thompson's long-lost map. It was the framework of all future maps of Canada; up until 1857 it was the best available and even as late as 1916 some parts of government maps were still taken from it.

And at Athabasca Pass he left a blazed trail. For the remaining years of the fur trade Canada's main transcontinental route crossed the Rockies at Thompson's second mountain gateway, and the thousands who made the arduous trek through the glacier-girt valley unwittingly threaded with moccasined feet the first sinews binding the nation from sea to sea.

4

TWO IN SEARCH OF A FORTUNE

The summer visitor to the resort village of Jasper sees to the south, dominant and serene against a deep blue sky, the snowy wedge of Mount Edith Cavell. Just beyond its blue-black buttresses the Whirlpool River rushes on its way to the Athabasca. The modern traveller can drive along the old Jasper-Banff highway to the mouth of the Whirlpool; in a few days he can hike or ride to Athabasca Pass where he finds, not desolation, but "beautiful meadows, trees, flowers and a deep, colourful mountain tarn."

Ah, yes, but he comes in summer; he hasn't walked for days through icy streams with frozen moccasins and snowshoes cutting his feet, nor is his larder empty hundreds of miles from civilization. Under those circumstances Mount Edith Cavell, the voyageurs' Montagne de la Grande Traverse, might not appear so serene—her massive presence might seem ominous.

On the scenic road to the foot of Mount Edith Cavell there is a lookout point with a breathtaking view toward the Tonquin Valley; the milky green Astoria River roars hundreds of feet below and across the narrow valley rises a fine mountain, its shoulders and summit splashed with red and umber. The valley, the mountain and the river at its feet all have historic names: Tonquin commemorates John Jacob Astor's ship which set out to build Fort Astoria at the mouth of the Columbia River; Franchère Peak is named for a young French Canadian fur trader who was one of Jasper's earliest visitors.

While David Thompson was approaching the Rockies in September of 1810, Gabriel Franchère sailed from New York on the ill-fated *Tonquin*. On March 22, 1811, while Thompson and his men were still building their boat at Boat Encampment, the *Tonquin* neared the estuary of the Columbia where the incredibly hot-tempered autocrat, Captain Thorn (whose "unspeakable cruelty" had already driven his crew almost to the point of mutiny), immediately ordered five of his men out in small boats to explore for a channel in the murderous waters. They were never seen again. Docking at last, he dumped men with provisions and building supplies and as soon as he could, sailed up the coast to trade. He never returned; the Indians he stopped to trade with found him equally obnoxious and in an episode of appalling carnage, murdered Thorn and all his crew.

Not only was this an inauspicious beginning for the Pacific Fur Company; it was also a serious crisis for the inadequately provisioned men left to establish Astor's post. However, by the time David Thompson's big canoe arrived in July they had gained a foothold; when, subsequently, the "partnership" crumbled (due to fantastically complex international and commercial rivalries), it was found that Astor had neatly out-manoeuvred the Nor'westers who were denied access to the mouth of the Columbia. But not for long.

The War of 1812 tipped the scales and the wily Nor'westers seized their chance, arriving at Fort Astoria in 1813 with the news that the British were blockading the coastline. Astor's ships wouldn't be able to bring supplies to his post on the Columbia! The Nor'westers came with a very reasonable proposal: would the Astorians accept their offer to buy the establishment? As the proposal was augmented by the news that British warships were coming to force capitulation of Astor's fort, the isolated men could hardly refuse. David Thompson's partners reigned at the mouth of the Columbia after all. To young Franchère this meant only one thing: "it was thus after having passed the seas and suffered all sorts of fatigues and privations, I lost in a moment all my hopes of a fortune."

Astor's men were offered positions with the new owners of Fort George (as it was renamed) or free transportation east if they wished. Franchère stayed, with the stipulation that he wanted to return home with the first brigade travelling to Boat Encampment. He left on April 4th, 1814, and after five weeks of arduous toil by canoe and portage, he and his companions reached the Canoe River at the western entrance to Athabasca Pass.

Twenty-four people, each carrying a fifty-pound load, struggled through swamps and dense forest, forded neck-deep in swift swollen streams and on the third day, stopping every few steps to take a breath on the final steep ascent, dragged themselves onto a plateau where they floundered through soft snow, "obliged to follow exactly the traces of those who had preceded us, and to plunge our legs up to the knees in the holes they had made, so that it was as if we had put on and taken off, at every step, a very large pair of boots." At last they reached the summit of Athabasca Pass: two frozen ponds on a snowy hump between "immense glaciers and ice-bound rocks . . ."

Early travellers' accounts vary as to whether there were one or two ponds there; they differ in a most dramatic way about the altitude as well, but all agree that it was awesomely impressive.

Franchère and his companions cleared away the snow for a camp and "supped frugally" on a few handfuls of "pounded maize"; admiring the surrounding ice walls "on which the rays of the setting sun reflected the most beautiful prismatic colours," they settled down for a bitterly cold night. The following day they continued along the Whirlpool, which rushed over its rocky bottom "in a thousand fantastic gambols." Making "a tiresome march" through forests Franchère seriously hurt his knee on a sharp branch of a fallen tree, but it "was impossible to flinch, as I must keep up with the party or perish."

Six days after leaving Boat Encampment they entered the Jasper valley, forded the Athabasca and camped at Prairie de la Vache where their supper still consisted of "corn parched in a pan." At least they were finally able to dry their clothing. The next day, passing the site of modern Jasper, Franchère thought the scenery was "the most charming that can be imagined . . . the beautiful river Athabasca . . . surrounded by green and smiling prairies and superb woodlands," and reflected that it was "a pity there was no one there to enjoy these rural beauties." As they proceeded, fresh venison became a most welcome addition to their diet. Franchère, whose knee was acutely painful, forcibly persuaded some Iroquois to take him in their canoe as they made their way toward the "high promontory, Millet's Rock" (today's Roche Miette), where those preceding them on horseback "were all at a stand, doubting whether it would answer to wade round the base of the rock which dipped in the water."

Until the railway builders, dangling on the ends of stout ropes held by their straining companions a hundred feet above, planted the dynamite which blasted away the nose of Roche Miette, it jutted into the river and at high water the ridge had to be crossed at what became known as Disaster Point. The top of the steep slope consisted of down-sloping slabs of slippery rock which, as the horses bunched at the top, often sent them hurtling over the precipice.

Franchère and his companions found a ford; "all passed round" and camped at Jasper House, at that time situated on the west side of the Athabasca at the foot of Brûlé Lake, where they enjoyed "an excellent supper of wild ducks." They didn't fare as well on many occasions during the three-month voyage across the continent to Montreal, and as they sometimes "supped on horsemeat," Franchère's fellow Astorian, Ross Cox, often on similar fare back on the Pacific, was beginning to chafe at being "so long debarred from the enjoyments of civilized life."

"Captivated by the love of novelty and the hope of speedily realizing an independence in the supposed El Dorado" (as he so quaintly puts it), Cox had joined the Astorians in 1811; when the fort capitulated he joined the Nor'westers. Perhaps his nostalgia became acute when some Nor'westers arrived with a supply ship from England. They produced "a few casks of bottled porter, some excellent cheese and a quantity of prime English beef, which they had dressed and preserved in a peculiar manner in tin cases impervious to air, so that we could say we ate fresh beef which had been killed and dressed in England thirteen months before!" But probably the determining factor in his decision to return to "the enjoyments of civilized life" was "another object" they brought, one which "strongly recalled to our semi-barbarized ideas the thoughts of our dear native home."

This was none other than "a flaxen-haired, blue-eyed" lively young barmaid who in "a temporary fit of erratic enthusiasm, had consented to become *le compagnon du voyage*" to one of the honoured gentlemen on board—a gentleman, Cox says (somewhat superfluously), "of rather an amorous temperament." At Fort George Jane Barnes found herself "the object of interest." The Indians "daily thronged in great numbers to our fort for the mere purpose of gazing on, and admiring the fair beauty . . . She had rather an extravagant wardrobe, and each day exhibited her in a new dress, which she always managed in a manner to display her figure to the best advantage."

A native swain, hearing that she was about to be sent home, "came attired in his richest dress, his face fancifully bedaubed with red paint, and his body redolent of whale oil," as befitted a son of a chief of the Chinooks. He proposed. If she would become his wife, "he would send one hundred sea otters to her relations; he would never ask her to carry wood, draw water, dig for roots or hunt for provisions; he would make her mistress over his other wives and permit her to sit at her ease from morning to night . . . and smoke as many pipes of tobacco during the day as she thought proper." These tempting offers, however, "had no charms for Jane" and the spurned suitor swept out, swearing he would never set foot in the fort while she remained. Jane went home (she returned for another visit later as the wife of a ship's captain) and in April of 1817 Ross Cox also left for home.

The brigade he accompanied started up the Columbia in a gale and proceeded in almost constant rain, fishing upset canoes out of rapids and dragging them with lines from shore, to arrive in five weeks at Boat Encampment where "with indescribable pleasure we bade a final adieu to our crazy battered canoe."

Carrying ninety-pound loads they trekked through the "gloomy valley" of the Canoe River in thick mist which rendered "the awful solitude" particularly impressive. "It appeared never to have been trodden by the foot of man, until the enterprising spirit of British commerce, after having forced its way over the everlasting snows of the Rocky Mountains, penetrated into this anti-social glen." Crossing the turbulent Wood River they "all advanced in line, the tallest and strongest mixed alternately with the lowest, each holding the other firmly by the hand," a precaution which saved the lives of those who lost their footing. Up the last steep slope which ascends "three thousand feet in seven or eight miles" they climbed, and over the hump onto the summit of Athabasca Pass, "situated between an immense cut of the Rocky Mountains."

"The sun shining on a range of stupendous glaciers, threw a chilling brightness over the chaotic mass of rocks, ice and snow . . . while at intervals the interest of the scene was heightened by the rumbling noise of a descending avalanche; which, after being detached from its bed of centuries, increased in bulk in its headlong career downwards, until it burst with a frightful crash . . . One of our rough-spun, unsophisticated Canadians, after gazing upwards for some time in silent wonder, exclaimed with much vehemence, 'I'll take my oath, my dear friends, that God Almighty never made such a place!'" The inference was clear to his awed companions.

Continuing down the Whirlpool next day, they found horses left for them "in a charming meadow" and, transferring their loads, resumed their journey "with great spirits." The valley widened, the snow was disappearing, and the next day when they crossed the Whirlpool, the water was running high. The horses were rafted over safely but when Cox and his companions launched their raft they were "carried instantly into the rapid." The passengers jumped overboard and seized the raft but they "might as well have attempted to arrest the flight of an eagle . . ." Before it was halted they had all sustained "severe contusions." Aboard again, they had scarcely time to "breathe thanksgiving" before they were dashing headlong into "a succession of cascades and rapids . . ."; at the last minute they swerved into shallow water and managed to get their battered craft across to the other shore. Only then did Cox realize that "the apprehension of instant annihilation" had momentarily "banished even the recollection of kindred home."

The Athabasca crossing was uneventful and they rode down the valley where "the country on each side presented a pleasing variety of prairies, open woods and gently rising eminences . . . a landscape that for rural beauty cannot be excelled in any country."

As they continued their journey the early morning mists drifted lazily up to snowy summits and disappeared "under the genial influence of a June sun . . . which imparted a golden tinge to the green savannahs, the open woods and the innumerable rivulets . . ." They passed "an old hunting lodge" near the mouth of the Maligne River where someone had thoughtfully left a freshly killed buffalo for them. "It was none of the fattest but to such half-famished devils it was an unexpected luxury." Taking some of the meat with them they rode on to Roche Miette, "a stupendous rock." The river was too deep to ford, so for three and a half hours they climbed over the shoulder; the horses made the ascent "with great labour; and the knees of the majority of our party were put to a severe test . . ." At sunset they camped in the shadow of the mountain and "succeeded in dispatching with wonderful celerity the remains of our buffalo."

Eleven days after leaving Boat Encampment they arrived at Jasper House on Brûlé Lake. The man in charge was "an old clerk," Jasper Hawes, who had trapped for years in the valley and for whom the park and town would one day be named. To the great disappointment of the weary travellers he could supply no meat. They plodded away from his "melancholy hermitage" and resumed their journey in birchbark canoes.

The long voyage over Canada's waterways ended at Lachine, Quebec, where Cox and his companions bought a keg of rum "which we presented as a valedictory allowance to our voyageurs . . . and drove off amidst their benedictions," for Montreal. After "a journey of five months and three days from the Pacific Ocean," Ross Cox was ready to resume "the enjoyments of civilized life."

A keg of rum also figured prominently in Sir George Simpson's crossing of Athabasca Pass.

A Toast to Their Honours

John Jacob Astor played every angle to regain the prize he had lost on the Columbia. But by the time the American government was ready to give him the necessary support, the Nor'westers were well entrenched and it would have taken too big a bite out of his prodigious fortune to dislodge them. For eight years the Nor'westers garnered the harvest from their Columbian Enterprise. Then they too went down to defeat. The ruinous rivalry of the fur trade mounted to a violent and bloody climax in 1821. Only amalgamation with the Hudson's Bay Company saved the day and with amalgamation, the proud and dauntless Lords of Northern Rivers, Lakes and Forests faded into oblivion—but in their passing they had laid the foundations for a nation.

To the helm of the world's greatest monopoly stepped dapper, brisk thirty-nine-year-old George Simpson. With unflagging energy and astonishing efficiency, he reorganized the business east of the mountains to the unbounded delight of his London superiors. Having done so, he wanted to draw a breath and respectfully requested leave to visit England—it was pretty well known that he hoped to bring back a bride—but he was ordered to sweep his new broom into the posts in the Columbia District.

In the late summer of 1824 he left Hudson's Bay on his first record-breaking dash across the mountains, having sent ahead Dr. John McLoughlin, the new chief factor for the Columbia District. With immense satisfaction he caught up to the big doctor who had a twenty-day start on him, especially relishing "his surprise and vexation at being overtaken" and his discomfiture at being caught still in camp at the late hour of 7 A.M.! In his coded "character book" Simpson caustically noted that his respected deputy's once fashionable clothes were covered with "a thousand patches of different Colors, his beard would do honor to the chin of a Grizzly Bear, his face and hands evidently Shewing that he had not lost much time at his Toilette . . ."!

Straining at the paddles his voyageurs hurried him from Fort Assiniboine up the Athabasca to Jasper House. When he first glimpsed the Rockies, a gentle undulation on the horizon mantled by the soft blue haze of autumn, they looked like the remembered hills of Scotland—an illusion soon dispelled as the brigade approached Roche Miette where the slate grey crags soared to the clouds. On October 12th they left Jasper House in its "wild and romantic" setting and made their way on horseback toward Athabasca Pass.

Game was plentiful and the governor tasted mountain goat and sheep; his "palate could not distinguish between them" but good business man that he was, he saw the possibility that the distinctive goat skins "might fetch a tolerable price." The matter was worthy of attention and on the spot he arranged to have one sent to London for appraisal. As they continued, the mountains rose to "a prodigious height"; the trail was "in many places nearly impassable"; the river had to be forded dozens of times and the horse carrying his "wardrobe" fell from a high bank and was swept a hundred yards down river before it was rescued "by the activity of the Driver." One can readily imagine that there was considerable activity on the part of the driver to save that particular bit of cargo!

The scenery became ever more impressive but the going became correspondingly arduous. As the impatient Simpson had business to attend to on the Pacific, it seemed to him that a capricious nature had placed this "formidable barrier . . . here for the purpose of interditing all commerce between the East and West sides of the Continent"!

In five days they reached the summit of the pass which was marked by a small circular tarn. From it trickled two tiny streams; one, the infant Whirlpool, joined the Athabasca to flow at last into the Arctic; the other joined the Columbia to reach the Pacific. Dr. McLoughlin was asked to ver-

*The fabled Committee's Punch Bowl, marking the summit of
Athabasca Pass, where travellers drank a toast "to their Honours"
whenever "a nabob of the fur trade" passed by.*

COURTESY WHYTE MUSEUM OF THE CANADIAN ROCKIES, BANFF (M517/42)

ify this extraordinary phenomenon. "That this basin should send its Waters to each side of the Continent and give birth to two of the principal Rivers in North America" seemed so remarkable that "I thought it should be honoured by a distinguishing title and forthwith named it 'The Committee's Punch Bowl' . . ." in honour of the governing committee of the Hudson's Bay Company.

The isolated peak-surrounded gap of Athabasca Pass became an imperishable memory for thousands of travellers. Three years after the christening of the Committee's Punch Bowl the quaint Scottish botanist, David Douglas, was to spend a momentous day there, unwittingly creating a far-reaching legend of two giant mountains.

Slithering down the Pacific slope, the governor's party reached Boat Encampment. It had taken just six days "to dispose of the celebrated Athabasca Portage." Embarking on the Columbia, in rain, fog and snow they covered a staggering one hundred miles a day so that the flamboyant governor could sweep up to the dock at Fort George in record time: eighty-four days since leaving Hudson's Bay—twenty days faster than it had ever been done before!

And a good thing he'd come! The Columbia District was "shamefully mismanaged": there was wasteful extravagance with the "gentlemen" enjoying "Eatables Drinkables and other *Domestic Comforts*"; officers were "amusing themselves Boat Sailing" and were not satisfied unless they had "a posse of Clerks Guides Interpreters & supernumeraries at their disposal . . . Everything" was on "too extended a scale *except the Trade.*" There'd be no more of *that*!

By the time he left in March of 1825 he was confident that matters were so arranged that the Columbia Department would show "handsome returns." Some of the "supernumeraries" were going back east with him; there were strict orders to make the posts self-sufficient by growing corn, fishing and raising cattle. Dr. McLoughlin was to abolish the trade in alcohol, build up the coastal trade and (to discourage American competition), denude the area south of the Columbia of fur-bearing animals. No wonder he was commended for "the masterly arrangements and decisive measures productive of the happiest effects" when he returned east.

The homeward trip along the Columbia "beats anything of the kind hitherto known . . .": sixteen hours a day in "much snow and rising waters," poling, paddling, dragging with lines and portaging. Food was in short supply and everyone "had long faces." The Little Emperor himself shot a deer to relieve the situation. At Boat Encampment at last, reading the mail which had been sent to him across the pass from Jasper House, he was distinctly testy: there were no provisions available so they would have "to fast for 4 or 5 days" and the horses ordered for the portage would not arrive for a week. There was only one thing to do: "we shall have to make use of our Legs, no joke after the labour & hardship we shall undergo . . ."

His forebodings were well founded. An hour "after concluding the water voyage" they were on their way, carrying ninety-pound loads over the gravelly valley bottom and wading through streams—sixty-two times one day. Some of the people simply couldn't keep up. Simpson bolstered them with "a Dram" and pushed on. Alexander Ross (another former Astorian) accompanied him on this journey and he noted that "despatch was the order of the day. The Governor himself, generally at the head, made the first plunge into the water, and was not the last to get out. His smile encouraged others and his example checked murmuring."

The brigade was bringing back an Iroquois "banished for Life from the Columbia for his uniform bad conduct," and on the second day of the trek the governor was informed that "the Blackguard Iroquois" had "broached a keg" and with six companions had proceeded to get gloriously drunk. He had then lightened his burden by throwing his provisions into the river. Such behaviour endangered the whole party, who would have to share their dangerously meagre rations with the malefactor or leave him to perish. Something had to be done lest there be a repeat performance. "Irritated exceedingly," Simpson acted. "I was on the impulse of the moment induced to descend to the disagreeable duty of chastising him on the spot with the first stick that came to hand." That attended to, he seized a hatchet and knocked a hole in the other keg, much to the distress of the people who really needed that dram in the days to come.

The next day they had to climb the "big Hill." Sinking in snow sometimes six feet deep, they plodded for nine miles before breakfast. Everyone was "drenched with perspiration altho' the Morning was very severe . . ."; on the final lap they hauled themselves up with the help of branches, sometimes scrambling on hands and knees. The climb had taken twelve hours so they camped before reaching the Committee's Punch Bowl. Erecting a platform of green logs for the fire, they rolled up in their blankets on the snow and slept with feet to the roaring blaze.

"Le feu! le feu!" They awoke to find that one poor soul who was sleeping with his feet too close to the fire had jumped up in terror and promptly slid into the deep pit which the fire had melted under the platform. Some of his bedfellows also slithered "with an easy descent into the fiery gulph." Fortunately they had dragged down so much snow that no one was seriously burned, but by the time their companions had extricated them (with many "jests and shouts of laughter") and "gathered up our odds and ends," it was 3:30 A.M. and time to go—according to Sir George!

They reached the Committee's Punch Bowl in time for breakfast where the governor initiated a ceremony which according to Ross was always observed "when a nabob of the fur trade passes by . . . This elevated pond is . . . dignified with the name of the Committee's Punch Bowl" and "his Excellency treated us to a bottle of wine" with which to drink a toast "to Their Honours" as they had "neither time nor convenience to make a bowl of punch; although a glass of it would have been very acceptable."

Having crossed Athabasca Pass, Sir George was keenly interested in alternative routes; at Boat Encampment he had carefully questioned Indians about the Yellowhead Pass and before he himself tried for a southern pass in 1841 he satisfied himself about the hazards of the Fraser and Thompson river routes—he had entertained a suspicion that their difficulties were exaggerated.

Descending the Thompson from Fort Kamloops in 1828, crashing into "the constant succession of rapids . . . the whitened countenances of the boldest among us, even that of our dark Iroquois Bowsman who is nearly amphibious, shewed that we felt anything but comfortable . . ." But "bad as Thompsons River is . . . Frazers River is infinitely worse . . ." Even though his crack voyageurs were using a bigger canoe and the river was not in flood as it had been for Simon Fraser's descent, the "foaming Waters" ran "with immense velocity . . . momentarily threatening to sweep us to destruction . . . our craft shot like the flight of an Arrow" through rapids and into "deep whirlpools . . ." The Indians, knowing that the river's hazards made it practically unnavigable, popped out of the forest to watch in amazement. He was forced to agree with their assessment. "Frazers River . . . was never wholly passed by water before, and in probability never will again . . . I should consider the passage down, to be certain Death in nine attempts out of Ten . . . I shall therefore no longer talk of it as a navigable stream."

In spite of these harrowing interludes Sir George chalked up another record on this, his second inspection of the Pacific trade; ". . . the longest Voyage ever attempted in North America in one Season," about seven thousand miles in less than six months. A young Highland piper, Colin Fraser, was making his maiden voyage with the demon traveller on that occasion; one wonders if he wasn't often too winded to unlimber the pipes!

Dr. McLoughlin had achieved great things in the Columbia District and Sir George returned east over Athabasca Pass. Some changes had been instigated in the Jasper area. Jasper House had been moved from Brûlé Lake to Jasper Lake just within today's park; Henry House, situated on the west side of the Athabasca at the junction of the Miette, was the point of departure for brigades travelling along Yellowhead Pass to service posts in present-day northern British Columbia. The origin of the name of this pass is uncertain; it commemorates a fair-haired trader, called "Yellowhead" by the Indians, who may have been the François Decoigne stationed at Jasper House when Franchère travelled through.

Sir George never crossed the mountains again after his history-making round-the-world trip in 1841. He had done all that he could to swell the company's coffers from the fur paradise on the Columbia and had pushed its frontiers to Alaska, California and Hawaii. American settlers thronging west posed an increasing threat to the Hudson's Bay Company's enclave on the Columbia—its future was uncertain and the establishment of a route through the southern Rockies was postponed. The brigades maintained the vital link with the Pacific by toiling over Athabasca Pass. The search for a pass in the south had never been pressed very hard, partly because the best fur-producing areas were in the north and partly because of the hostility of the Indians on the plains.

Four years after Sir George's journey through Simpson Pass a very different type of early traveller crossed the mountains in the Banff area. He was not bent on setting speed records or finding new passes; nor was he concerned with increasing the profit margin on beaver pelts. But by establishing friendly relations with the Indians he and a tiny remnant of like-minded men played important roles in providing easier access to the southern Rockies.

6

AMONG THE BLACKFOOT

Since 1838 Father Pierre Jean De Smet had travelled extensively in the American Pacific Northwest, winning the friendship of many Indian tribes. (In years to come the Belgian Black Robe would gain respect as a mediator between the white man and the natives; in 1868 when the Sioux and their allies threatened to kill every white man, he walked alone into the camp of Sitting Bull and secured at least a temporary truce.) But the Blackfoot Indians had begun to make "frequent incursions" into the territory where Father De Smet had established missions and the bloodshed was a source of distress to the Jesuit priest. In 1845 he crossed the Rockies from the west on a mission of peace to the Blackfoot.

With two Kootenays who had offered to guide him to the country of their enemies and another Indian acting as hunter and interpreter, Father De Smet travelled along the Columbia River and, passing through "country that was highly picturesque and agreeably diversified by beautiful prairies," rode north to Lake Windermere where he camped on September 4th. Following the route along which Sir George Simpson had been so maddeningly impeded in his headlong dash to the Pacific four years earlier, they went on through "dark alpine forests," crossed Sinclair Pass and followed the Kootenay River to the mouth of another stream, where they were faced with ascending "the stupendous chain which appears as an impregnable barrier." Over "circuitous paths" they climbed, surrounded by "colossal walls . . . with the most beautiful scenery in nature spread out" before them. They left behind "the birches shining like magnificent silver columns supporting diadems of golden autumnal leaves amidst purple-berried juniper" and arrived on September 15th at the summit of White Man Pass, where "all was wild sublimity." As he was now entering the country where he hoped to accomplish his mission of peace, De Smet and his men erected a cross of peace. Because of that symbolic act the stream they had followed to the summit has since been named the Cross River.

At the lonely little summit camp he probably saw Mount Assiniboine, the highest mountain in that part of the Rockies, for he wrote: "The monuments of Cheops and Cephren dwindle into naught before this great architectural cliff of nature." They then descended into the Spray River Valley, "jeweled with enamelled meads," and made their way through burnt forests where windfall and broken rocks formed "obstacles and contusions" for men and horses.

Beside the Bow River they pitched their solitary tent. The remains of a recent encampment alarmed his guides and De Smet was reminded that he was approaching the land of the Blackfoot "from which, possibly, I shall never return!"

What had been taken for signs of a Blackfoot camp were actually those of some Mountain Stonies, whom they encountered near the entrance to the mountains as they followed the Bow onto the prairie. Camping with these friendly people, Father De Smet forgot to barricade the door of his tent with boughs and awoke one morning to find that the ravenous camp-following dogs had eaten his moccasins and the leather collar of his cassock, and that he "was minus one leg of my cullotes de peau!!!" It was not the first time that he travelled in tattered habiliments; he started one journey with two hundred shirts and on his return had not one left. He'd given them all away.

He parted from the Stonies and went in search of the Blackfoot, but it seems that his guides were none too anxious for an actual encounter with them; instead of heading for the prairies they kept to the wooded foothills on their way north. Here the portly priest was not only kept from meeting the Indians but learned a great deal about travelling through western forests. After nineteen days he was experienced enough to issue some advice. "Anyone who thinks of visiting them should render himself as slender, as short and as contracted as possible; to learn how to cling to a saddle and

Father Pierre Jean De Smet, "the Belgian Black Robe."
COURTESY THE LATE MAJOR FRED BREWSTER, JASPER

avoid the branches ever ready to tear him to pieces and flay his face and hands." One day he found himself "in a singular and critical position": attempting to pass under a tree that inclined across the path, he noticed a stout hooked branch above and instantly "extended myself upon the neck of my horse." A mistake. For "it caught me by the collar of my surtout, the horse still continuing his pace. Behold me suspended in the air—struggling like a fish at the end of a hook. Several respectable pieces of my coat floated, in all possibility, a long time in the forest . . ." Then it began to snow and he discovered something else. "Woe to the first pedestrians! The least rubbing of the hat, the least touch . . . and a deluge of snow showers down upon the shivering cavalier."

When they emerged at last the battered father sported "a crushed and torn hat—an eye black and blue—two deep scratches on the cheek," giving him "the appearance of a bully issuing from the Black Forest . . ."

By early October he had been conducted to the fort at Rocky Mountain House where he hoped to meet the Blackfoot. When they came they greeted De Smet with stately courtesy and one old chief, "decorated from head to foot with eagles' plumes . . . embraced me tenderly, rubbing my cheek with his scarlet-painted nose." He accepted the invitation to visit them later at their camp but by then the only guide available proved unreliable—he left the wandering priest to fend for himself in the wilderness. Winter was closing in and although he had hoped to recross the mountains, there was no one to guide him; he proceeded to Fort Edmonton where he might be able to spend some more time with the Blackfoot. He was disappointed, for all winter they were skirmishing with their enemies and scarcely visited the post. In the spring he had to return west.

On March 12, 1846, he left Fort Edmonton with three Métis guides, travelling by dogsled for six days to reach Fort Assiniboine and then up the Athabasca River to Jasper House where Sir George Simpson's former piper, Colin Fraser, was in charge. Probably the missionary had decided to return home this way in order to minister to the handful of Iroquois who had made the valley their home ever since they had been brought from the East by the Nor'westers. They and Colin Fraser's native wife were delighted to see a priest of their own faith. Since it would be some weeks before the spring brigade arrived and as game was scarce at the fort, De Smet went with the

Indians for a month to what he calls "the Lake of Islands" where there were plenty of fish. Experienced travellers at Fort Edmonton had expressed serious misgivings about the genial Jesuit's ability to make the arduous portage over Athabasca Pass because of his ample girth, so he now sought "to remedy the inconvenience of my surplus stock by a vigourous fast of thirty days."

Still rotund in spite of these drastic measures, on April 25th he was ready to leave with the westward-bound fur brigade. At Jasper House his little flock gathered round to bid farewell and "begged leave to honor me with a little ceremony . . . Each one discharged his musket in the direction of the highest mountain, a large rock jutting out in the form of a sugar loaf, and with three loud hurrahs, gave it my name." Thus a range and a conspicuous mountain above Jasper Lake commemorate an "American tourist."

They trekked toward the pass amid "prodigious" mountains which sent avalanches thundering on every side with "a frightful rapidity." Near the summit they met the eastward-bound brigade escorting "old friends" with whom the priest had camped the year before at Kalispell. British army Lieutenants Warre and Vavasour had been on a mission too—a secret military mission urged by Sir George Simpson who was concerned about defending the Oregon Territory.

Crossing the Rockies by a southern route (probably by White Man Pass) they had outfitted themselves with superfine beaver hats, frock coats, figured vests, tobacco, fine wines and whiskies, extract of roses, silk handkerchiefs, razor strops and nail brushes, and travelled through the territory in a style befitting "gentlemen enjoying field sports and scientific pursuits." Their work completed (they reported the mountain passes unsuitable for troop transport), they were on their way back to England and gladly took Father De Smet's mail for Europe with them.

Gladly also they threw away their snowshoes and mounted horses. Those going west fastened on the snowshoes and the poor priest soon confessed himself "a most clumsy and awkward traveller." In single file they trudged over snow sixteen feet deep, "alternately ascending and descending—sometimes across plains piled high with avalanches—sometimes over lakes and rapids buried deeply—now on the side of a steep mountain . . . then across a forest of cypress trees, of which we see only the tops."

"I cannot tell you the number of my summersets . . ." The voyageurs may have been hard put not to smile at the stout Black Robe spread-eagled in many a snowdrift, but with customary good humour they helped him up and urged him on. At night, snugly wrapped in a buffalo robe on his bed of green logs beside the fire, "under the beautiful canopy of the starry heavens," he almost forgot the trials of the day. But as they approached the Columbia, fording streams as many as forty times in a day, frequently immersed to the shoulders, Father De Smet's legs swelled painfully and eventually he lost the nails of all his toes.

In eight days they reached Boat Encampment. Four times he had found his strength gone. "I should have perished in that frightful region if the courage and strength of my companions had not roused and aided me in my distress . . ." Three weeks later he arrived safely at his mission near Fort Colville.

At Rocky Mountain House and Fort Edmonton Father De Smet had worked amicably with the Reverend Robert Rundle, a Wesleyan missionary who had come from England to Canada in 1840. In February of 1841, Mr. Rundle bundled up in lamb's wool hose, woollen drawers, thick, lined trousers, leggings, gaiters, flannel shirt, waistcoat, coat, pilot coat, shawl and moccasins; tying his sealskin cap under his chin, he tucked a buffalo robe around him in the dogsled his drivers had waiting and set out on the seven-day journey from Fort Edmonton to Rocky Mountain House. At night only the howl of wolves "broke the fearful solitude."

When they had passed Gull Lake, Alberta, the young clergyman eagerly searched the western horizon for his first glimpse of the Rockies. But when he saw them, they "didn't excite in my mind those feelings I had expected for the circumstances were rather trying." Following the tracks of the sled which was far ahead of him, he was walking alone over a strange, vast countryside; he thought of home and friends. Blood on the trail—evidence that the men were mistreating the dogs—distressed him. Exhausted, he actually fell asleep beside the track several times and then in desperation hurried after the men as night approached. When he finally caught up they revived him with beef-steak tea. He had eaten almost nothing all day.

As they approached the fort they saw a delegation of Indians coming to meet them; Rundle's guide informed him that these were the Crees they were expecting to find at the fort. Gravely, with stately ceremony the natives greeted him. For a moment the little missionary was almost overwhelmed. With quiet courtesy the tall Sons of the Plains surrounded him. These were Blackfoot!

"Blackfoot, Piegan, Blood . . . These were the Indians so blackly painted in history and whose name alone is enough to cause alarm . . ." They gathered in large numbers at the fort while Mr. Rundle was there. "Clean, beautifully dressed . . . They loaded me with kindness and by their conduct completely won my affection."

He apparently won affection and regard in return. Among the natives he was remembered with goodwill in many camps for more than forty years after his departure from the West.

Having accepted an invitation to visit the Blackfoot camp on the Bow River in the spring, he rode for weeks over "the ocean-like plains spread at the base of the Rocky Mountains which rose sublimely in the distance . . ." When he and his companions had exhausted their provisions a Blood Indian family saved them: "hungry—they fed us—strangers, they took us in." Scouts carried the message that the distinguished visitor was approaching as he neared the camp; two chiefs were sent to meet him with a handsome white horse on which he was ceremoniously welcomed into their midst.

Mr. Rundle had not only a passion for his calling but a passion for the mountains. In June of 1842 he returned to the Indians of the southern plains. Riding toward Old Bow Fort, just west of present-day Calgary, he found the proximity of the Rockies tremendously impressive. "What would my friends in dear old England give to witness them?" From the site of the fort he wandered toward the outlying range but, "after fatiguing myself, I was obliged to return . . . how deceptive the distance is! The mountains are still a long way off . . . What a spectacle to see them painted on the western sky at sunset!"

In November of 1844, ministering to a few isolated families of Mountain Assiniboines, he rode "at last right into the midst of the Rocky Mountains." The surrounding peaks beckoned irresistibly. Leaving his two native travelling companions, Mr. Rundle set out to climb a mountain, alone. Hours later with the summit still far above him, he turned back; beneath his feet loose rocks impeded his progress; beside him "steep slopes fall away into nothingness." The descent took longer than expected and as he had eaten nothing all day he nearly fainted from weakness and exhaustion as he crossed a projecting ridge. When he had negotiated the last hazard he wondered how he would find his way back to camp before nightfall. Fortunately his companions found him.

In four days he was in "a beautiful valley" where he sketched Devil's Head Mountain, then rode back onto the plains.

Three years later he returned to the Rockies. On June 27, 1847, he held religious services with a tiny congregation of Indians; their place of worship "a small plain ... quite in among the mountains ... The scenery is most magnificent." It is assumed, with good reason, that Mr. Rundle's "never-to-be-forgotten" Sunday was spent on the site of modern Banff. During the next few days he rode to Lake Minnewanka where he met another band of natives; as the moon rose above the silent peaks, he held evening services. It was his last visit to the mountains he loved. On the morning of his departure he blazed a tree "RTR July 1, 1847" and, proceeding "through an opening in the mountains, left them."

The year before, another chronicler of the mountains had met Mr. Rundle at Fort Carlton and recorded an amusing episode. Artist Paul Kane and Mr. Rundle were leaving for Fort Edmonton with Chief Factor Rowand and the departing travellers were being accorded a rousing Indian farewell. Mr. Rundle had brought his cat from Edmonton, fearing that it might be eaten in his absence. He now had it safely concealed "in the breast of his capote" and tied to the pummel of his saddle with a four-foot string. The Indians were vigourously shaking hands with the little party ("a practice to which they have taken a particular fancy") and "Mr. Rundle, a great favourite, was receiving a large share of their attention." The general uproar excited the horses—and the hidden cat. To the Indians' complete astonishment (they couldn't understand where it had suddenly come from) it leapt from its concealment, bit and scratched Mr. Rundle's plunging horse which promptly threw the poor minister over its head. He wasn't hurt, and "everyone was convulsed with laughter"; the Indians joined the merriment with great "screeching and yelling" which "rendered the whole scene indescribably ludicrous." The little missionary was more concerned with the fate of his pet than with the amusement of his companions; it was with great regret that he consented to leave her behind to be brought up later in the boats.

In 1847, however, as he was returning to Fort Edmonton from Banff, Mr. Rundle suffered a more serious fall from a horse, breaking his wrist. Never in robust health, he had for eight and a half years selflessly faced the hardships of frontier life, but when the fracture didn't heal properly he had to return to England. Perpetuating the memory of the gentle missionary, Mount Rundle towers serenely over the valley of the Bow at Banff.

AN ARTIST'S GLORIOUS ADVENTURE

Since his boyhood days in eastern Canada, Paul Kane had dreamed of travelling in the wild Northwest where Indians hunted buffalo on the great plains, where mighty rivers flowed from snow-capped mountains. A period of study and painting abroad only sharpened his taste for the glorious adventure. Carrying a sheaf of sketches, he sought out Sir George Simpson at Lachine, Quebec and explained his desired project. Favourably impressed with the young artist's work and his eagerness to paint the North American scene, Simpson commissioned twelve paintings immediately and arranged passage for him with the westward-bound canoes.

The brigade was already on its way to Sault Ste. Marie on May 9th, 1846, when Kane and Sir George left Toronto to overtake them. The steamer stopped overnight at Mackinaw and Kane was assured by the ship's master that he could stay ashore, but when he arrived at the appointed time for departure next morning, Sir George and the steamer had left without him! Since there wouldn't be another boat for four days this was "a damper of no ordinary magnitude." A frenzied search produced a skiff and three teenage boys willing to attempt the forty-five-mile voyage across Lake Huron and the "forty-five miles on a river with which we were totally unacquainted . . ." In a stiff wind with only a blanket sail, they paddled furiously over the lake and toiled all night against the stiff current. At dawn they caught up to the steamer near Sault Ste. Marie. Great was Sir George's astonishment to find the abandoned passenger on board again!

However the brigade was still a two days' journey ahead and Sir George, setting out in his state canoe, had no room for a passenger. (It is difficult to know which sentiment was uppermost in the busy governor's mind: admiration for the young man's persistence, or impatience with the extra responsibilities he presented.) In any event he himself had to be off and advised his determined protegé to catch the company schooner and meet the brigade at Fort William. Kane arrived there a day late! "I was compelled to trespass on the kindness of a gentleman with a canoe . . .": once again paddlers raced to catch the westward-speeding governor. They made it. Sir George congratulated Kane "on overcoming the difficulties of starting"! An exciting beginning to what must surely be one of the most interesting sketching expeditions ever undertaken.

Weeks later, having left the canoe brigade near Fort Garry, Paul Kane rode slowly over the western plains where he found it "indispensably necessary to wear a veil" against the plagues of mosquitoes. He was on his way to hunt the buffalo.

Riding with the Métis into the midst of a herd of "four or five thousand," the scene "became one of intense excitement." In full pursuit, Kane's mount tripped in a badger hole, throwing its rider "with such violence, that I was completely stunned . . . I was speedily remounted . . . and coming up with a large bull" brought it down with his first shot. He charged after another and wounded it. Facing him, the great beast pawed the earth, "bellowing and glaring savagely . . ." It looked "so fine" that the artist dismounted to sketch it! It charged. He had to dash for his life.

Travelling from Fort Pitt, "during the whole of the three days that it took us to reach Edmonton House, we saw nothing else but these animals covering the plains as far as the eye could reach, and so numerous were they, that at times they impeded our progress, filling the air with dust almost to suffocation." In the evenings he sketched, enjoying the "soft warm haziness of Indian summer . . . the unbroken stillness, the enchanting repose . . . the golden prairie with sleepy buffalo grazing on undulating hills."

At Fort Edmonton he was told of the Indians who had found a keg of rum in the river and were about to make the most of this good fortune, when one of them begged his companions to consider a moment. Suppose it were a trick? After all, the white man was rather annoyed because some Indians had shot at the brigade last year; maybe he had poisoned the rum and left it here in a spirit of revenge! They were persuaded to exercise due caution and eight old women were recruited as official tasters. As the only effect produced by this test was that "they commenced singing with great glee," the warriors soon stopped "their potations." Obviously the contents of that keg were too good to be wasted on old women!

On October 6th, five months after leaving Toronto, Kane left with the fall brigade of sixteen men travelling with sixty-five horses to Fort Assiniboine and on to Athabasca Pass. Making "slow and fatiguing" progress through the thick woods, they were overtaken by Colin Fraser who was on the way to his post at Jasper House. He enlivened the monotonous journey for Kane with accounts of his experiences as Sir George Simpson's piper when they had travelled "among Indians who had seen few or no white men." Colin, very stately in his Highland uniform, had "carried the pipes" and when Sir George swept up to the isolated forts "the bagpipes were put in requisition, much to the astonishment of the natives who . . . of course never beheld so extraordinary a looking man, or such a musical instrument, which astonished them as much as the sound produced"!

Colin hurried ahead to his post; at Fort Assiniboine the cavalcade took to canoes on the river and followed him. They were packing along five thousand of the finest otter skins—annual payment Sir George had arranged to make to the Russians for trading in their territory. The water was low and dragging this precious cargo with lines from shore delayed them seriously.

On October 29th, "their outline scarcely perceptible" in the haze, Kane had his first view of "the sublime and apparently endless chain of the Rocky Mountains." The next day the men greeted this fine view "with a hearty cheer." Two days later they camped at the mighty fortress of Roche Miette where a howling blizzard raged; ". . . it is scarcely possible to conceive the intense force with which the wind howled through a gap formed by the perpendicular rock called 'Miette's Rock' and a mountain opposite . . ." Before the force of the gale the tall pines waved "like fields of grain."

Kane had heard the story of the voyageur for whom the mountain is named. In French Canadian folklore Miette had become a legendary figure

Roche Miette (with Disaster Point at extreme left) where, according to legend, the French Canadian voyageur dangled his feet from the beetling summit and enjoyed "de nice smoke wit St. Peter on de gate."
COURTESY WHYTE MUSEUM OF THE CANADIAN ROCKIES, BANFF (M517/42)

with prodigious capacities for travelling in the Northwest; none could excel his gifts as a fiddler and spinner of yarns with which he enlivened many a campfire. And no one matched his feats of daring. According to legend, Miette and some companions passed the great mountain on the Athabasca one day and his companions laughingly pointed to its beetling summit with the taunt: "You tell us next how one time you smoke de pipe on top!" So he climbed it and sat on the edge dangling his feet over the frightful abyss. When he rejoined his friends he remarked casually: "I been have de nice smoke up dere wit St. Peter on de gate"!

The tale may not be the absolute truth but Miette was an inhabitant well known in the valley. In the 1830s he was "a Company servant" who hauled coal from the Roche Miette area to Jasper House and to Henry House at the mouth of the river also named for him; he lived from time to time where today's Jasper Park Lodge nestles beside Lac Beauvert.

When the men who had been sent ahead to Jasper House for horses returned to Roche Miette, Kane and the brigade forded round Disaster Point with water and ice floes at saddle height and, "cold, wet and famished," arrived at Jasper House where a blazing fire and five or six pounds of roast mountain sheep soon set things right. Colin Fraser's establishment offered hospitality and a high degree of togetherness. "The dwelling house is composed of two rooms, of about fourteen or fifteen feet square each. One of them is used by all comers and goers: Indians, voyageurs, and traders, men, women, and children being huddled together indiscriminately; the other room being devoted to the exclusive occupation of Colin and his family consisting of a Cree squaw, and nine interesting half-breed children."

Preparing for the portage, Kane had an Indian make enormous snowshoes for him. On November 5th they started out with thirteen loaded horses; for the next few days their route "lay sometimes over almost inaccessible crags and at others through gloomy tangled forests." The cold increased and the snow became so deep that they had to stop a day and fashion snowshoes for the rest of the party. Already delayed by attempting to transport the otter skins, they were now really worried: the men with boats and provisions awaiting them at Boat Encampment might despair of their coming and leave, with "disastrous consequences" for the party advancing slowly through Athabasca Pass.

A woman was making the arduous trek; one of Chief Factor Rowand's men was accompanied by his Métis wife and, when the cavalcade donned snowshoes, Mrs. Lane soon proved to be "one of our best pedestrians." Some years before, a young wife had been climbing this same route, going to join her husband; she lagged and no one noticed until camping time that she was missing. Her track was followed back to "a perpendicular rock overhanging the roaring torrent." She had lost her footing and plunged to her death over the precipice.

It took Kane and his companions seven days to get to the summit of the pass. In "intense cold" the platform of green logs was again raised beside the Committee's Punch Bowl and weary travellers slept with feet to the fire.

On the final stages of the steep descent to the Columbia, Kane stayed behind to sketch for a time. Resuming his journey, he came to a river which he could scarcely believe the party had crossed until he saw their tracks on the opposite shore. He soon learned how he must travel for a time: snow-shoes off, wade across the icy stream; emerge and struggle to replace frozen moccasins and unwieldy snowshoes; run to restore circulation to numbed limbs and then plunge in again. At the deepest fords the travellers went shoulder to shoulder and carried Mrs. Lane. After three days they staggered in to Boat Encampment at five o'clock in the afternoon; they had eaten nothing all day but a bit of pemmican soup. The brigade with whom they were to rendezvous had been waiting nine days and was preparing to leave next day.

With "heartfelt satisfaction . . . we exchanged the wearisome snowshoe for the comfortable boats, and the painful anxiety of half-satisfied appetites for a well-stocked larder." True, the twelve hundred-mile voyage ahead with the perils of the Columbia's "innumerable rapids" would have its dangers, but "we no longer had to toil on in clothes frozen stiff, . . . half-famished, and with the consciousness ever before us, that whatever our hardships and fatigue, rest was sure destruction in the cold solitudes of those dreary mountains." In fifteen days they reached the Columbia District, where Kane wandered and sketched until the autumn of 1847 when, in cold wet weather, he made his way with the brigade back to Athabasca Pass.

This time they had to wait at Boat Encampment for the westward brigade coming across the mountains on horseback. For eighteen anxious days they waited as provisions dwindled and the men "performed charms to hasten the arrival of the brigade" by erecting crosses with one arm pointing to the east. The day after its arrival the entire party took to the river and hurried south along the Columbia, leaving Kane to cross the pass with four Indians. On October 31st he started out, in charge of returning the fifty-six horses brought over by the Columbia-bound party.

It was a remarkable ascent. The horses became mired in river beds; they stuck fast with loads wedged between trees; they were unloaded, forced through and reloaded; they brushed the packs off in their heaving efforts on the narrow track or ran "helter-skelter through the woods," scrambling up steep hills. The forests rang with eloquent French profanity—"there being no oaths in the Indian language . . . I never passed such a busy, tiresome, noisy, and disagreeable day in my life." One day a packhorse fell over a twenty-five-foot cliff and had to be rescued. Strangely, his load was not deranged, nor was he hurt, but he "certainly looked a little *bothered*"!

At the summit the animals wallowed in deep snow. There was no feed for them at the Committee's Punch Bowl and the weather turned bitterly cold. Kane's long red beard was a solid mass of ice, but they scarcely dared to stop, even to eat. They "pushed on to the utmost of our power" under the threat of a sudden snowstorm which would mean almost certain death to such a tiny contingent in the desolate Whirlpool valley.

The temperature dipped to fifty-six below zero but the storm didn't strike until they reached the Athabasca, six days after leaving Boat Encampment. The blinding blizzard obscured the opposite bank but they managed the crossing with the horses—Kane's precious sketches were carried on the riders' shoulders. The next day the storm continued unabated; hurrying on toward Jasper House, they were forced to dismount and run to ward off serious frostbite. Reaching their destination at last, "we soon forgot our trouble over a good piece of mountain sheep . . ."

Kane's trials were not over. As usual there was little food or game at the post and he had to make his way to Fort Edmonton. With two natives he set out, the three of them "cheering ourselves with the idea that none know what they can bear until they are tried."

Tried they were. It was an incredibly rigorous trek to their first stop, Fort Assiniboine. Often perilously close to starvation, struggling over great masses of ice heaved up on the frozen river, they took bone-chilling plunges into the frigid water; with feet cut by the strings of moccasins in which perspiration formed razor-sharp films of ice, they left behind a trail of blood. Long days spent on snowshoes left them with mal de racquet which made their insteps feel as "if the broken and sharpened bones were grinding together at every step . . ." The hardships were borne.

They reached Fort Edmonton in plenty of time for Christmas festivities, doubly enjoyable after their gruelling journey. Kane had by then recovered sufficiently to put on a spirited performance at the dance in the great hall. "The dancing was most picturesque . . . Occasionally I . . . led out a young Cree squaw, who sported enough beads around her neck to have made a pedlar's fortune, and having led her into the centre of the room, I danced round her with all the agility I was capable of exhibiting, to some highland-reel tune which the fiddler played with great vigour, whilst my partner with grave face kept jumping up and down, both feet off the ground at once . . . I believe, however, that we elicited a great deal of applause from the Indian squaws and children, who sat squatting round the room on the floor."

A few days later he went by dogsled to Fort Pitt with a colourful wedding party. In six graceful one-passenger carioles, each pulled by four dogs gaily decorated with embroidered and fringed saddle cloths, pompons, feathers and tiny bells, they skimmed over the frozen river, the bride travelling in her own specially made, beautifully painted cariole. Soon "the wedding tour" was interrupted by "a diverting occurrence." They unexpectedly overtook a herd of buffalo and "notwithstanding all the efforts of the men, the dogs went in furious pursuit." As "all the sledges, carioles, dogs and men" raced across the river, the buffalo, in alarm, dashed for the steep banks and clumsily tried to scramble up. The foremost slipped, rolled, and knocked those behind on top of one another into the snowdrift below where they were entangled with men, dogs, smashed sleds—and somewhere in "the wild scene of uproar and confusion," a bride! Miraculously, no one was hurt; the sleds were repaired and the wedding party continued on its way.

Kane returned to Fort Edmonton and journeyed to Rocky Mountain House to sketch the Indians there, then left for home with the spring brigade in May. When he at last reached Sault Ste. Marie where he'd made his desperate dash to catch the outgoing canoes more than two years before, his "greatest hardship was trying to sleep in a civilized bed."

He worked for eleven years to finish his paintings and in 1859 his book, *Wanderings of an Artist*, was published. The same year a westward-bound visitor called on him. Undoubtedly Kane's paintings and reminiscences about his glorious adventure were of unusual interest to his distinguished guest—the Rockies' first aristocratic big game hunter.

A Patrician Hunter

The tall thirty-two-year-old Earl of Southesk had been ill and restless after the death of his wife and expressed to friends a desire "to travel in some part of the world where good sport could be met with among the larger animals, and where at the same time I might recruit my health by an active open-air life in a healthy climate." Canada was recommended by an influential Hudson's Bay Company official who made arrangements for the handsome Scot to travel under the patronage of Sir George Simpson. Leaving for the West in the spring of 1859, their journey together held its share of dash and drama.

Seventy-two years old, in poor health and nearly blind, the governor was, as usual, going west for the annual meeting of the company's Council of the Northern Department, travelling this time by rail and steamer to St. Paul, Minnesota—he wanted to examine the possibility of transporting goods from there to Fort Garry. The escort ordered to meet him was delayed by floods but if the earl expected the Little Emperor to wait for travel conditions to improve, he was soon disappointed. "There was no help for it," Southesk observed; "We were all bound to obey our leader, even if we thought his decisions doubtful or mistaken." On three hours' notice Sir George was dashing ahead in a covered cart—he was going to meet the tardy escort. Menacing Indians clamoured for presents, tried to overturn his cart and fired shots over his head. They didn't deter him.

The earl, so elated at the thought of being freed from the constrictions of civilization, soon discovered that it wasn't to be an unmitigated blessing. He awoke one stormy night to find himself immersed in an icy pool in his flooded tent. Stoically he decided that little could be done until daylight; he "improved matters by turning my india-rubber bath bottom upwards, with a pillow on top of it, so as to form an island," donned a waterproof over soaking garments, lit a candle and wrote in his journal.

When Sir George left him at Fort Garry he offered valuable advice, the services of one of his best voyageurs, Toma, and alerted all the posts ahead to provide the distinguished traveller with every convenience.

Lavishly provisioned with a wagon, three carts, two large tents, a portable table and stool, all manner of tools and utensils, presents for the Indians, delicacies such as sugar, jam, biscuits and eggs (but no wine or liquor) and a specially fitted cart loaded with an elaborate armoury for the hunt (and to "bid defiance to any parties of Indians"), Southesk left the fort on the fifteenth of June, 1859, accompanied by seven men—including a gamekeeper from his estate—and fifteen horses.

Soon they overtook the Métis going on their semiannual buffalo hunt. In long columns, hundreds of carts moved over the prairie: wild dogs dashed in and out; wives and daughters travelled in carts "of every hue." Beside them, gay in blue brass-buttoned capotes and beaded belts, the hunters rode "their showiest steeds. Everything sparkled with gaiety and life." However, the discriminating earl did not fancy "the cotton gowns of the women, shapeless, stayless, uncrinolined, displaying the flatness of their unprojecting figures."

Leaving them, Southesk's party made its way slowly westward over the seemingly endless prairie which was broken here and there with bluffs and little lakes. Tiger lilies, wild roses, strawberry blossoms and bluebells made "a vast oriental carpet thrown upon the plain."

Like his master, the earl's favourite buffalo-running horse, Bichon, was something of a gourmet, wandering off the path to browse on tufts of the choicest flowers. Slightly less engaging was Bichon's reluctance to be separated from his companions—he neighed so loudly and incessantly on these occasions that he frightened off the game and "means were taken to break him of this habit. At length he has learnt that this is a forbidden practice, so he takes great pains to check himself, and at any moment of forgetfullness or

James Carnegie, Earl of Southesk, dressed for "sport . . . among the larger animals."
COURTESY SIR CHARLES ALEXANDER CARNEGIE, EARL OF SOUTHESK, KINNAIRD CASTLE, SCOTLAND

strong temptation, changes his incipient neigh into the funniest little muf-
fled squeaks, ending in a sort of low, appealing sigh." Poor Bichon's creamy
coloured sides often streamed with blood as they rode through insect-
infested plains and woods: "venomous eye-blinding, hard-skinned little
sandflies . . . bulldogs with scissory clippers . . . mosquitoes on the wet
ground . . . ants everywhere—it is maddening"!

At the end of the day the earl sat at his tent door watching the sunset and
the animals while the men told tales or sang round the fire; the frogs croaked
and cranes uttered their lonely cries as he wrote in his journal. And then he
settled down in his own tent and by candlelight enjoyed his volumes of
Shakespeare. One rainy afternoon after a session with *Two Gentlemen of
Verona*, he wrote: "This open-air life suits me well, though, when one con-
siders it bit by bit, it does not seem so very charming. Long wearisome riding, indifferent monotonous eating, no sport to speak of, hard bed upon the
ground, hot sun, wet, no companion of my own class; nevertheless I am
happier than I have been for years."

Soon there was "sport to speak of." Buffalo covered the plains. "The deep
rolling voice of the mighty multitude . . . like the booming of a distant ocean
. . . Putting spurs into Bichon's yellow sides I sailed after the cows . . ." With
Bichon straining every nerve in the excitement of the chase, Southesk stood
in the stirrups and "fired into the heaving mass." He got the cow they needed
for food. Now, for "a large and perfectly unblemished head" as a trophy. He
picked a bull with "long perfect horns, most luxurious mane and beard" and
with Bichon going gallantly, stuck to him for two miles, "moving in a sort of
triangular enclosure of living walls . . . I closed on him, down went his head,
onward he came in full charge . . ." Bichon cantered out of the way and
approached again. Up went the bull's tail in sign of battle. Bichon slipped
neatly round and Southesk sent a bullet through the great beast's heart. "I
got off my panting pony and took a long look at my bull, feasting my eyes on
his noble proportions . . ."

One day after dinner, "without the slightest warning, a storm of noise
broke upon us—bells jingled, whips cracked—the tramp of galloping horses
resounded close at hand . . . In a semi-circle which completely hemmed us
in, a number of armed and mostly naked warriors were rushing down the
slope." Blackfoot! Everyone in camp reached for guns—but they had been

63

put away because it was Sunday! When the approaching riders were only a few feet away, they stopped, stared, and then trotted up with friendly smiles. They were Crees, who supposed they had come upon a camp of Blackfoot. "They planned to surprise us—and so indeed they did!"

At Fort Edmonton the leisurely trek across the prairies was at an end. Exchanging carts for pack saddles, on August 17th Southesk and his men rode into the difficult terrain to the west—the earliest recorded travellers to follow approximately the route of today's Edmonton-Jasper highway. The usual trail had been via Fort Assiniboine; Henry Moberly of Jasper House had opened the more direct trail just the year before. The earl's bold plan was to go from Jasper House south along the mountains to Kootenay Plains, but in two days he met Mr. Moberly who reported that there was no game in the Jasper valley and advised the aristocratic hunter to travel up the McLeod River instead, then proceed south to Kootenay Plains. This would provide "about a ten day's march with a view of the highest peaks in a country which he believed no European had ever seen . . . where bears and wild sheep were certain to be abundant."

The vicissitudes of the trail soon became very apparent. The track was barely wide enough for a loaded animal to pass between the trees, and the horses "were forever trying to escape from the treacherous boggy ditch . . . leaping to one or the other side of the trench as they endeavoured to make their way along the firmer margin, but there was seldom much room there, so after a struggle that displaced or scattered their packs, down they inevitably plunged and continued their floundering in the mire . . . By the end of the day my knees were one mass of bruises from cannoning off the fir stems, when Rowland made sudden dashes for the bank, or attempted to rush into some opening where the trees grew wide enough apart to allow passage for himself, though none for his rider's limbs . . . If ever I get home I shall know how to appreciate comfort. Still, health is better than comfort."

In the evening he read. "I believe intellectual reading in moderation, to be a rest for the body after hard labour; it seems to act as a counter-irritant, drawing off fatigue from the muscles to the brain."

After many trying days—"One solitary gleam of consolation enlivened this weary day: an unexpected far-distant view of two grand peaks of the Rocky Mountains over which a thundercloud cast a solemn, leaden shade. It was but an imperfect view, but so marvellous was the contrast between the damp, confined darkness of our track through the dripping fir-trees and the sudden freedom of an open sky bounded only by the magnificent mountain-forms, that for a moment I was quite overwhelmed . . . All weariness vanished away, and I felt myself ready for any labours that might bring me nearer to so splendid a goal."

One evening, eleven days after leaving Fort Edmonton, the clouds that had obscured the mountains disappeared to reveal that "most glorious sight—the Rocky Mountain Ranges stretching along the horizon as far as the eye could reach . . . Below us rolled the river among dark pines; hills, also covered with pines—some black and scorched with fire, some green and flourishing—filled up the prospect for many miles; then came flat bare eminences, the footstools of the loftier range, and then uprose the mountains themselves, rugged in form, peaked and tabled, and scored with gashes . . ." The sight left him with feelings "almost too deep for utterance."

Antoine, his old Métis guide from Fort Edmonton, now led them through very rugged country; the nights turned cold and even though Southesk wrapped his head in three blankets and piled on all his clothing he was unable to keep warm until the sun rose above the surrounding peaks. Fortunately he had obtained a black stallion from a hunter they'd met. Jasper, "an admirable horse," was "expert at crossing deep ravines and cared nothing for muskegs, however deep and bad; even when sinking in a swamp he would take the opportunity to snatch a bite of grass if his nose got near enough the surface." Scrambling over fallen timber on steep hillsides he would sometimes, "while drawing himself over a log, stop half-way and begin eating any tempting mouthful that happened to lie handy."

At the dinner halt, "in the midst of noble scenery," Southesk spent a very pleasant hour reading *Macbeth* as the men chatted good-humouredly and prepared new delicacies for their noble master's discriminating palate: moose, "excellent but tough"; porcupine, which Toma called porty-pig, "rich and fat when roasted but like delicate mutton when boiled"; beaver back-bone—"exquisite, better than suckling-pig"; beaver tails, "like pork fat sandwiched between layers of Finnan haddock"; the hind leg of siffleur—"a miniature haunch of venison." An Iroquois family who travelled with him for a time introduced another culinary adventure—skunk done to a turn on a spit. It was white and tender, but "a suspicion of skunkiness" kept him from cleaning his plate.

Pierre, the Iroquois father, interrupted the earl's reading one evening, urgently appealing for help with his sick baby. Southesk found the mother crying over the nearly naked baby and "hoped Heaven would enable me to do their child some good and soothe the parents by some show of active measures . . . I dared not give medicine, knowing that pills and powders fit for men might kill a ten-month baby—fearing, besides, lest if the child died, I should be held by these untaught people the cause of its death . . ." Putting on "an air of decision," he sent to his camp for a pot of weak tea, asked to have the fire built up and the baby wrapped in blankets. Then he had the mother hold the baby near the fire and spoon tea down its throat. "With perfect confidence in my skill," she fed the poor shrieking, struggling infant. Gradually it lay quiet, flushed and relaxed; in the morning he was relieved to learn that the baby was almost well.

Before reaching Edson on today's Edmonton-Jasper highway, Southesk left the usual trail (dim though that was) and struck into country that was not to be mapped in detail for many years. Sixty-five years passed before surveyor-historian J. N. Wallace laid down Southesk's route through the Rockies, assisted by mountain sketches in the earl's book.

By early September he was travelling amid the peaks which form the eastern boundary of Jasper Park, camping for a time beside present-day Medicine Tent River where he and his men climbed a mountain and erected a cairn. "I am the first European who has visited this valley, and if I might have the geographic honour of giving my name to some spot of earth, I should choose the mountain near which the two rivers rise." He felt, however, that this prominent peak near the source of today's Southesk and Medicine Tent rivers might be visible from another valley and be therefore already "appropriated." But no one could dispute the one he'd climbed. It is now Southesk Cairn Mountain and the fine mountain which was his first choice is, rightly, Mount Southesk.

Southesk rode along the valley amid "scenery of surpassing magnificence." His men broke camp and as they came to meet him "they formed a bright picture . . . all life, dash, rattle and glitter . . . so grandly backgrounded by the stately rocks: ribbons streaming, guns swaying, whips flashing, gay colours sparkling in the sun; some approaching at a quick trot, others dashing after vagrant steeds, or urging the heavy-laden pack-horses, who jogged along like elephants with castles on their backs . . ." McBeath, a tall Scot with dark moustache and beard, military belt and sword, red blanket saddlecloth on his coal black horse; Toma, the earl's personal attendant ("a most faithful and excellent fellow"), massive, swarthy, black eyes twinkling with humour; Lagrace, "that original and amusing old man . . . who enlivened our halts after the weariest marches," colourful in purple shirt and white camp decorated with scarlet streamers and an ancient eagle's feather—the mountains they rode beneath that day are now named for them.

The aristocratic hunter had travelled an enormous distance in search of "good sport . . . among the larger animals." At last he saw them—a fine herd of bighorn sheep, stately old rams with "handsome" horns. Southesk got one. But old Antoine, with a gun the earl considered "a most extraordinary little implement, so short and small, so bound up and mended with leather, brass-headed tacks and altogether so worn and weather beaten," bagged a beauty! With his own superb weapon, Southesk dashed off in hot pursuit of one equally fine. He wounded the one he wanted and hurried to finish it off. Whisky insisted on following.

Whisky had been befriended by the earl on the prairie. "A sleigh dog, fat as a pig" with a four-inch tail; "one look at him dispelled melancholy; every movement he made was a farce . . . With his cunningly timorous countenance and sleekly rounded plebian body, he was a true Sancho Panza of a dog . . ." But as a hunting companion he left something to be desired. He either ran ahead excitedly or lagged, "squeaking loudly, if I make any threatening movement." When Southesk whipped out his telescope to find the ram, Whisky yelped horribly, thinking his master wielded "some whip of dangerous new design."

The earl's chase took him down a steep mountain side, with scree and rock sliding treacherously while Whisky whined above in terror and sent down showers of stones. He scrambled down somehow at last, to where the earl had found the magnificent ram silhouetted on a cliff thirty feet directly above. The hunter took careful aim and fired two shots. The great beast leapt in an arc and crashed at his feet. It was his finest trophy, the horns measuring 38-1/2 inches round the curve. But in its fall it had nearly crushed poor

Whisky, "who must have entered this day in his journal as one of horrors"!

Five more excellent trophies were taken from that hunt but it was not "an unmingled pleasure." The successful hunter had twinges of conscience about the "slaughter"; however, he consoled himself with the thought that apart from the animals taken for trophies, they had only killed what they needed for food and probably that herd would "never again be alarmed by the sight of man."

The next day a snowstorm struck; the men sang round the fire in their tent and Southesk wrote in his journal. "To be storm-staid for an indefinitely long time in the heart of the Rocky Mountains, with winter stealing on apace, and a long and difficult journey before one is not an encouraging prospect. Nor, disguise it as one may, is it very enlivening to sit, with wet feet, under a thin canvas covering that does not quite exclude the keen north wind." However, it was better than "wallowing in luxury and feeble indolence" and manfully he turned to *Titus Andronicus*—"a most disagreeable play," he decided.

Heading toward the Brazeau River, it became equally disagreeable to learn that Antoine now didn't know the route. Overhearing anxious discussions among his men, Southesk was convinced that they were trying to get him out of the mountains "by the quickest and easiest road, instead of exploring the finer and less-traversed routes, according to my frequently-expressed desire." Outraged, he turned back and the chastened men joined him. He explained and "cordiality seemed quite restored."

And a "less-traversed route" they certainly found! They missed today's Job Pass and came instead to "an impassable rock wall that stood right across our path." Clambering over steep ridges and burnt timber, men and animals were badly cut; then, cutting steps in the almost perpendicular frozen slope and dragging the horses with ropes, they made "an incredible ascent" to the summit. "I doubt if any human being ever came to the place by our road," Southesk declared.

It was mid-September and "fiercely cold"; their tents and blankets were always sheeted with ice; no one was certain of the road ahead. Their predicament was serious. At last they found a stream which eventually took them down to the warmer Kootenay Plains, where they rafted over the North Saskatchewan and made their way along the Siffleur River to Pipestone Pass.

Along that high, bleak valley they rode in snow and mist with "only enough of the surrounding rocks and mountains visible . . . to show how much noble scenery was being lost to me forever." Food was getting very low; Southesk was desperately weak and exhausted. The candles were gone, but Toma improvised with hardened sheep fat so that his master could at least read *Romeo and Juliet.* One man was in agony with cramps and they had to plod along slowly. Southesk was shocked to find that without consulting anyone the sick man had been rash enough to "swallow a whole charge of gunpowder with water" as remedy for what ailed him. He recovered.

Weak as he was, Southesk made a desperate attempt to get mountain goats—these animals had up to now been so elusive that he had become obsessed with the "Enchanted Beasts." When they finally spotted some, the two he killed were not very good specimens; even so, in attempting to get them he and Antoine were threatened with a cold night on the mountain, "like flies on a wall." The old guide managed to get his master down. When the party emerged into the Bow Valley their situation was serious indeed for they had only two days' provisions left.

Then one evening they were surprised to hear the sound of Christian hymn singing in the lonely valley. They came upon a little band of Stoney Indians, a fortunate encounter, for a gun, ammunition, tobacco, clothing and blankets, trinkets for the women and a fine-toothed comb ("certainly it seemed needed") changed hands and Southesk's larder was filled with moose meat. Two of the band's young men were taken along to Fort Edmonton to bring back more blankets, ammunition, knives, kettles and clothing for these good and needy people. After camping at today's Cascade Mountain, the patrician traveller made his way out of the mountains. At his last mountain camp he pronounced the moose nose dinner "very good."

On October 12th he was back at Fort Edmonton where, after a short rest, he parted with Whisky (who preferred "the ignoble ease" of the fort) and started a two-month winter trek to Fort Garry. When they reached Fort Carlton on the way, he and his party equipped themselves for winter travel, the earl in "a cap of marten with mink under earpieces, fingerless gloves" and a special luxury of his own invention, "immense buffalo-robe boots reaching to the knee." All the men enjoyed the luxury of enormous caps of fur, some made of whole fox skins—even Duncan, the impeccable Scottish gamekeeper usually so conservatively turned out in his "grey shooting suit," was resplendent in "a white capote with hood . . . I hardly knew him!"

Before that, in agonizing cold with his beard "hung with icicles," storm-bound on the featureless prairie, the earl had reflected beside the guttering candle in his tent. "Why am I enduring this? For pleasure—was the only answer, and the idea seemed so absurd that I laughed myself warm. Then as the circulation returned, I remembered that I was taking a lesson in that most valuable of human studies—the art of Endurance; an art the poor learn perforce, and the rich do well to teach themselves . . ." On the other hand, "I often think of the story of an officer who was so anxious to harden himself before a campaign against the Kaffirs, that he used to leave his comfortable quarters and sleep uncovered in the open air during the worst of weather . . . When marching orders came he was too rheumatic to go with his regiment."

The doughty earl seems not to have suffered such afflictions from his trials in Canada. In fact his health was apparently well "recruited" for he returned home, married a second time, had eight more children and lived to the respectable age of seventy-eight.

When he was leaving the mountains he saw evidence of events foreshadowing momentous changes in the Rockies. At Old Bow Fort he met six Americans going to search for gold in the Fraser River; when he emerged from the valley of the Pipestone he found a tree blazed a month before by Dr. James Hector. The two Scots, undoubtedly the only Europeans travelling in the area, just missed each other along the Pipestone. Both were homeward bound: Southesk with his trophies after a successful hunting expedition, Dr. Hector after a far-reaching exploration of mountain passes.

Probing the Barrier for Rails and Roads

Civilization was inexorably closing in on the far-flung boundaries of Sir George Simpson's Hudson's Bay empire. The influx of American settlers had wrenched away the profitable Columbia River domain when the international boundary was settled in 1846; a mere twenty-two years later Vancouver Island had also been relinquished and soon British Columbia would join it as a crown colony. At Fort Garry pressure for free trade mounted and in Britain the Hudson's Bay Company's age-old monopoly was being seriously opposed before a parliamentary committee set up in 1857. The Little Emperor rushed to the defense.

But even as the old warrior fought for the company's right to retain its privileges, a handsome young Irish sportsman was preparing for an expedition which would strike another blow at its exclusive reign in the Northwest.

Captain John Palliser's proposed expedition got the backing of the British government, which needed facts about the company's territories. Could settlers be sent there or was most of it, as Sir George stoutly maintained, unsuitable for cultivation? What about the possibilities for roads and railways across that vast extent of country stretching between the eastern provinces and the colony on the Pacific—could they surmount the great barrier of the Rockies?

The four scientists on the Palliser expedition compiled the first comprehensive report on conditions in what was to become western Canada, and for three years, with their adventure-loving leader, they made the first large-scale incursion into the territory of the Blackfoot Indians.

That they encountered almost no hostility from the Indians—and they were often surrounded by as many as two thousand of them—can be attributed largely to Palliser's notable prowess as a hunter and horseman and to the reputation of the expedition's youngest member, a twenty-three-year-old Scot with the ink hardly dry on his medical diploma, who was as well a most enthusiastic and competent geologist.

Dr. James Hector earned fame as a great "medicine man" by ministering to the needs of the natives (a service which Palliser acknowledged as facilitating the expedition's excursions into their midst). Equally important (as his Métis guide Peter Erasmus fondly remembered years later), his brisk, affable manner, his ability to ride or tramp on snowshoes with the best of them and his readiness to pitch into all the tasks and hardships of frontier life, "won him admiration in many teepees that never saw the man." He penetrated deeper into what are now Banff, Jasper, Kootenay and Yoho parks than any white man preceding him and ventured into country rarely if ever visited by the Indians.

The Palliser expedition's westward push was halted for the first winter at Fort Carlton and from there in January of 1858 Hector skimmed by dogsled the 393 miles over the ice-bound wilderness to Fort Edmonton. After a brief stop he made a six-day dash to Rocky Mountain House. Sleeping outdoors, even two huge fires failed to cut the bitter north wind when the temperature fell to twenty below. But as his party neared David Thompson's old fort in the cold light of dawn Hector got his first glimpse of the Rockies. "The effect was quite exhilarating as they became lighted up rapidly by the pinky hue of morning . . . We got quite excited with the view and went on without halting for about thirty miles . . ."

For two days he searched in the woods for the famous Stoney hunter and guide he'd come to hire for the spring excursion into the mountains; this Indian's name meant "the one with the thumb like a blunt arrow," and as Hector couldn't pronounce it, he called him Nimrod. Arrangements completed with him, Hector returned to Edmonton, mapping the Saskatchewan River and geologizing as he went. Peter Erasmus, son of a Dane and a native woman, was engaged for the spring work also, as were Métis from Lac Ste. Anne. With this important business attended to, he returned to Fort Carlton—skimming along on skates part of the way!

In June of 1858 the whole expedition moved toward the mountains.

For weeks they rode over the plains under the great shallow dome of the western sky. At last, in August, the monotonous trek was over. The Rockies rose starkly before them.

Their reconnaissance of the mountains was to include all possible passes between the international boundary and Athabasca Pass. At Old Bow Fort the expedition divided into three groups. Palliser started for a pass he named Kananaskis, one he'd been told about in 1848 when he was hunting on the American plains—his informant was James Sinclair who had taken the Métis emigrants across White Man Pass in 1841.

In 1854 Sinclair had taken one hundred white people (including his own family) from Fort Garry to settle in the Oregon Territory. Incredible as it seems, twenty-eight men and eleven women with children and infants apparently crossed Kananaskis Pass. Maskepetoon, the guide who had been with Sinclair in 1841, led them from Fort Edmonton, the women and children going in carts, the men driving livestock before them. At the base of the mountains a halt was made—a baby was born but died in twenty-four hours. Here too, they abandoned their carts (seen later by a member of the Palliser expedition) and started on foot to the height of land. This time their guide got lost. They trudged in frosty autumn weather through burnt forests; they bridged streams and crossed fearful abysses. In a gruelling trek they stumbled over shale and boulders and three feet of snow to the summit. It took them thirty days to make the crossing. The emigrants had expected to reach Washington in September—they staggered in on December 16th.

Palliser crossed Kananaskis Pass (presumably, North Kananaskis Pass), descended what is now the Palliser River to its junction with the Kootenay and made his way back east across the mountains by North Kootenay Pass. Another expedition member, Lieutenant Blakiston, travelled south from Old Bow Fort, named the Livingstone Range for the famous African explorer and crossed the Divide by North Kootenay Pass. Returning via the Waterton River (which he named), he camped beside the beautiful lakes in what is now Waterton National Park.

Dr. Hector and the expedition's botanist, the beloved little Monsieur Bourgeau, were instructed to proceed into the mountains by whatever route they found the most promising for their work. So at Old Bow Fort they too left their screeching carts behind and on August 7th, 1858, rode with their men toward the Gap, gateway to Banff National Park.

Free as a breeze, adventure-bound—with what mounting excitement they must have approached the Rockies! The valley narrowed and they entered a dense forest, so cool after the arid plains: emerging, they found themselves in a wide valley hemmed in by ever higher precipices. It was a geologist's paradise! And the dedicated little botanist was in seventh heaven—son of the high Alps, he had longed for this moment. They scrambled up a mountain and like two delighted boys playing Robinson Crusoe, explored an ancient high-roofed cave. They named their first ascent Grotto Mountain, performed their "morning ablutions" where a sparkling waterfall splashed into a clear pool, and around its emerald green margins examined the delicate alpine plants which reminded them of home.

Bourgeau decided to linger with his men in these happy botanical hunting grounds but Hector, eagerly anticipating more geological treasures round every bend, continued up the Bow accompanied by Nimrod, Erasmus and two Red River Métis. Sketching, measuring mountains and mapping, he camped across from the striking Three Sisters and rode toward a fine grey limestone peak. The Indians called this the Mountain Where the Water Falls and Hector named it Cascade Mountain. While they camped "at a beautiful little prairie" where modern Banff nestles, an old Stoney told them he had guided the Reverend Mr. Rundle to Lake Minnewanka and Hector named Mount Rundle for the pioneer missionary.

The little party had brought no food, only some grease, tea and tobacco as Hector had been assured that game would be plentiful. While Nimrod went hunting to replenish the larder and the men cleared the trail ahead, Hector climbed on Cascade Mountain.

Resting on the way, a brilliant pinch of feathers flew into his face—a humming-bird. As he scrambled up he was startled by a "flock of white objects darting away" where he'd seen only rocks; he marvelled at how well the mountain sheep blended with the rocks on which they perched. Only when they fled with white rumps flashing did they become visible, vanishing again as "they wheeled in a mass for another look." He slithered down over scrub timber and with Nimrod visited Bow Falls.

Next day they travelled along the Bow, past a mountain to the north of

Simpson Pass which Hector named for Bourgeau. The old Stoney they'd met at Cascade Mountain had told them that high water in Healy Creek would make it difficult to reach that pass, so they continued on up the Bow Valley. Naming the Sawback Range on the eastern edge of the valley, they approached the massive rocky bastion of today's Mount Eisenhower; its great towers and battlements suggested to Hector the name Castle Mountain, and so it was known for many years.

Nimrod, returning from a successful hunt, reported that the trail ahead needed clearing. While that was done and the meat dried, Hector and one of the men enjoyed a twelve-hour climb which took them to within two thousand feet of the summit of Castle Mountain. On August 20th the Bow was crossed and in a surprisingly short time, they reached the summit of the Divide at Vermilion Pass. Cree war parties on occasion had crossed there years before; over it would run the first highway to be built through the Rockies, the Banff-Windermere road.

On the western slope the weather immediately became wet. The five men made their way down the valley of the Vermilion River to the plain where Hector inspected the yellow ochre mud in curious circular clearings. Nimrod told him that the Kootenays used to fire it until it turned bright vermilion, making a valuable trade article, war paint; he told them too, after they reached today's Marble Canyon in the rain-soaked forest, to take away some of the soft white stone to manufacture pipes.

As they continued along the Kootenay River Valley the forest thickened; the rain continued and what faint trails there were became very hard to find. More serious, there was no game. Hector surmised that the absence of game accounted for the lack of recent Indian trails. The country was certainly not familiar to the guides—as they proceeded Nimrod thought they were among mountains bordering on the North Saskatchewan. Their situation worsened for they discovered that the constant wet weather had rotted nearly all of their dried meat and the forests provided no pasture for the horses.

On short rations, they made their way to the source of the Kootenay and turned northwest up the Beaverfoot, with Hector still hoping to find a way across the mountains to the Columbia. But the western wall seemed impregnable. It was clear to him that a road could easily be built over the Divide and along the Kootenay, but the challenge to the west had to be abandoned for now—they had to find their way back to the eastern slope of the mountains where there was game. Continuing along the Beaverfoot Valley, "The going was rugged": in deep ravines they fought through a labyrinth of down timber amid violent storms. They were averaging less than five miles a day.

On the morning of August 29th they came to a large stream thundering beneath the high precipices which hemmed it in. In escaping the fallen timber on its banks one of the pack horses plunged into the cataract and was rescued with great difficulty. In the excitement Hector's horse dashed into the forest and when approached, wheeled and lashed, hitting Hector full in the chest. He was unconscious for several hours. When he came to, he was in great pain but was able to assure the anxious men that he was not seriously hurt. On his instructions Erasmus prepared some pain killer and prudently had Hector sign a brief account of the accident, as suspicion might have fallen on the men had their leader failed to recover.

Sometimes this historic accident near today's Wapta Falls has been dismissed as trivial. The incident which resulted in the naming of the Kicking Horse River was in fact a crisis. The isolated little party was without food except for five pounds of dried meat which Hector rationed for three days; in that time they would have to make their way over unknown terrain to reach the eastern slope or their plight would be desperate. And Hector's accident made it impossible to travel for at least a day.

Poor Nimrod. So much depended on him now. If only he could find something to hunt! When at last he sighted a flock of goats he was trembling with weakness and the urgency of the situation. He got one. But it tumbled over a cliff and in attempting to reach it, he ran a sharp branch into his foot. The great hunter had to return to camp, humiliated and lame.

On the last day of August they started off, even though travelling was extremely painful for Hector. Following the raging Kicking Horse River, at nightfall they camped in its magnificent canyon. The next day Nimrod tried again for game but, impeded by his lame foot, he failed and they struggled ahead with nothing at all to eat. They crossed the river as it boiled and leapt through the narrow channel, its bed treacherous with wet mossy boulders, and for eight hours climbed a steep slope through the forest. Luscious blueberries stilled the pangs of hunger momentarily and eventually the slope widened and levelled out. Near two little lakes where there was, at last, pasture for the starving horses, Hector found a stream flowing east. They camped on the summit of Kicking Horse Pass.

Hector shot a grouse and to celebrate their discovery of the pass, they prepared a watery stew, adding the ends of a few candles to provide nourishment for five men who had been on starvation rations for four days and fasted for one. Next day they followed the eastward-flowing stream down into a wide valley where Nimrod shot a moose. To add to his glee, he was able to announce that at last he knew where he was! They were back on the Bow where they enjoyed their moose steaks. Not until they sat down to eat did they realize how weak they were and how depressed they had been. Desperation had kept them going.

As they were having their meal a Stoney Indian popped out of the trees and Nimrod was further overjoyed to find that his friends were camped nearby. When they moved to the Stoney camp next day the women immediately took over the weary travellers' affairs: they unpacked the horses, put up tents, lined them with spruce bough beds, cut firewood, stacked it neatly nearby and prepared a feast. The first snowstorm of the season swirled among the peaks as they rested for a few days while the women dried the moose meat for the next stage of the journey. In spite of the lateness of the season, Hector wasn't ready to follow the Bow back out of the mountains. Although he had just crossed the Divide twice by passes new to the white man, he wanted to examine David Thompson's Howse Pass before returning to Edmonton House.

With the forest a blaze of autumn splendour, they rode north along the Bow and camped beside a fine lake; above them towered a lovely mountain. Today they both bear Hector's name. Next day, rounding a conspicuous peak, Hector had his first close look at the glaciers which straddle the Divide for miles. At Bow Lake the great Wapta Icefields broke through the mountain wall; a massive glacial tongue crept down to the turquoise water. Reaching the summit of Bow Pass, just north of the lake, the magnificent vista of the Mistaya Valley, heavily forested, lake-gemmed, stretched for twenty-five miles to the North Saskatchewan. Nimrod told him that the prominent mountain on their right, at the head of the valley, was the highest one known to the Indians and Hector named it for his patron, the distinguished geologist, Sir Roderick Murchison.

Slithering down the "break-neck" slope, the party went on to camp at peaceful Waterfowl Lake; three days after leaving the Stoney camp, they reached the historic valley of the North Saskatchewan. The white man had made the first recorded crossing from the Bow to the North Saskatchewan along a route which would one day be world famous.

Hector set out in search of Howse Pass. At the camp on the Saskatchewan there were well-marked Indian trails, but going west they encountered "the densest forests" they'd ever seen. Instead of readily finding their way to the pass (Thompson's map was not available at that time), they ended up at a lovely secluded lake—Glacier Lake, Hector named it, for before them lay an immense snowfield and glacier. Tight schedule notwithstanding, the young geologist couldn't resist exploring it. Nimrod stoutly refused to venture there; dreadful disasters awaited Indians rash enough to set foot on a glacier, he insisted—at the very least they would be unlucky in hunting forevermore. And success in the hunt was vital at the moment for their moosemeat was almost gone.

From their camp above the lake, Hector and Sutherland found a way up the icy slope of the Lyell Glacier (named by Hector for a famous geologist) and climbed among the crevasses—on moccasined feet with no socks! One such giant fissure blocked their way and they threw stones into its blue green depths; calculating the interval it took for them to crash to the bottom, Hector estimated its depth at sixty feet. It was four feet wide. They leapt across. Up a steep rocky ridge on the side of the valley they struggled, crawling at some points, and with "dangerous climbing" made their way around "abrupt nicks in the knife-like edge." They reached the summit at three o'clock where they were rewarded with a "splendid view."

Below, the lake "reflected beautifully" the surrounding mountains; in the distance the valleys lay deep in floating mist through which the peaks rose "like islands through the icy mantle." Beside the lake, rising from mighty spurs and buttresses, a magnificent black pyramid towered more than a thousand feet above its neighbours. Hector named it for a Scottish scientist—Mount Forbes.

When Hector had completed the scientific observations for his map, he and Sutherland started down in a snowstorm. At one place they had to pass a wall of rock and ice by knotting their leather shirts together and proceeding on their bare feet! Their moccasins were frozen by now anyway. They got back to camp at eight in the evening. Supper still consisted of dried moose-meat, "as nourishing as parchment"; in spite of avoiding the glacier, Nimrod and the hunters had been unsuccessful.

They had to press on to Kootenay Plains for game and with winter fast approaching Hector only had time for another quick try for Howse Pass. Following the right stream this time, he rode to approximately the place where, fifty-one years before, David Thompson had camped "amid the stupendous and solitary wilds . . . impatiently awaiting the melting of the snows . . ."

Hector turned back and rode away from the historic valley. Perhaps he wasn't sorry he hadn't had time to examine the pass. It gave him a perfect excuse to come back the next year.

After an arduous journey back to Fort Edmonton he allowed himself only a brief respite before returning to the mountains in the vicinity of Devil's Head Mountain, mapping as he went. He made the 536-mile round trip in twenty-nine days to get back to the fort in time for Christmas.

On January 12th he was off again. Accompanied by Erasmus and two other men he left for Jasper House, travelling by dogsled via Fort Assiniboine. It was a beautiful clear, cold day when he started out and the company factor, Mr. Christie, went along part way—bringing provisions for a picnic! After "a very merry evening" Hector continued on snowshoes along the Athabasca. Emerging from thick forests on January 31st, he saw the Rockies again, in "bolder outline here than I have seen elsewhere." The last forty miles were covered in a day, for the ice was now clear of snow and they could skim along unimpeded by their snowshoes, which they were relieved to discard after travelling on them for seventeen days.

Reaching a place on the Athabasca opposite Roche Miette, a crossing at Disaster Point confronted the travellers. It was dark when they arrived; the black, swiftly flowing open water was fringed with ice. At a shallow place, "without taking the harness off the dogs (we) unfastened them from the sleds, and pitching them into the water, pelted them with pieces of ice, so that they swam to the other side of the river. We then got off the edge of the ice ourselves, and found the water took us above the waist, and getting the sleds, loads and all on our shoulders, waded through the rapid, which was about one hundred yards wide, and so reached the left bank. The wind, which had changed at sunset to N.E. was bitterly cold, so that the plunge into the water felt warm at first, but on re-emerging, we at once stiffened into a mass of ice, for as I found half an hour afterwards, the thermometer stood at -15 degrees."

Hector was too modest to mention it but Erasmus said later that Hector insisted on crossing the river first in order to build a fire for the men. When they emerged he made them strip and give themselves a brisk rub down, remarking, "Peter, our people in England would be shocked at the discomfort of your western dressing rooms!" Then they "again tackled the dogs, that were all frozen into a lump with their harness, and after a run of two miles through the woods we reached Jasper House at 10 P.M."

This lonely outpost he described as "beautifully situated on an open plain . . . completely encircled by mountains . . . The little group of buildings . . . have been constructed in keeping with their picturesque situation, after the Swiss style . . ." With Mr. Moberly, the Hudson's Bay man at the post, he tried to climb Roche Miette but the massive summit block defeated him. However, from his vantage point at thirty-five hundred feet above the valley he could see "the ugly place" where they had crossed below Disaster Point and concluded that if they had been able to see where they were going they might have hesitated!

On February 10th, 1859, accompanied by Mr. Moberly and guided by Tekarra, a local Iroquois, Hector set out for Athabasca Pass. The weather had been mild but as they travelled along the Athabasca it turned bitterly cold; they camped among "the sand hills" opposite the sharp escarpment of the Colin Range which Hector named for Colin Fraser. Probably from today's Old Fort Point, he took readings for his map, naming Pyramid and Tekarra mountains and marking the Miette River—the route to Yellowhead Pass, now "abandoned for many years." (Mount Edith Cavell must have been hidden by clouds, for so prominent a landmark would have appeared on his map.) They went on to camp at Prairie de la Vache and on the 13th made their way to the mouth of the Whirlpool River.

Here, however, Hector had a severe disappointment. Tekarra had injured his foot; as it was badly inflamed, he had to turn back. Without a guide, a traverse of Athabasca Pass was too hazardous. But Hector couldn't leave without at least looking at the famous pass and marking it on his map.

From camp he climbed a ridge to the east. Round the summit of Mount Edith Cavell the clouds swirled; south of it rose Whirlpool Peak and in the cleft between lay the old trail to the Committee's Punch Bowl. Hard-pressed voyageurs and distinguished travellers no longer halted there—the mountain solitudes had reclaimed it. Hector named the Whirlpool River, which the fur traders had thought was the main Athabasca, and on his map placed as well two legendary peaks which botanist Douglas had placed on earlier maps, flanking the summit of the pass. "Having been directed by Tekarra, I easily recognized Mount Brown and Mount Hooker . . ." He was wrong.

Up the Athabasca he travelled and camped at the foot of Mount Kerkeslin, the beautiful peak which dominates the east side of the valley. Alone he wandered upriver to "a precipitous cañon . . ." Ahead, the great river flowed; beside it on the west, forested slopes rose to snow-capped precipices marching into the remote distance toward the Athabasca's unknown source. He named a conspicuous mountain on the right for Mr. Christie and one on the left for another company factor, Mr. Hardisty—and turned back. Almost forty years would go by before the white man explored the magnificent reach of country between Athabasca Falls and Saskatchewan Crossing—country spanned today by the Jasper-Banff highway.

On very short rations at times, Hector returned directly from Jasper House to Fort Edmonton along the forest trail Mr. Moberly had opened the year before. Largely because Hector was so enthusiastic about completing the examination of Howse Pass, Palliser applied for and received permission to continue the expedition's work for another season.

In the spring the expedition members finished their work east of the Divide and headed for Kootenay Pass on their way to the Pacific; Hector was to cross the mountains to the Columbia and, if at all possible, find a way from there across to the Fraser and Thompson rivers before joining his companions for the voyage home.

At a Stoney camp on the Highwood River he engaged William to assist Nimrod, who agreed to accompany Hector only on condition that he be allowed to bring along his wife and child—he refused to leave his wife with friends, insisting that he couldn't return through the mountains without her. The Indians were to go as far as Howse Pass; from there Hector and two

*Sir James Hector, left, with Sir Edward Whymper. Mary Schäffer
photographed them together when Hector returned to the Rockies in 1905 to
ride over the gleaming rails thrust through Kicking Horse Pass, the route
he had pioneered more than forty years before.*
COURTESY GLENBOW ARCHIVES, CALGARY (NA334-2)

Americans he'd met on the plains intended to continue with only James Beads, one of Sir George Simpson's old guides, who had served the expedition from the beginning.

Once again Hector climbed, geologized and mapped in the autumn sunshine as they travelled to present-day Banff; Cascade Mountain was even more beautiful than he remembered. William led them over Pipestone Pass to the North Saskatchewan River where Nimrod was persuaded to leave his wife and child in William's care for two days while he guided Hector over Howse Pass. Next day, on the pretext of going hunting, Nimrod left. Rejoining his family and William, they retraced their footsteps to the Bow where they met Southesk's party. Nimrod was one of the Stonies the earl took to Fort Edmonton to bring back gifts.

Without a guide who knew the country Hector found that he "needed all the little experience I had picked up of the Indians' tact in threading through forest country in a given direction; and I daresay . . . we often followed a roundabout bad line of route when a better existed." They did just that as soon as they began their search for Howse Pass. After passing the spot Hector had reached the year before, they went up the wrong valley and found themselves at the dead end of today's Freshfield Glacier. They retreated and followed the Howse River. Once again the white man rode through David Thompson's long-neglected gateway to the Columbia. The undisturbed forest had crept over the trail.

Descending the "narrow tortuous valley" of the Blaeberry for twenty miles, they emerged into the valley of the Columbia and turned north, hoping to find a cleft in the Selkirk Range which would provide a passage to the Fraser and Thompson rivers. For ten days the little party strenuously forced a trail through the dense forest; wet weather rotted their dried meat; trails, pasture for the horses and campsites were almost nonexistent. With one axe they fought their way through the timber-choked valley. The wall of the Selkirks appeared impenetrable. When they met a Shuswap Indian he told them that it was much too late in the year to attempt a crossing to the Fraser and Thompson rivers, even if they managed to reach Boat Encampment through the heavily obstructed forest. Reluctantly, they turned back and made their way south to Lake Windermere where they followed the old fur trade route to the Pacific.

The findings of the Palliser expedition established the feasibility of settling immense tracts of land in what are now the prairie provinces—and that historic development would mean the end of the Hudson's Bay Company's exclusive reign in the great Northwest. Practicable passes had been found through the Rockies but the mountain wall west of the Columbia remained unbreached. For twelve more years the barrier was virtually unbroken. Then the white man returned—a handful at first, swelling to a mighty army in another ten years. When the toiling, sweating battalions dispersed, Hector—by then Sir James Hector, a distinguished geologist in New Zealand—came back.

Along the steep hillside where, forty-five years before, he'd picked blueberries to stave off hunger, astride the precipices beside the foaming river, a black panting locomotive carried the old man over the gleaming rails thrust through Kicking Horse Pass.

10

THE EL DORADO OF OUR HOPES

The Palliser expedition aroused interest in the western territories of British North America; another stimulus to the westering urge was a discovery made while Palliser and his men were probing the passes of the Rockies. Gold was found glittering in the sands of the Fraser River.

The news spread like wildfire. From south, east and west the ever-hopeful came in thousands; by sailboat, rowboat, canoe and steamer, over unknown and dangerous terrain, novices and grizzled veterans slogged hundreds of miles, drawn irresistibly by dreams of fabulous and instant wealth. No one will ever know their numbers, the extent of their hardships, their triumphs and disappointed hopes . . . or how many lost their lives.

Several large groups came from Canada's eastern provinces and some of these left records of their journey. Instead of making a long and hazardous sea voyage they decided to cross the continent by what advertisements called "an easy wagon road through a lovely country unequalled for its beauty and salubrity of climate." Along a route "constantly" travelled "with perfect safety" they would cross the Rockies. Then they need only drift easily along the Fraser to the Cariboo gold fields.

A party of over a hundred Overlanders left Ontario in the early spring of 1862, going by rail to St. Paul and on to Fort Garry where they provisioned themselves for what they were confident would be a sixty-day excursion. There they were joined by the only woman known to have made the trek. Her belongings included two basket cradles for her youngest children; her husband tended their three-year-old. Well concealed by her voluminous clothing was the fact that she was expecting her fourth baby. Joining them there as well was another remarkable traveller—the most notorious "humbug and n'er do well" ever to tramp the Canadian West.

Felix O'Byrne was an Irishman between fifty and sixty years old with a long face, large features and a receding mouth with almost no teeth; "a curious mixture of the cleric and the rustic," he wore a long alpaca coat of "ecclesiastic cut, fustian trousers," a wide black hat and carried an enormous stick. Pipe in hand, in a rich brogue liberally larded with impressive Latin quotations he held forth at great length about his fascinating career. He had studied law, edited a paper in India and acted as secretary to a wealthy Louisiana planter—a position which terminated abruptly when his employer brought the good news that he'd just had him elected to the Home Guard. Mr. O'Byrne took to his heels and for a time taught classics in a small northern college until (according to him) it closed for lack of funds. Eventually he turned up at Fort Garry. Delighted to have such a distinguished scholar in their midst, local parents paid him well to conduct classes for their children in his hotel room but, as he frequently disappeared without notice for a day at a time, leaving his students to raise an uproar, that soon came to an end. He stayed on, borrowing money, visiting and maintaining toward his long-suffering hosts an attitude of insulting condescension. The townspeople saw hope of deliverance when the Overlanders arrived, and foisted him off on them as a chaplain.

In June the long line of screeching ox carts started across the plains. In such a large group of the most widely divergent ages, backgrounds and degrees of responsibility, strict rules had to be drawn up for the order of marching. Even so laggers would lose their place in line and find the mudholes deepened by those preceding. The day often started with anxious pedestrians "running with cups of tea and pancakes in their hands, eating on the run" and dragging tents and pails of unwashed dishes as they hurried to catch up—a scene which more punctual travellers found hilarious. Inevitably there were shirkers; tempers flared and the hotheaded came to blows. But at night they rallied around campfires, organized "a musical association" and enjoyed singsongs accompanied by "four violinists, 2 fluitests and a number of others who played small Instiments."

It didn't take long for the Overlanders to size up their chaplain ("always interfering with everyone's business"), and younger lads added a spot of excitement by dashing up suddenly, firing guns and yelling wildly that Indians were about to attack. Mr. O'Byrne would disappear with alacrity behind the nearest tree, enjoining anyone within earshot: "I'll mind your axe and you take my gun and shoot them!" At Fort Carlton they'd had enough. They dumped him.

Mr. Woolsey, the Methodist missionary there, put up with him for the winter, but by spring he confessed to his fellow missionary, the Reverend Mr. McDougall: "John, I'm about tired of Mr. O. B. Could you not take him to Edmonton and leave him there?" Mr. McDougall obliged and they set out by dogsled. The river had flooded over the ice in places and Mr. McDougall waded in the icy water trying to steady the sled carrying his passenger, who repaid him for his trouble with robust oaths. "When he continued his profanity I couldn't stand it any longer so just dumped him right out into the overflow and went on. However, when I looked back and saw the old fellow staggering through the water and fending his legs with his cane from the sharp ice, I returned and helped him ashore . . ." At Fort Edmonton O'Byrne made himself at home with customary aplomb until two notable travellers arrived the following year.

On the next stage of their journey from Fort Carlton the Overlanders marched for days in constant rain. Many of the swollen streams were unfordable so they worked waist-deep in water to build bridges; they waded for hours over flooded meadows until someone wondered if this was really "an *overland* route." The sight of Fort Edmonton was "the signal for a hearty and tumultuous cheer . . ." During the preceding eleven days their clothing had never been dry and their "toil-worn, jaded, forlorn and tattered appearance" was in striking contrast to their appearance on starting out. They had been much longer on the road than anticipated. "Yet we had full confidence in our ability to reach the El Dorado of our hopes."

At the fort they learned that "the Boundary, Cootanie and Sinclair passes" were easier, but the Yellowhead was recommended as the most direct way to the Cariboo, although "some of them represented the road as nearly impassible, and foresaw difficulties and dangers which they considered almost insurmountable." André Cardinal, a Hudson's Bay Company employee who had been born at Jasper House, was taken on as guide over the mountains; oxen were exchanged for pack horses and on August 1st the cavalcade started west.

Very soon they could see that the journey was to be "totally different from what we had passed through." Swamps and hills, streams and dense forests replaced the open prairie; work parties had to cut trails and clear fallen timber. At river crossings, baggage was ferried over in canvas boats made of tents and ropes but getting the livestock across presented problems: the streams were filled with many "a bewildered equestrian making a vain attempt to guide his steed across the stream . . . while yonder another bold navigator astride an ox, sometimes in the water and sometimes out, was boxing the compass in his ineffectual endeavours to persuade his boon companion to shape his course toward sundown."

When at last they saw the Rockies, "lofty snow-clad peaks, standing out in bold relief against the blue sky beyond and glistening in the sunlight, the company was enraptured at the sight of them; for whatever dangers or difficulties might possibly be in store for us among them, all were heartily tired of the endless succession of hills and streams and swamps . . . and were willing to face almost any danger that would be likely to terminate or vary our toils."

Their toils were by no means terminated when they reached the mountains; they were varied by increasing hardship.

When they camped at Roche Miette a thunder storm raged spectacularly about "its cold and craggy cliffs, crowned with eternal snows." Over Disaster Point—"a very narrow pathway, with a perpendicular wall of rock on one side, and a steep declivity down to the edge of a precipice several hundred feet high on the other"—the long cavalcade made a wearying climb. Below they could see "Jasper House, a perfect picture of loneliness and solitude . . ."

It was only open in winter now. Across the river from it they camped and enjoyed their last "musical evening," thinking that their music must be a novelty in the quiet valley. Other fiddles and songs had echoed here. But the presence of the white woman and her children was probably unprecedented.

Rafting over the Athabasca, they went on to Yellowhead Pass. Along the Miette they discovered "that anything we have seen is about child's play compared to this": obstructed by interlaced fallen timber, what path there was lay first on one, then on the other side of the river, so that "in the short space of two hours we waded through it no less than seven times, while the water threatened to sweep us off our feet."

Once across the Divide they hoped that the worst part of their trek would soon be over. But after following the Fraser for several days they were forced to make a decision. They had expected to be at their destination a month before and their provisions were almost gone; the scarcity of pasture had weakened their livestock so that one or two had to be abandoned every day; it was autumn and no one knew how much longer it would take to reach their goal. The guide knew little about what lay ahead and was allowed to return. Some killed their cattle and most went on short rations supplemented with birds, porcupines, squirrels and skunks.

Travelling in groups, some arriving west of the mountains before others, the Overlanders now chose to continue their journey by separate routes. One group elected to follow the Fraser River. True, the river flowed north, away from the Cariboo, but it would (they hoped) take them to Fort George; from there they could proceed to Quesnel and make their way to the Cariboo. Building cumbersome rafts forty by twenty feet, they enclosed them with high railings and constructed stone fireplaces so they could prepare meals without stopping to set up camp. Some of the party procured from Indians or fashioned their own dugout canoes. Livestock and goods were loaded; passengers thronged aboard the clumsy rafts and, preceded by the canoes, the flotilla set out on the Fraser—blissfully unaware of what lay ahead.

The footsore travellers were elated; this was much better than slogging through timber! For two days they drifted happily toward Fort George. In the Grand Canyon of the river the turbulent water leapt and frothed between the rocky walls. The canoers heard the roar—too late. They were sucked into the maelstrom.

Among the Overlanders were men who had never before pitched a tent, wielded an axe or paddled a canoe. Nonswimmers were attempting to navigate the Fraser. Of three men in one of the canoes that preceded the rafts into the canyon, only one could swim; exhorting his companions again and again not to loosen their hold on the capsized craft, he struck out for shore. He perished in the raging water. The two nonswimmers were washed onto a sandbar with the canoe and were rescued by the oncoming rafts. At least one other man in the canoes that attempted the passage was lost. His companions found his diary on shore later; with a strange premonition his last entry recorded his own death in the rapids of the Fraser. There is no certainty about how many others may have died there. Incredibly, the rafts wallowed through the rapids.

Along the Yellowhead route other Overlanders were still straggling west. One tiny group faced a difficult crossing of the infant Fraser after a torrential rain. Their "guide" found the water too high and they decided to wait until it was lower in the morning; one man, however, didn't intend to wait and secretly bribed the guide to carry him over. Their companions watched with astonishment as the two of them hurried off along the trail without a backward glance! Not willing to be so callously abandoned, they stripped, tied packs and clothing on their backs and stepped into the rushing stream. They were immediately swept off their feet and managed to get back on shore only after great difficulty. Everything they had was lost in the river— an older man made a desperate effort and recovered his clothing and wallet, but his exertions brought on a chill and he was delirious with fever all night. His companions refused to leave him; they waited four days with almost nothing to eat until another party caught up and rescued them. Undoubtedly there were many other unrecorded incidents of human frailty and quiet heroism.

When the decision was made to proceed to the Cariboo by different routes, thirty-six people, including the Schubert family, decided to start for the Thompson River. They hoped to reach Fort Kamloops (which they thought must be about two hundred miles south), then travel the old fur trail west to the Fraser River which they would follow to the gold fields.

They entered the virgin forests along the Thompson, driving ahead of them more than a hundred head of livestock. For over two weeks the men slashed a trail through timber. The party advanced only sixty miles—at that rate, disaster faced them, for winter would trap them in the valley. They too must take to the river. Slaughtering their animals (at what they named Slaughter Camp) they built rafts and embarked on one of the most dangerous stretches of river in the Northwest. At Hell's Gate on the Thompson the rafts had to be abandoned. Accompanying those making the wearisome three-day portage to get past the rapids was Mrs. Schubert with her three children. At the end of the portage, new rafts were built and the Overlanders set out again. More rapids awaited them; some of the exhausted group left the river and, in driving rain and sleet, slogged ahead on foot. All were in pitiful condition. In mid-October they reached Fort Kamloops. At least one man had met his death in the Murchison Rapids.

The raft bringing the Schuberts was hurried ashore in time to erect a tent where in a few hours an Indian midwife announced the birth of little Rose—the first white girl born in the interior of British Columbia. The indomitable woman had persevered on an expedition (as one of her companions said) "which few men would have the courage to undertake."

Most of the people in this group of Overlanders made the fifty-mile trip west to Cache Creek; hardly any continued north to the Cariboo. Like those who had followed the Fraser, they turned away from the "El Dorado of our hopes." A few journeyed from Quesnel, a few from Cache Creek to the gold fields to see for themselves, but the majority accepted the evidence presented by weary and dejected men returning from the Cariboo: for every one who found gold, nine "merely stayed and starved."

The Overlanders had made a five-month journey, enduring many hardships; some had lost and all had risked their lives; many had used their life savings or sacrificed economic security to search for gold. Winter was at hand when they were at last within reach of their destination and most were unable to provision themselves. They hurried to the coast where they hoped to find work.

There is no record that any of them ever found the fortune they thought would be theirs for the taking. But like thousands of other prospectors they stayed to swell the population of British Columbia.

THE INCREDIBLE JOURNEY

By all odds the journey of the first tourists to travel by the Yellowhead route should have ended in disaster. The prospects for a successful venture seemed very unpromising: a pampered, sickly twenty-three-year-old aristocrat attempting to penetrate almost untouched mountain and forest wilderness with the help of one able-bodied man and a one-handed trailbreaker taking along his wife and young son, the country beyond the Rockies unknown to any of them. When one learns furthermore that they were ill-equipped, inexperienced and encumbered with that most ineffectual of hitchhikers, Mr. O'Byrne, the whole undertaking appears wildly improbable.

Fortunately Lord Milton's companion, personal physician and tutor was not only able-bodied—twenty-seven-year-old Dr. Cheadle, a husky good-humoured former Cambridge oarsman, was a tower of strength. Like the Earl of Southesk, Milton and Cheadle were in search of a glorious adventure in the far West, hunting the buffalo and grizzly, but unlike the literary-minded earl, who would probably have scorned such a diversion, they were lured as well by the gold of the Cariboo.

Arriving in Quebec in July of 1862, they travelled through American territory on the way to Fort Garry. Weeks later they learned that the stagecoach on which they had ridden part of the way had been attacked by a Sioux war party who had massacred all on board—two days after their own passing. When they reached the Red River the steamer was late, so in a fine spirit of adventure they decided to paddle the five hundred miles to the fort. "Jolly feeling of independence, quietly paddling along . . ." That was on the first day. During the next fifteen, they stopped time and again to patch their leaky canoes. The paddling became monotonous as they made their strenuous way in stifling heat amidst swarms of tormenting mosquitoes—Milton's face and arms were painfully swollen and he blossomed with a flaming sunburn. Thinking to avoid the heat and mosquitoes by travelling at night, they sat midstream as a fierce lightning storm crackled around them. Many times they set to work wringing out trousers, shirts and blankets and cleaning rusting guns, "sulkily enough."

But with considerable gusto they also enjoyed the novelty of baking bread and doing their first laundry—their "white ducks," no less! Eating wild game and catching gold-eyes was great sport until all their food ran out, and eventually the game too; when the steamer unexpectedly came round a bend, they paddled frantically toward it and in their eagerness were almost sucked into its churning paddlewheel.

At Fort Garry in early August Dr. Cheadle bought supplies, attended to the thousand and one details for their westward trip, answered urgent appeals for his medical services and accompanied Lord Milton to the many social engagements expected of visiting gentry. Lord Milton packed and repacked—he was to be a maddeningly slow starter from now on—and when the doctor thought he had him on his way at last, he sneaked back to a wedding party where there was "much violent fiddling" and dancing, and corn whisky flowed freely. Poor Dr. Cheadle . . . his trials were just beginning.

Proceeding west, by mid-October they realized it was too late to cross the mountains. Nothing daunted, they decided to winter with their two native guides in the wilderness about eighty miles from Fort Carlton. They built a shack with spaces between the logs through which a hand could be slipped, installed parchment windows, thatched it with marsh grass and earth, "lit a fire in the embryo chimney and part tumbles down; consternation!" The logs were chinked eventually, Fort Milton got a new chimney and there in Indian country they trapped and hunted.

Their Indian neighbours expected frequent hospitality (and rum) at Fort Milton, and proffered their own: very soon an old chief offered his lively daughter as a wife. They declined, but even the circumspect Dr. Cheadle observed, "not bad looking though." Two days later Lord Milton went calling on the chief's ménage—"to flirt with La petite sauvagesse," Cheadle suspected. When the doctor returned home a few days later from a buffalo hunt, she'd moved in. He persuaded his charge to send her packing but in spite of exhortations, Lord Milton romantically enlivened the long cold winter with the dusky Dalilah while Cheadle trapped, fended off starvation and cold, sent the guides hundreds of miles to replenish supplies, worried about Milton and longed for spring. Cheadle "shed no tears" when they departed from their winter quarters in April but Milton, in happy anticipation, drew plans for the cabin he intended to build when he "comes out again to this place!"

At Fort Carlton they engaged Baptiste Supernat who knew the route as far as Tête Jaune Cache, just beyond Yellowhead Pass, and at Fort Pitt they met Louis Battenotte. This competent Métis, known as Assiniboine because he had lived for a time with that tribe, was anxious to cross the mountains; although Milton and Cheadle were reluctant to burden their weak party with the wife and son he insisted on taking along, they were sufficiently impressed with his reputation and agreeable manner to accept his offer of help. In spite of the fact that he had only one hand, Assiniboine and his family turned out to be Cheadle's invaluable assistants.

At Fort Edmonton Mr. O'Byrne awaited them. After his arrival with Mr. McDougall he had lived for a time in a hut on the brush-covered river bank and the factor was obliged to keep him from starving. As O'Byrne was absolutely terrified of wolves and bears, he moved to a lodge nearer the fort and when it blew down, was gratified to find that Milton and Cheadle had arrived. He threw his lodge cover over their cart, satisfied that this would provide at least a temporary home. In short order he presented himself to Dr. Cheadle as a fellow Cambridge man and "nearly knocked my head off with Latin quotations and crammed birth and aristocracy down my throat in nauseating doses"—not forgetting ample references to his own grandfather, the bishop.

He wanted to cross the mountains with them and he pursued his purpose with remarkable tenacity. At great length, and repeatedly, he poured out his desperate need to escape from the wilds "so uncongenial to his classical tastes." As usual, someone took pity on him. "Poor fellow," wrote Cheadle. "I wish we were not so short of carts or we would willingly give him a lift, although he is an ungrateful dog." O'Byrne persisted: he would walk, provide his own food, ask no wages and would be useful. At last, they "hadn't the heart to refuse him" and he congratulated them on "deciding so wisely." The good people at the fort, delighted with this satisfactory turn of events, took up a subscription and presented him with a horse.

On June 3rd, 1863, the pitifully inadequate party started for Jasper House. The people at Fort Edmonton had little hope that they could overcome the difficulties ahead, but warnings of dangerous rivers, rapids and impassable forests fell on deaf ears. To the Cariboo they intended to go—they would follow the year-old trail of the Overlanders. Fortunately they never knew the fate of that perilous trek. Probably the knowledge wouldn't have deterred them from making a start and later, when their own situation was desperate, they might have made the one fatal decision: accepting the fact that they were beaten.

Not many days out of the fort it should have seemed prudent to abandon their project. The trail was an eye-opener—"no one but a Hudson's Bay voyageur would dream of taking horses into such a region!" The animals wallowed in quivering muskeg; Lord Milton slept poorly and petulantly refused to get up in the mornings; he quarrelled with Baptiste, the only one who knew at least part of the route, and the guide promptly left with one of their best horses. However Assiniboine thought he could find the way and Milton eagerly panned for gold in every stream. Cheadle had now to assume an even bigger burden of the heavy work, including the lifting of 180-pound loads onto the horses, for O'Byrne's promised assistance consisted of good advice, generously distributed. He refused even to pack his own horse, issued orders to the Assiniboine family like "an emperor" and at day's end, when camp was being set up, he was hidden in the bushes "quietly smoking and diligently studying the last remnant of his library, Paley's *Evidences of Christianity.*"

One evening while he was reclining by the fire "divested of his boots," a horse trampled embers into a dead tree nearby. In minutes the camp was ablaze. Cheadle seized an axe and began chopping down trees to cut off the fire; a horse rolled in the fire and had to be rescued. While that was going on, "the fire had again got ahead and I set to work with the axe and shouted to the rest to bring water, and Milton's activity and presence of mind in helping me at once saved us . . . Whilst I was energetically cutting down trees and crying for water, I observed O'Byrne sitting down, tugging away at a boot. I shouted to him very angrily, 'Mr. O'Byrne, what on earth are you doing? Why the devil don't you bring some water?' 'I can't, I've only got one boot on'"! When Cheadle retorted hotly that he'd burn as well with one boot on as with two, he did his bit by limping up with half-filled pans.

As they proceeded, he lagged behind and then, because of his terror of bears, the woods rang with cries for help. Assiniboine one day hid beside the trail until O'Byrne had passed, then growled like a bear; this tactic produced a gratifying burst of speed, but soon the party just ignored his urgent appeals. Before long he gave it as his considered opinion that, although he had travelled in many lands, he had never known until now what travelling meant.

Their progress was frustratingly slow and Cheadle and Assiniboine scoured the woods looking for moose to eke out their provisions. They returned empty-handed. Milton, who had been putting in his time panning for gold, had heard a big animal thrashing about; assuming it was one of the horses, he whistled and yelled. A big moose took off into the forest. Anyway, as usual, he'd given his gun to someone else to carry!

Eventually they reached the Athabasca River and from its high banks saw the heavily forested hills, soft in the blue haze, and beyond, the sun shining on the snowy Rockies. Even the Assiniboines cried out with delight at the majestic sight. "A cleft in the range, cut clean as with a knife, showed us what we supposed to be the position of Jasper's House and the opening of the gorge through which we are to pass across." It was their first glimpse of Roche Miette, the great sentinel of the mountain gateway to modern Jasper Park.

When they arrived at its base the river was in flood and they tackled the steep ridge of Disaster Point. As everyone was trying to cope with this laborious climb, O'Byrne hove into view—without his horse. The fat lazy chestnut stallion, heaving and puffing, had momentarily refused to budge. So O'Byrne just left him there and of course, the delighted horse turned back. "Poor beast," he announced, "it's no use attempting to fetch him, he's *much* too exhausted to proceed further anyway!" Someone else had to go back for it.

They had all been anxiously looking for Jasper House; until they found it they couldn't be certain that they were on the right road. At last they saw it, a tiny speck in the valley below. Assiniboine and Cheadle had spotted mountain goats and scrambled on the rocks for a successful hunt. Descending with all the meat they could carry, they looked back up and could scarcely believe they'd made such a precipitous climb; in the excitement of the chase they had thought nothing of it. Although Cheadle had never in his life endured "such an awful grind" as on that crossing of Disaster Point, it had been well worth it—they'd had no fresh meat since leaving Fort Edmonton.

A raft had to be built to cross the Athabasca and when the doctor and Assiniboine had cut down enough trees, everyone started carrying the logs down to the water for assembly. Cheadle found O'Byrne in the shade and "apologized for interrupting his studies," but would he perhaps help Lord Milton? Yes, indeed! "He'd been 'looking forward with eager impatience for an opportunity of giving my assistance.'"

The doctor and Assiniboine staggered under enormous loads. Lord Milton managed to hoist the end of a small log onto his shoulder; O'Byrne held the other end in his hand and, complaining of his awful burden, dropped it every few yards. When he was persuaded to get it up onto his shoulder, he "uttered the most awful groans . . . 'Oh dear, Oh dear, this is most painful—it's cutting my shoulder in two—not so fast, my lord . . . I shall drop with exhaustion directly . . . !' And then with a loud 'Oh!' and no further warning, he let his end of the tree down with a run, jarring his unhappy partner most dreadfully."

Mr. O'Byrne's "assistance" came in for some discussion. Overhearing it, he ("with the imperturbable confidence he always displayed in all social relations") said it was all very well for the doctor "with the shoulders of a Durham ox," but "work like that would soon kill a man of his delicate constitution." When it was pointed out that Lord Milton was not strong but had done his share, he replied, "Oh, yes! I have been lost in admiration of his youthful ardour all the day!"

The next day a man arrived from Jasper House and advised them that a much better crossing place existed upstream and that Mr. Macaulay, who was in charge of the fort, would assist them on his return to the valley. Milton was unwell anyway and not able to travel, so they moved camp to a nearby lake where they could fish. On the way they had to cross a stream and O'Byrne, who had by now acquired a decided distaste for riding, was crossing with the help of his stick. "Oh dear! Oh dear! I shall be carried off!" Someone rode back and, clinging desperately to his rescuer's stirrup, he managed the ford.

In the evening they enjoyed the grandeur of the Athabasca Valley—the towering peaks, lonely little Jasper House in its garden of wildflowers across the river, the setting sun painting the snowy summits pearl rose, and at nightfall, under a velvety sky, two Indians in a canoe spearing fish by torchlight.

On the fourth of July Mr. Macaulay accompanied the travellers upriver and the next day helped them construct another raft. Mr. Macaulay had listened sympathetically to the doctor's complaints about O'Byrne and had administered a stern lecture, so that this time O'Byrne strolled up and asked solicitously: "Oh Doctor, *can* I be of any use?" Unfortunately the work was already finished.

Macaulay had also advised Cheadle to take on an Iroquois who knew the road as far as Tête Jaune Cache; Milton was enraged at the extra expense— a runty horse! But the doctor stood firm; they had already taken twice the usual time to get this far and to make better progress he needed at least "one able-bodied man" for "hauling Milton and O'Byrne to the Cariboo." When Mr. Macaulay had seen them safely across the river, they were so relieved to be on their way they didn't bother to go back for their one good axe which they'd left behind on the other side. Had they known what lay ahead that axe would have been fetched.

Like the Overlanders, the little party soon discovered the trials of the track along the Miette. Cheadle considered it "The worst road I ever saw." Fire had littered the valley with timber so that it was "like walking amongst a game of spillikins"; they had to dismount, "whack and chivy" the horses; leaping, rushing and scrambling, the animals were in danger of breaking their legs; the stream had to be forded incessantly. It was all too much for O'Byrne—"his face grew very long" and he refused to mount at all. It took four days to reach the Divide.

It was a "glorious morning" when they left Yellowhead Lake. Soon there was "a great bawling" in the rear and Cheadle rushed back to meet "a very disconsolate" O'Byrne whose horse had shied and thrown him over its head. They continued their struggle with muskeg and flooded streams. O'Byrne "halloa'd" in distress again and this time staggered up leading his horse, its saddle dangling under its belly—it had fallen in a bog and rolled on him. "A most *awful* journey!" Sympathy and exhortation brought on an unusual burst of enthusiasm and "he elected to lead . . . In a few minutes, of course, . . . horses got all wrong and a pretty bother" it was to straighten things out. He was "blown-up" and sent to the rear. Attempting to make some progress through the thick woods, Milton was dragged onto the tail of his horse and "scrambled up like a monkey"; Cheadle's mount rammed into a tree, giving the doctor a tremendous whack on the head and "scratching my face hand-somely . . . The memorable 10th of July!"

Continuing to Moose Lake on another "glorious morning" they forded a swiftly flowing stream. The water streamed over the horses' shoulders and a reluctant O'Byrne was forced to mount. With Milton and Mrs. Assiniboine riding on each side of him he sat rigid with terror; "clutching the mane with both hands, he did not attempt to guide his horse, but employed all his pow-ers in sticking to the saddle, and exhorting his companions: 'Steady, my lord, please, or I shall be swept off . . . Oh dear, Oh dear, what an awful journey! *Do* speak to Mrs. Assiniboine, my lord; she's leading me to destruction; what a reckless woman!'" Reaching shore he proclaimed: "Narrow escape that, my lord! Very narrow escape, indeed, Doctor. We can't expect to be so lucky every time you know."

Along the steep trail beside the lake the horses either took to the water, soaking all the supplies, or somersaulted over precipices. In between, the travellers admired "the very handsome" surroundings, but Milton was forced to admit that negotiating the trail required horsemanship that "beat hunting in Ireland!" O'Byrne strode up carrying his pack and saddle. He would ride no more. The weather grew oppressively hot; the horses stuck fast, straddled over fallen trees, and at best proceeded only by "a succession of jumps." Milton insisted that they camp early; when it was explained that it was imperative to keep going until they found pasture for the horses, he quar-relled with the guide and "in an awful passion . . . abused" him. Everyone "perspired at every pore" and O'Byrne was "very confused." He swore he'd never forget the horrors of that trail as long as he lived!

At the Grand Forks where "the boiling impetuous" Fraser dashed over its rocky bed, the scene was "grand and striking beyond description . . . On every side snowy heads of mighty hills crowded, whilst immediately behind us, immeasurably supreme, rose Robson's Peak . . . A shroud of mist rolled away . . . the upper portion was trimmed by a necklace of light feathery clouds, beyond which its apex of ice, glittering in the morning sun, shot up far into the blue heaven above."

The soul-uplifting moment was brief. Tempestuous days followed. Milton quarrelled again with the Iroquois guide; Assiniboine said he and his family would leave if his lordship was so discontented. Cheadle was thrown from his horse and in the confusion two horses behind him jumped into the river. Assiniboine, with astonishing speed and bravery, rescued one from the boiling cauldron, but the other was lost. It had carried their papers, Milton's passport and cheque book, watches, some valuable gunpowder, revolvers, caps, tea and tobacco and Milton's clothing. He was left with one pair of "dirty, holey canvas trousers, a leather shirt, one pair of worn out moccasions, no boots and no coat." The Iroquois quietly disappeared, taking as payment O'Byrne's horse.

A few straggling Shuswaps took them across the Fraser in dugouts (with O'Byrne "loosening his cravat in case he should be upset") and they pushed on to the crossing of the Canoe River. With the one little axe they had left they cut trees for the necessary raft. As soon as it was launched it tore down the stream "at a fearful pace, it appearing certain that we must run foul of a tree overhanging the bank on the side we started from . . ." Poling desperately, urged on by the frantic shouts of Assiniboine, they just escaped it. But the current clutched the craft and flung it toward the far side of the river, "straight for a little rapid which we passed over like an arrow, and then to what seemed certain destruction, a large pine closely overhanging the water and through the branches of which the water was rushing and boiling like a mill-stream at the wheel. Assiniboine shouted 'Land with the rope!', jumping himself with one, up to the shoulders in the stream, and catching a small tree round which he whipped the rope like lightning; but it snapped like a thread, and the other, which I had leaped ashore with as the raft neared the land for an instant before rushing under the pine, was dragged out of my hand in a moment. The raft rushed under the tree . . ."

By some miracle O'Byrne had stuck to the careening raft. The boy had jumped with Cheadle and seeing his mother clinging to the tree, far out in the water, dashed off in search of his father. Cheadle managed to free Milton, who also clung to the tree, but they needed a rope to reach Mrs. Assiniboine. Seeing O'Byrne striding along shore they shouted for him to get a rope. He held up his hands in despair, but none the less gallantly surrendered his neckerchief to the frantic boy. Assiniboine had hauled the raft to shore, unfastened the rope and with his help the poor woman was rescued. Fortunately she wasn't hurt. Recriminations were heaped on O'Byrne's performance, to which he replied that he couldn't remember a thing from the time the raft rushed under the tree.

Everyone was tired and irritable when they came to the Thompson River. Food was dangerously low (O'Byrne's private supply had been exhausted long before); the horses were failing for lack of pasture. They faced a serious decision. The dim trail of the Overlanders petered out where they had taken to the river at Slaughter Camp.

O'Byrne was horrified at the thought that they might do the same and called Dr. Cheadle aside. "Doctor, I hope that you and Assiniboine will be very careful indeed in crossing the river, for you know I think you managed very badly indeed last time, I may say, disgracefully so . . . Now, if you will take my advice, you will keep perfectly cool and collected . . . and not shout at one another as you did before . . ."

An anxious council was held. Should they cast their fate with the river too, or should they try to cut trail through the forest to Fort Kamloops? Overruling Milton's objections, the dream of the Cariboo was abandoned. They decided to try the forest; that way they would at least have their horses for food if starvation threatened. Assiniboine was encouraging: they "would get out of this mess."

Their prospects were bleak. It had taken the Overlanders approximately four weeks to reach Fort Kamloops from the Fraser; they had had the services of more than thirty potential axemen and a supply of meat. Milton and Cheadle thought their provisions would last for ten days, in which time they hoped to be at the fort. They had two axemen (one handicapped) and one little axe.

They began their trek through the forest. The giant cedars hid the sky;

Lord Milton after his arrival in Victoria, B.C., and the end of his "incredible journey."
COURTESY B.C. ARCHIVES, VICTORIA (A-02651)

dank ferns rose shoulder-high and the tangled undergrowth was rank with devil's club—that abominable plant with great thorny stems which puncture the skin and leave festering wounds.

"No one," wrote Cheadle, "who has not seen a primeval forest, where trees of gigantic size have grown and fallen undisturbed for ages, can form any idea of the collection of timber or the impenetrable character of such a region . . . trunks prostrate, trunks reclining, trunks horizontal, trunks propped up at different angles, . . . timber of every size in every possible position, entangled in every possible combination." Allowing themselves only two meals a day, they struggled ahead, making about three to five miles a day. At night they sat down to a watery stew made of a scrap of pemmican, a partridge or two, an occasional fish and sometimes a few berries. Game tracks were scarce and the hard-pressed party didn't dare halt long enough to hunt in earnest.

On the twelfth day, they realized that at the rate they had travelled the fort was nowhere near; their food supply was down to pemmican the size of a fist. A horse would have to be killed but no one was willing to do it. Assiniboine returned from an unsuccessful hunt saying he'd found a dead Indian. Cheadle went to see.

"The corpse was in a sitting posture, legs crossed, arms clasped over knees, bending forward over the ashes of a miserable fire of small sticks. The ghastly figure was headless . . . the skin brown, shrivelled, stretched like parchment . . . a tattered blanket still hung round the shrunken form . . ." Nearby was a small axe, a fire bag, a large tin kettle and at the skeleton's side, fragments of a horse's skull "which told the sad story of his fate. They were chipped into the smallest pieces, showing that the unfortunate man had died of starvation, and prolonged existence as far as possible by sucking every part of nutriment out of the broken fragments . . ." Cheadle walked silently back to camp.

Physically weak, nagged by anxiety, they were all "greatly depressed by this somewhat ominous discovery. The similarity between the attempt of the Indian to penetrate through pathless forest, his starvation, his killing the horse for food, and our conditions was striking."

Assiniboine had to kill the horse. They ate with mixed feelings, dried the remaining meat and continued their desperate trek. In the days that followed, there were times when Cheadle thought their chances slim, and Assiniboine would rally everyone; at other times, Assiniboine considered it useless to go on—Cheadle and Milton would struggle ahead and he came up to help them out of their difficulties. O'Byrne became more helpful but was sunk in gloom and no longer read Paley—he said he'd lost his faith and the book sickened him. But when the last of their dried meat was gone, Mrs. Assiniboine produced a private cache she'd hoarded, scraped the flour sack and made "a handsome rubbaboo"; O'Byrne once more perched his one-eyed glasses on his nose and "resumed his theological studies."

For five weeks they saw "no human being, nor for the last three had we seen the smallest evidence of man's presence at any time in the wild forest in which we were buried." Another horse had to be killed; Assiniboine's hand was so lacerated that he couldn't cut trail and Cheadle was weak and ill. Mrs. Assiniboine ably cut trail. Still the valley confined them.

Ten days after finding the headless Indian they heard a crow, "that bird of ill omen which to us proclaimed glad tidings"—open country ahead! Four days later Milton astonished everyone by getting up first and making fire—at daybreak! They came at last to a faint blazed trail; the valley expanded and, with shouts of joy, they emerged from their gloomy forest imprisonment onto a beautiful prairie. While their famished beasts grazed on the first good grass they'd had since leaving Tête Jaune Cache, the exhausted, starving stragglers "at one accord lay on the green turf and basked in the sun."

They met a few Indians on the trail as they continued, and traded the remnants of their belongings for potatoes, fish and berries. After a few more trying days they reached Fort Kamloops. Clothes in tatters, the legs of Milton's trousers torn off above the knees and Cheadle's in ribbons, feet covered only by shreds of moccasins, "faces gaunt, haggard and unshaven, hair long, unkempt and matted"—they feasted. "Our troubles were over at last—at last!"

Their hosts were "anxious to know who we were, where from . . . whether intending to mine or seek employment, and seemed rather incredulous when informed that we were a mere party of *pleasure!*"

As a party of pleasure they resumed their journey with the delighted Assiniboines as their guests. In Victoria they were driven about in a buggy drawn by "a pair of dashing horses," with Milton and Cheadle as chauffeurs "on the box and Assiniboine and family behind inside, to their immense satisfaction"; Milton and Cheadle took them to the theatre and to dinner with the governor! Then the two young adventurers rounded out their Canadian journey with a visit to the Cariboo.

At Fort Kamloops O'Byrne had resumed his overbearing ways, confidently expecting to continue his freeloading. He was sent packing. Before departing, however, he called Dr. Cheadle aside and asked for socks, silk necktie, tea, sugar, bread and money. Lord Milton supplied letters of reference, tea, tobacco and matches and the man in charge at the fort donated "cakes and bacon." With his habitual lack of gratitude he buttonholed the doctor again and "in the coolest manner" repeated his request for money. When he got an indignant refusal, he amicably bid farewell, saying "he bore us no ill will!" Years later they heard that he had arrived in Australia, where he enlivened bush campfires with tales of his daring exploits during a terrible crossing of the Canadian Rockies.

Back in England, Dr. Cheadle served his profession with distinction. Lord Milton returned briefly to Fort William, Ontario, in 1872 with his wife, where he lived for a time in a wilderness cabin—until it burned down. Perhaps it had been built according to the plans he'd so enthusiastically made when they left Fort Milton!

Within a quarter of a century "parties of pleasure" would stream to the Rockies. The way was paved for them by equally daring and persistent men—thousands humble and forgotten; a handful, men of wealth and power, memorable.

12

ACHIEVING THE IMPOSSIBLE

1860, the year Palliser returned from his expedition, marked the end of an epoch. Sir George Simpson died. And with his passing the Golden Age of the fur trade was over. The days of monopoly rule by The Company of Adventurers of England Trading Into Hudson's Bay were numbered; that venerable institution underwent a metamorphosis from which it emerged as a many-tentacled financial giant, under the command of a flinty-eyed, bearded, bushy-browed Scot. He hadn't risen from the ranks with the lightning speed of the Little Emperor. In fact, knowledge of unfolding events would have caused that little autocrat to turn over in his grave.

Sir George, in 1830, had finally made his visit to England to bring back a wife—his lovely cousin, twenty-six years his junior. In 1838 when the young matron was at the gubernatorial mansion-office at Lachine, Quebec, sandy-haired eighteen-year-old Donald Smith arrived from Scotland; Sir George put him at a clerk's desk. Other young apprentices had toiled there and as the young chatelaine was lonely when Simpson was away, she took a friendly interest in the lads so far away from home, sometimes entertaining them at tea. When the master of the house found out he flew into a towering rage. "I am not going to endure having any upstart quill-driving apprentice dangling about a parlour reserved to the gentry and nobility!" he thundered. Donald Smith was promptly banished to a lonely post on the Labrador coast—for twenty-seven years. That was the apprenticeship of the man destined to become one of the most powerful men in Canada, governor of the Hudson's Bay Company, multimillionaire railway baron and future Lord Strathcona.

Donald saved his money at his bleak fur trade post. He invested the savings of his men at their request and they paid him interest. His tall handsome cousin, George Stephen, who had come to Canada in 1850 as a draper's apprentice, made a fortune in woollen and cotton manufacturing and soon became a prominent shareholding official in the Bank of Montreal. Stephen, fashionably dressed (he even had a valet), lived as befitted his station in life; his seedy-looking country cousin Donald didn't impress him particularly when he came on occasional visits. However, Stephen gave him valuable advice about investing his money and when canny cousin Donald came out of his long exile, he was only a hairsbreadth away from being the principal stockholder of the Hudson's Bay Company (he'd taken advantage of a drop in the value of their shares) and one of the Bank of Montreal's wealthiest patrons.

Not only had there been great changes in Donald Smith's fortunes. Canada was changing too. In 1867 Prime Minister Sir John A. Macdonald had presided over the giant step of Canadian Confederation; the Hudson's Bay Company's ancient land rights in the West were transferred to the new dominion in 1870. The fur empire on the Pacific had changed to an isolated crown colony and the growing settlement at Fort Garry had sent Sandford Fleming to petition Britain for a railway. The Canadian West was bound to be settled, but by whom—the fledgling Canadian nation, or the emerging giant to the south? Canada's only hope of holding the western territories lay in linking them to the East by rail. But where were the vast sums required for a transcontinental railway to come from?

Donald Smith began to gather a clan of shrewd acquisitive businessmen—they were empire building. On a trip to St. Paul, Minnesota, Smith found former Canadian J. J. Hill defying the Hudson's Bay Company monopoly on shipping into Fort Garry. In the true spirit of the old fur traders Smith responded by putting up a stiff fight; a boat was built for Norman Kittson, former Canadian, Astorian, free trader and now the Bay's shipping agent on the Red River, and Smith ordered him to battle Hill for control of the shipping trade. Protracted competition, however, promised to be expensive and Donald Smith took another look: if it was going to be too costly to lick 'em—he'd join 'em. He arranged for amalgamation. Smith, Kittson and Hill then lowered their rates and ruthlessly drove all others from the field.

On his travels in the United States, Smith also watched with interest the fate of a bankrupt railway and tried persistently to persuade cousin George (who was now president of the Bank of Montreal) that it would be a good investment. The more cautious Stephen pooh-poohed such a rash venture. But eventually, he agreed to look into the matter; with R. B. Angus, the bank's general manager, and Smith he visited the area served by the line. Stephen was impressed with the number of settlers flocking in; the railroad might be worth a try after all. Smith, Kittson, Hill, Stephen and Angus were in the railway business. After ten months of operation, the St. Paul, Minneapolis and Manitoba Railroad (as the reorganized company was called) realized profits which raised eyebrows in financial circles, and George Stephen as president was the wealthiest man in Montreal. They never looked back.

Sir Hugh Allan, steamship tycoon, wanted a share of the current railway bonanza and manoeuvred to cash in on the gold expected to flow from a government charter to build a Canadian transcontinental railroad. He got carried away as the prize dangled within reach. Sir John A. Macdonald was waging an election campaign and Sir Hugh contributed substantially to his party. Sir John's Conservatives won but correspondence relating to the "donations" had been filched; when the gleeful Liberal opposition broadcast the news that Allan, with his charter for the railway pending, had "bribed" the government, the fat was in the fire.

In the ensuing scandal Sir John was fighting for political survival. It promised to be a near thing, but at the last minute Donald Smith, a now influential Conservative member of the House, was expected to save the day. Before a hushed assembly Smith rose and announced that he would be glad to vote confidence in the government—could he "do so conscientiously." He had thrown Sir John to the wolves! That worthy Scot was enraged: "I could lick that man Smith quicker than hell could frizzle a feather!" he shouted. He felt that Smith had privately promised his support, so the outburst was understandable. But Smith maintained that Sir John had been too far gone in his cups to remember what had been said at the time. Sir John had been drinking heavily. He had even more reason to do so now. His government had to resign.

Sharing his defeat was the first Canadian Pacific Railway Company. Sir John began the long struggle to return to power; Donald Smith and his associates continued to rake in their profits. Across the continent in British Columbia, Walter Moberly had been trying to overcome another formidable obstacle to an all-Canadian railroad—the mountain barrier.

Paul Kane had interested Moberly in the Pacific coast; armed with a letter from Sir George Simpson, Moberly arrived in British Columbia in 1858 where he scoured the wilderness as surveyor for that colony's government. In the winter of 1859 he met Captain Palliser, who told him that all hope of finding a route through the mountains of the Gold Range west of the Columbia River would have to be abandoned. "They present an unbroken and impassable barrier," he maintained. Moberly thought not, and five years later set out to prove it.

From the south arm of Shuswap Lake he came to a valley running east into the Gold Range. Disturbing an eagles' nest, his interest was aroused as he watched the birds soar far up the valley. He followed and successfully penetrated the armour of the Gold Range at what he named Eagle Pass. He then attacked that other obstacle, the Selkirks, which Hector had found impassable. He ascended the Illecillewaet River Valley, east of present-day Revelstoke, but winter was approaching and the Indians guiding him refused to continue; he had to turn back without finding the pass. That dramatic discovery was not to be made for another sixteen years.

Sir Sandford Fleming was put in charge of the railway surveys which began in 1871, when British Columbia joined Confederation—under the terms of union the Canadian government had agreed to start a transcontinental railway within two years. Thousands of men fanned out all over the country, looking for the best line, and Walter Moberly was charged with finding the way across the Selkirks and the Rockies. He favoured following the Big Bend of the Columbia around by Boat Encampment, skirting the Selkirks; the narrow valleys and snowslides he'd seen in the Illecillewaet Valley six years before indicated that the railroad there would be expensive and dangerous.

But which pass should he choose across the main chain of the Rockies?

In 1871 he had his headquarters near the mouth of Blaeberry Creek. Long-silent Howse Pass echoed to the ring of axes, and chains snaked through the dark forest as surveyors examined the route of their great predecessor, David Thompson. Moberly intended to try again for a better route through the Selkirks, but in 1872 he was ordered to move camp to the Yellowhead. Once again the "rapids, riffles and canyons" of the Columbia carried laden canoes. Horses carrying three hundred-pound packs laboured through the primeval forests at its shores; men and supplies moved along the old fur trade route of Thompson's Athabasca Pass to set up headquarters near the present townsite of Jasper. The bleak solitude at the Committee's Punch Bowl was broken by the steady tramp of heavily burdened men and heaving horses as the white man resumed the search for the best way across the fastness of the Rockies.

In 1872 Sandford Fleming came to see the Yellowhead for himself. Approaching present-day Jasper Park, the mountains towered "in a grand silver-tipped line . . . all their grandeur presenting as it were an impenetrable wall." But rounding Roche Miette, "an easy ingress" into the mountains was revealed. As they rode toward the Miette Valley Fleming's party felt that "nature had united all forces here to make this the natural highway into the heart of the Rocky Mountains."

Lulled into false optimism by the placid-looking Miette River, they thought at first that early travellers had exaggerated the difficulties of the Yellowhead route. They changed their minds. Indeed, as they continued along Milton and Cheadle's trail "down the frightful North Thompson," they marvelled at the pluck and hardihood of those two young men who had refused to accept defeat. Fleming's journey was not without its own hardships but he continued to favour the Yellowhead for the railway. By 1880 surveyors had located the line from Fort William through Yellowhead Pass and along the Thompson, and a brilliant young American engineer, Andrew Onderdonk, had started on his contract to build the Pacific section. Elsewhere the road was being built at a snail's pace, in bits and pieces.

But in 1880 lethargy vanished. Pent-up forces were about to be unleashed. Sir John A. Macdonald was back in power, refurbishing his dream of a transcontinental line and Donald Smith's syndicate was ready to invest its millions. They applied for the railway charter and got it, although Donald Smith's name was not on the contract—to mollify Sir John. However, he was down for five thousand shares and his grey eminence loomed in the wings.

The new Canadian Pacific Railway Company and Sir John A. Macdonald were now committed to achieving the impossible. The infant dominion had a population of four million (the United States had forty million people when it undertook its first transcontinental); between the settled East and Fort Garry there was nothing but forest, granite, lake and muskeg, and the tiny scattered settlements in the West were cut off from the Pacific by the rocky backbone of the continent. Across this immense and sometimes apparently impassable terrain the road was to be flung and the settlers brought in to make it pay. In a colossal act of faith the C.P.R. and Sir John undertook to overcome those tremendous obstacles in ten years.

To William Cornelius Van Horne obstacles were merely challenges. This fantastically dynamic American had forged a reputation as impressive as his physical stature—son of a distinguished Knickerbocker family, a boy telegrapher who rose to the power and prestige of railroad manager, ruthlessly efficient, a born gambler—at thirty-eight he threw away security and plunged with astonishing energy into the task of translating Canada's impractical dream into reality.

As general superintendent he set up headquarters in Winnipeg (formerly Fort Garry) in 1881 and announced that he intended to build an unheard-of five hundred miles that year. "Nothing is impossible," he said to engineer J. H. E. Secretan. "Just show me the route, that's all I want, and if you can't I'll have your scalp." He built four hundred and eighty miles that year. At his bidding, with army-like precision, thousands of men, mules and horse-drawn scrapers tore the unbroken soil and graded it. Loads of hand-hewn ties were heaved into place; a black belching locomotive steamed up and loads of shining rails clanged down—the air rang as they were hammered into place. Just ahead went the surveyors and locators; sometimes the ink was scarcely dry on their plans when the army of tracklayers was at their heels. And as the silver snake wound westward, no acceptable route had yet been found across the mountains.

Like Sir George Simpson the C.P.R. wanted the shortest route through paying territory. They discarded Sandford Fleming's Yellowhead Pass—it was too far north. Recently it had been definitely established that the southern plains were suitable for farming and cattle raising; syndicate member

J. J. Hill was believed to have coal interests in the south and furthermore, if the rails went too far north of the boundary, American lines would throw up spur lines and cut into C.P.R. profits. Where, then, should the line be threaded through the more southerly mountains?

J. J. Hill had been responsible for hiring Van Horne. Impressed by another American's ingenuity in discovering economical railway locations, Hill recommended him for the job of finding the best way through the mountains. Major A. B. Rogers, fifty-two years old, a Yale engineering graduate and onetime ship's carpenter, was a "short, snappy little chap" with enormous flying Dundreary whiskers. In the field he wore an old pith helmet and canvas suit—it was said that with a sea biscuit and some bacon rinds in one pocket and a few plugs of tobacco in the other he could travel for weeks in the wilderness. He spared neither himself nor man nor beast and his brusque staccato speech was liberally adorned with the most picturesque profanity, earning him the nickname of the Bishop. His scientific instruments consisted of a compass and an aneroid slung around his neck.

After consulting Walter Moberly, the major decided to attack the Selkirks first, from the west. Sending equipped engineering units of 125 men to Bow River Gap at the entrance to Banff Park, he left St. Paul, Minnesota, on April 1st, 1881, travelled by rail to San Francisco (the shortest route at the time) and made his way to Fort Kamloops. This took three weeks, but characteristically, he had every confidence that he could now cross mountain terrain unknown to him and join his men east of the Rockies by July 1st.

Accompanied by his twenty-one-year-old nephew, Albert Rogers, he bought supplies at Fort Kamloops and with the help of Chief Louie (whom he "subsidized") and the priest in charge of the mission, he "enlisted ten strapping young Indians on rather an ironclad contract"; they were to serve him "without grumbling until discharged, and if any came back without a letter of good report his wages were to go to the church and the chief was to lay on 100 lashes . . ."

Proceeding to Eagle River by boat, they spent fourteen days getting their supplies through the Gold Range by Eagle Pass, built a raft to cross the Columbia near present-day Revelstoke and took up Moberly's unfinished task of finding a pass by ascending the Illecillewaet River.

For two weeks, with food strictly rationed, the major pushed his men

*Major A. B. Rogers. Standing in triumph at the summit of the pass he
had discovered for the C.P.R. through the Selkirks, Rogers and the stately
Sir Sandford Fleming celebrated with a game of leapfrog!*

COURTESY B.C. ARCHIVES, VICTORIA (A-01857)

until they were all "as lean as greyhounds" and only fear of the lash kept the Indians from deserting. It took five days to cover the first sixteen miles! This took them to the point where Moberly had been forced to turn back. Carrying one-hundred-pound packs, they forged ahead in deep snow; wading in icy streams and struggling through dripping underbrush, they were soaked to the skin. Avalanches crashed down, churning the forest into matchwood in their wake. When the snow became too soft for daytime travel, they walked at night, and on the 29th of May they reached the backbone of the Selkirks.

In the shade of a towering pyramid that they named Syndicate Peak (today's Mount Sir Donald), they climbed until four in the afternoon when they reached what appeared to be the summit of the range. The major ordered the immediate ascent of a mountain to the south to see what lay ahead. For tension-filled hours they "crawled along the ledges, getting a toe-hole here, a finger-hole there"; four Indians fell over a precipice—mercifully they were not hurt and made their way back to the valley. Late in the evening the rest of the party pulled themselves onto a crest high on present-day Mount Avalanche.

"Such a view! Never to be forgotten!" wrote Albert Rogers. "Our eyesight caromed from one bold peak to another for miles in all directions . . . Everything was covered with a shroud of white, giving the whole landscape the appearance of snow-clad desolation." Below lay Major Rogers's Pass.

They spent the night on their eerie perch, stamping their feet to ward off frostbite and taking turns whipping each other with packstraps to keep up circulation. With only eight days' rations left they had to turn back without crossing the Selkirks, but the major had seen enough to convince him that a feasible pass had been found.

Making an arduous dash along the Columbia he went to Spokane, rode the old fur trail up through Idaho, followed the Kootenay with two Indian guides, crossed Kananaskis Pass and arrived to meet his men at the Gap on July 15th—just two weeks behind schedule!

He now examined the passes through the Rockies in the vicinity of the Bow. Men sent to report on Howse Pass pronounced it an unfavourable route and by the end of 1881 he'd satisfied himself that it was to be Hector's Kicking Horse Pass. American locators tolerated steeper grades and sharper curves than Sir Sandford's more cautious engineers and the C.P.R. was made up of men in a hurry—caution could be thrown to the winds.

Crews surveyed east and west of the Rockies' summit that winter and in the spring of 1882, starting from the mouth of the Kicking Horse River, the major completed his exploration of Rogers Pass; he and Albert Rogers reached the summit of the pass from the east. The way was clear. But the mountains were not yet vanquished. The rails had still to pierce the ridge-pole of the continent.

When Sir Sandford Fleming was recalled from England to give his opinion of the proposed route, he got a vivid impression of the magnitude of the task ahead. The rails had reached Calgary when he arrived in August of 1883 but he was astonished at how little the engineers in charge of the survey east of the mountains knew about the road west—he didn't realize that long stretches of it had still to be surveyed. He was even told that Rogers had not yet found the pass through the Selkirks.

Sir Sandford was apparently unaware of the fact that the brisk major had made an official announcement of his discovery of the pass and, incidentally, had made it in his own fashion. One evening during the dinner hour the doorbell had rung at George Stephen's new Montreal mansion. His butler protested to the "unheralded and dilapidated" visitor that the master could not be disturbed. The little caller stood firm, however, and Mr. Stephen was summoned. Major Rogers conveyed his momentous news and, so the story goes, was taken in hand by the butler, suitably clothed and welcomed to dinner.

In the late summer of 1883 Rogers was back at the Kicking Horse River; Sir Sandford's party travelled west from Calgary to meet him and get first-hand information about the proposed route through the mountains. On the way they had to negotiate the canyon of the Kicking Horse. The travellers "moved forward down and up gorges, hundreds of feet deep, amongst rocky masses, where the poor horses had to clamber as best they could amid sharp points and deep crevices, running the constant risk of a broken leg . . . A series of precipices run sheer up from the boiling current to form a contracted canyon. A path has therefore been traced along the hillside, and on the steep acclivity . . . there is scarcely a foothold; nevertheless, we have to follow for some miles this thread of a trail, which seemed to us by no means in excess of the requirements of the chamois and mountain goat. We cross clay, rock and gravel slides at a giddy height. To look down gives one an uncomfortable dizziness, to make the head swim and the view unsteady, even with men of tried nerve . . . We are from five to eight hundred feet high on a path of from ten to fifteen inches wide, and at some parts almost obliterated, with slopes above and below us so steep that a stone would roll into the torrent in the abyss below. There are no trees or branches or twigs which we can grip to aid us in our advance . . . I do not think that I can ever forget this terrible walk; it was the greatest trial I ever experienced."

When they caught up to him the jubilant major announced that he had indeed found the pass through the Selkirks and escorted them to the summit himself. On the meadow crowning Rogers Pass the triumphant major received congratulations from Sir Sandford; lacking wine they drank a toast to his discovery from a clear mountain stream and feasted on the abundant berries. Then, as their men watched gravely, the stately Sir Sandford and the curt little major played leapfrog!

The rough and ready Rogers was very proud of finding the pass which bears his name—he carried the C.P.R.'s bonus cheque of five thousand dollars for years until Van Horne waved an engraved gold watch under his nose, saying it was his when he cashed that cheque. Still scouring the continent for railway lines, in 1887 he was thrown from his horse in the Coeur d'Alene mountains. He never recovered. Two years later he died.

Sir Sandford gave qualified approval to the route (his was the first party to make a continuous traverse along the actual line of the railway from Lake Superior to the Pacific) and Van Horne hurled his rails into the mountains. Peaks threw back the sound of rock drills, giant powder thundered and men ducked for cover, axes gashed sylvan forests, spidery bridges spanned deep chasms, miles of snow sheds were slung up the mountain sides in Rogers Pass and the rails crept along the precipices. Forging east, Onderdonk's sixty-five hundred Chinese from Oregon, California and Hong Kong worked with thousands of white men, blasting grades out of the naked cliffs and packing in supplies along canyons where Simon Fraser had seen the Indians' spindly ladders clinging precariously above the boiling water. By the end of 1883 it appeared certain that the titanic task would be finished well before the deadline.

Then, grim as the peaks it skirted, the spectre of financial ruin loomed before the C.P.R. Construction costs were devouring the syndicate's millions; depression struck and the threat of bankruptcy sat like a wolf on the railway barons' doorsteps. Against all odds, Smith and Stephen refused to throw in the sponge and Sir John A. Macdonald fought desperately to rescue his cherished dream.

The railway project was vehemently opposed in many influential circles in Canada; it was regarded as an immensely expensive gamble which would only serve to enrich a handful of tycoons. A government loan was imperative, but Sir John's proposal to grant one met serious opposition. By a narrow margin he managed, at last, to push the relief measure through parliament.

In a matter of months the additional millions were gone. Stephen and Smith now pledged their own personal assets and scoured the international money market for loans—without success. The payroll couldn't be met and in Rogers Pass three hundred armed men went on strike for pay that was thirteen months in arrears. The C.P.R. was about to go under, only months from completion.

A frantic Stephen hounded Sir John and again the prime minister promised to do what he could to snatch the enterprise from the jaws of defeat. Stephen sent Donald Smith a famous telegram, a reminder that their kinfolk in the ancient Clan Grant used to rally before battle at a great rock, Craigellachie, in the valley of the River Spey—it was their rock of defiance. The wire read only: "Stand fast, Craigellachie!" For there were still dark days ahead.

Sir John ("Old Tomorrow" to the harassed Stephen) had every reason to put off requesting another loan; there were strident admonitions against any more "handouts" to the C.P.R., even among his ministers. He waited, manoeuvred, delayed; ruin hung over the syndicate like a pall.

Salvation came from an unexpected quarter. The West was threatened with a second Métis and Indian uprising; fifteen years before it had taken three months to get troops west. But Canada now had a railway—with gaps. Van Horne said he would transport the militia. Packing them into flat cars, hauling them with farm sleighs where the rails hadn't yet been laid, he got them west in a matter of days—in time to snuff out the Riel Rebellion. The C.P.R. had proved its worth to the nation.

*Donald Smith driving the Last Spike, November 7, 1885. A bareheaded
Major Rogers stands far left; William Cornelius Van Horne and the tall,
square-bearded Sir Sandford Fleming stand beside Smith.*
COURTESY CANADIAN PACIFIC RAILWAY ARCHIVES, MONTREAL (NA1960A)

Sir John took a bit more time to let this lesson make its impression on public opinion; clamouring creditors stood ready to take over the railway. Harried and exhausted, President George Stephen managed to prolong the life of the C.P.R. from day to day. At a directors' meeting he made what Van Horne called the finest speech he'd ever heard. "Donald," he concluded, "when they come they mustn't find us with a dollar." An inventory was taken of the silver, paintings, furnishings and statuary at Stephen's mansion. Disaster seemed imminent.

Gradually Sir John's cabinet came to realize that if the C.P.R. "went down the Government would fall the day after." When the prime minister at last applied for the loan he was successful. Stephen's persistent appeals in the international money market also bore fruit. The line could be completed.

Just west of Revelstoke, B.C., on November 7th, 1885, a cold grey mist clung to the cliffs over Craigellachie. A great locomotive throbbed, waiting to thunder west over the unused rails. A knot of workmen clustered round an iron plate which had been placed to join the rails running west to those running east. Beside it stood a peppery little man with flamboyant whiskers; next to him, top-hatted, bulky Van Horne and towering, square-bearded Sandford Fleming watched solemnly. A commanding figure with piercing eyes, unbelievably bushy brows and jutting beard picked up the great hammer—and drove the Last Spike.

That hammer blow by the austere man in the tall silk hat marked the completion of one of the greatest railway projects ever undertaken. And Donald Smith symbolized in that act something more: the fur trader of long ago had closed the last link in a chain tenuously begun and relentlessly forged by his adventurous, rock-ribbed predecessors—men who had refused to be daunted by the barrier of the Rockies.

A few months after that historic day an old man boarded the Transcontinental. The Architect of Confederation was going to see, for the first time, the extent of his dominion. Past eastern lakes and forests, round rock and muskeg, Sir John A. Macdonald travelled; on to bustling Winnipeg, then westward—for days the vast empty plains unrolled beside him. Soon he would see the Pacific. As the long voyage mounted to its climax, from a special seat on the cowcatcher of the locomotive Sir John saw the Rockies.

Perhaps it was not only the wind streaming into his face that brought tears to his eyes.

Mount Stephen stands guard at Kicking Horse Pass; the Van Horne Range marches along the skyline beside the Kicking Horse River; Mount Macdonald and the white pyramid of Mount Sir Donald tower over Rogers Pass. They stand as enduring monuments to men who achieved the impossible.

INITIATING A NEW AGE

At staggering cost civilization had at last breached the Rockies. But the barrier presented yet another challenge. "The mountain section won't pay for the grease on the axles!" an early opponent of the railway taunted.

Van Horne had assessed the situation during construction. Crossing from Revelstoke to the summit of Kicking Horse Pass in the autumn of 1884, conditions were even worse on the abominable tote road than they had been for Sir Sandford Fleming. Sinking to the hips in slush he slogged with his party up to Rogers Pass; over the unfinished trestle spanning Mountain Creek the men crawled on hands and knees—a few days before, six men had crashed to their death in the swirling current 160 feet below. Imperturbably Van Horne walked across on the two loose planks balanced precariously over the chasm. Through bog and mud they foundered, reaching the next work camp mud splattered and drenched.

Stopping for a day to dry his clothes, Van Horne stomped cheerfully about his business in a borrowed flannel shirt and overalls which were split up the back and inelegantly laced together with clothesline to accommodate his ample girth. Then, as the party proceeded east, provisions ran out. Going without food for two days was a real hardship for Van Horne, who had a prodigious appetite, but his cultivated palate rebelled at bannock made from flour which had leaked into the cook's saddlebag, where it was copiously mixed with "curry-comb leavings, etc." As he toiled up to camp he announced that he'd just made a momentous discovery: a hungry man could smell boiling ham ten miles away!

Inspection of the route indicated clearly that construction, maintenance and operating expenses would eat up profits. At Rogers Pass, thundering avalanches meant building miles of snowsheds as protection against their destructive power; giant rotary plows would be needed to clear the tracks and monstrous auxiliary locomotives would have to haul the trains over the steepest grades. One way to pare costs was to avoid hauling heavy dining cars over steep grades, so Van Horne planned small inns for Siding 29 in the Bow Valley, at Field below Kicking Horse Pass and at Rogers Pass. But it wasn't merely a matter of keeping down the overhead. The mountain section must be made to pay.

Once again Van Horne was equal to the challenge. This surprising tycoon, perfectly at home with his hardbitten, sweating workmen, organizing footraces and boisterously playing cards the whole night through, also had a cultivated artistic sense (his collection of paintings and delicate Japanese porcelains was world-famous) and a keen appreciation of natural beauty. When he had approached the Rockies from the east for the first time in 1883, Lac des Arcs was perfect in a setting of new-fallen snow, frosted spruce and soaring peaks. The burly railroader was enchanted and immediately on his return east urged the dominion government to create a national park there. The C.P.R. had insisted on the shortest direct line through the mountains; Van Horne had found that the route chosen ran through some of the finest alpine scenery on the continent. "We can't export the scenery— we'll import the tourists!" He set out to introduce the Rockies to the world.

With characteristic vigour and flair he recruited scores of artists, photographers and writers; they came, were captivated by what they saw and prepared elaborate brochures proclaiming the Canadian Rockies as "the Mountain Playground of the World." Parlour and sleeping cars were designed for comfort and aesthetic appeal; the cuisine was above reproach. "Parisian Politeness on the Canadian Pacific" Van Horne's posters boasted, and his line lived up to the promise.

Some of his own advertising copy evoked smiles: "'How high we live,'" said the Duke to the Prince, "on the Canadian Pacific Railway.'" But it worked. Soon dukes and princes were coming from every corner of the world and Van Horne's staff served them with pride and finesse. Only his own beloved and devoted personal porter could, without reprimand, commit the endearing faux pas of consistently addressing Her Royal Highness, the Princess Louise, as "Your Succulency"!

Visitors not only came in increasing numbers to see the Rockies; they wanted to stay awhile. So at Siding 29 (renamed Banff for the Banffshire birthplace of President George Stephen), Van Horne selected a superb site on the heavily wooded slopes of Sulphur Mountain and engaged an American architect to design a French-style chateau in memory of the voyageurs who had helped to pioneer the mountain passes. Arriving to inspect its construction, the usually even-tempered Van Horne staged "a magnificent explosion." The builder had turned the plans around so that the kitchen faced the breath-taking panorama! On the spot Van Horne designed a rotunda to provide the coveted view for his guests. When the building was finished he proudly advertised the Banff Springs Hotel as "the Finest Hotel on the North American Continent."

The government had established a national park in the Banff region (partly because of Van Horne's enthusiastic recommendation and partly because of the hot mineral springs discovered there), and soon paths and carriage roads were being cleared. For the convenience and enjoyment of visitors the railway provided saddle horses and carriage rides. As their livery business grew, they looked for an enterprising local man familiar with the area to take it over and build it up.

John Brewster, an Irishman, had brought his family from Ontario; when he saw the hot springs gushing from Sulphur Mountain he decided that Banff would some day be a mecca for visitors. He settled down, working as a blacksmith, and with the help of his family established a small dairy which supplied the Banff Springs Hotel; his sons acted as fishing guides when they were mere striplings. The C.P.R. persuaded Brewster to accept the company's backing for a ten thousand-dollar bank loan to buy their livery business—like Smith, Kittson, Stephen, Angus and Hill, the Brewsters never looked back. The way they parlayed that loan into a fortune would have won the admiration of those early tycoons! The Brewsters too became transportation czars; with their diversified enterprises this colourful family built an empire which made their name world-famous and young Jim, a genial westerner

The old Banff Springs Hotel, commissioned by Van Horne in 1884 and advertised by him as "the Finest Hotel on the North American Continent."
COURTESY WHYTE MUSEUM OF THE CANADIAN ROCKIES, BANFF (V92/NG3-2)

with a gift for showmanship, became an outstanding promoter of Banff.

Shrewdly the railway realized that another local man would also be "a distinct asset," as one of their officials put it. Tom Wilson, a pioneer with "extensive knowledge of the area and an interesting and romantic past," was a charming raconteur; they thought he would "stimulate interest in the mountains." Their assessment was accurate. For many years Tom did for the C.P.R. and the Rockies a job that would do credit to a highly paid public relations man.

He had come west from Ontario as a member of the Northwest Mounted Police but resigned to pack supplies for the C.P.R. mountain survey, working for a time with Major Rogers. Camped with the pack-train at Laggan (today's Lake Louise Station) on a cloudless night in 1882, young Tom was startled by the crash and rumble of distant thunder. Stoney Indians camped nearby told him that the noise came from a great white mountain above "the Lake of Little Fishes." From the heavily wooded valley there was no sign of either a snowy mountain or a lake and Tom's curiosity was aroused.

Next morning he persuaded one of the Indians, Edwin the Gold Seeker, to take him to the great white mountain. Together they climbed through the quiet forest until they emerged suddenly on the shore of a peacock blue lake. The dark green forest "which had never known an axe" mantled the beautifully coloured mountains springing sheer from the water's edge; the gleaming gable of the great white mountain formed a magnificent backdrop, and over all lay the exquisite peace of those places "untouched by the hand of man."

That memorable day when Tom became one of the earliest, if not indeed the first white man to gaze on the matchless beauty of Lake Louise, he recalled time and again to the end of his long life. Fascinated visitors heard him tell too of the time he'd wandered from a survey camp at Kicking Horse summit, searching for a strayed horse until its tracks led him to lovely, isolated Emerald Lake. Only the Stoney Indians had penetrated here and there into the surrounding mountain wilderness and from them he got information which would soon be eagerly sought by patrons of the C.P.R. To the outfitting and guiding business Wilson established came Bill Peyto, Jim Simpson, Fred Stephens, Ralph Edwards, Billy Warren, the Tabuteau brothers and other adventurous men destined to play an important part in the next phase of exploration in the Rockies.

While guests enjoyed the luxury and exclusiveness of the Banff Springs Hotel, strolling on peaceful paths, riding in carriages and dressing for dinner; while Victorian ladies, elegantly gowned, daintily shod and with frothy hats atop high-piled coiffures ventured to the foot of the great glacier at Glacier House (near the summit of Rogers Pass), across the Atlantic an Irish clergyman was eagerly anticipating a more strenuous vacation in the Selkirks. The visit of the Reverend Mr. William Spotswood Green had far-reaching consequences.

His interest in the Rockies was aroused by his cousin, the Reverend Mr. Henry Swanzy, who in 1884 attended the meeting of the British Association for the Advancement of Science, assembled that year in Winnipeg. Van Horne persuaded some of these distinguished visitors to see the West, offering to send them in a special car to the end of steel in the Rockies. A few members of that august assembly decided to continue west over the unfinished part of the line and like Van Horne, they arrived at a work camp mud caked and soaked. They too were outfitted in overalls, and afforded the rail crew unintentional amusement by sprinting after chipmunks in vain endeavours to capture specimens of mountain fauna.

The hardships of their journey to Kamloops did nothing to diminish their enthusiasm for the grandeur of the scenery. When the Reverend Mr. Swanzy returned to England he could hardly wait to tell his cousin about the wild, rugged alpine country he'd seen. Untrodden peaks! Valleys that had never known the foot of man! Magic words to that young clergyman, who like so many members of his calling had been scrambling in the Alps for years.

Four years later, Mr. Green realized "the visionary desire" his cousin had kindled with his descriptions of "vast pine forests with their background of glacier-clad peaks." The two parsons spent six weeks in the Selkirks and with instruments supplied by the Royal Geographical Society, they mapped and photographed (using the wine cellar at Glacier House for a dark room), and compiled the first topographical map of the Selkirks in the immediate vicinity of the railway.

Van Horne's publicity was about to be enthusiastically augmented, but to a different audience—one which was to make a far greater impact on the development of the Rockies. Mr. Green's papers to the Royal Geographical Society and the British Alpine Club as well as his charming book, *Among the Selkirk Glaciers*, were full of glowing accounts of "a perfect alpine paradise . . . with dark green forests, rushing streams, purple peaks, silvery ice and cloudless skies . . ."

Swiss and English alpinists came to see. It was true! Here were miles upon miles of virgin peaks! On their heels came an American, Professor Charles Fay of Tufts College. The tall, heavily bearded president of the Appalachian Alpine Club came almost by chance. Stopping at Glacier House on the way home from California, he had only a few hours to spare. But there soared the challenging summit of Mount Sir Donald! Up he climbed, far enough to see "the chaotic upheaval of billowing summits, crags and ridges extending beyond the utmost bound of vision." Unlike his native mountains, these were glacier-capped and snowfields abounded—here, right beside the railway was terrain to challenge the true alpinist. It was the beginning of a long and happy association with the Canadian Rockies for him and his climbing associates; forty years later, at eighty-four, the majestic and beloved veteran was still tramping about happily at the Canadian Alpine Club camp.

The Irish clergymen, the English and Swiss climbers and the American professor were the advance guard of a small band of pioneers who, like a handful of men in every age, needed to see "what lies back of beyond." Sombre professors, professors gay and witty, earnest and inspired men of the cloth, scientists quaint and dedicated, carefree adventure-loving undergraduates, eminent business and professional men, a little Quaker widow—they wrote exciting chapters in the Canadian Rockies' Golden Age of discovery.

They journeyed into an unknown land, and when their work was done they cherished "the memory of long days on the trails of northern forests, of peaks and sunlit icefields, of campfires in the purple twilight, of snow-capped ranges clothed in the glory of early morning." In Canada's great alpine wilderness they wrought a transformation.

TANTALIZING GLIMPSES INTO THE UNKNOWN

To encourage the growing popularity of mountaineering the railway brought two professional Swiss guides to the Selkirks in 1899. By 1901 these heavily booted, pipe-smoking stalwarts were even shepherding a lady to the top of Mount Sir Donald, which had formerly looked so frightfully inaccessible.

It was no rugged female veteran who made that ascent but a dainty little Englishwoman who'd never climbed a mountain in her life. Mrs. Evelyn Berens's climbing plans created a great stir and the matter of suitable wardrobe required careful consultation with other lady guests; her husband's best knickerbockers were considered most appropriate. During the climb she found herself unconsciously grasping them delicately between thumb and forefinger as though they were a gown!

Van Horne's promotion of Canada's scenic wonderland was certainly paying off; when Mr. Green and his cousin stayed at Glacier House in 1888 they found it bursting at the seams—on several occasions they arrived back after a few days' absence to find that their rooms had been rented temporarily and their extra tent requisitioned for the overflow of guests.

On their way home Mr. Green and Mr. Swanzy hoped to round out their season's explorations with the ascent of Mount Temple which J. J. McArthur, then surveying for the first detailed map of the area bordering the railway, had found to be the highest peak in the immediate vicinity. As he couldn't take time to show them the way to what he considered the best approach for their climb, they decided at least to get a good look at it from Lake Louise.

At Laggan a timber contractor who had been to the lake warned them that they could easily get lost, but they set off confidently along the dim trail Tom Wilson had cut through the forest since his first visit there. Separating at one point where the track was uncertain, Mr. Green arrived on the shore first. "I was quite unprepared for the full beauty of the scene . . . nothing of the kind could possibly surpass it!" How many thousands have echoed his words!

Expecting his companion to join him momentarily, he built a raft of floating logs in happy anticipation of an exploratory sail on the silver-rippled water. He photographed and sketched. Still there was no sign of Mr. Swanzy. Then with startling swiftness a terrible storm broke; ominous clouds swirled about the peaks, the placid water was lashed to white fury and peals of thunder rang from crag to crag. "The very mountains seemed about to crash around my ears." Crawling into his little tent, which the gale threatened to tear from its moorings, he listened to the roar of the forest and worried about his friend. By nightfall Mr. Swanzy hadn't put in an appearance. Calm returned to the lake; the wail of a solitary loon accentuated the awesome loneliness.

Sleeping fitfully as avalanches crashed from the glaciers, Mr. Green rose at dawn and hurried down to Laggan. He found that Mr. Swanzy had returned to spend the night there rather than attempt to find the lake in the storm; in the morning he had dashed back up to the lake looking for his cousin. Mr. Green went up again to meet him but they returned separately to Laggan, for so thick was the forest that they had unknowingly passed each other on the way.

Five years later Yale undergraduate Samuel Allen of Chicago and another young climber-explorer, Walter Wilcox from Washington, D.C., climbed together near Glacier House. Then they too went on to Lake Louise. The tiny rustic chalet the C.P.R. had built there in 1890 had burned to the ground and Wilcox and Allen camped in the primeval solitude surrounded by "peaks hitherto, no doubt, undisturbed by human foot." They failed in their attempts to climb Mount Victoria and Mount Temple but returned home eagerly looking forward to a whole summer of hunting, photographing, exploring, climbing and mapping in their alluring mountain hideaway.

Lake Louise and the first chalet, as they were in 1890.
COURTESY ERNEST BROWN COLLECTION, PROVINCIAL ARCHIVES OF ALBERTA, EDMONTON (B9785)

In 1894 the five-member Yale Lake Louise Club (as they grandly called it) found the manager, Mr. Astley, putting the finishing touches to the C.P.R.'s new little log chalet, where they paid the handsome sum of twelve dollars a week which included meals and the use of horse and boat. Mr. Astley's managerial duties were very diversified—after every storm the trail to Laggan was blocked by windfalls and his skill with an axe was required to open up the track so that baggage, mail and food supplies could be brought up for his guests.

After browsing through a book on the techniques of mountain climbing, the inexperienced members of the club felt ready to storm the heights. The intrepid trio of Wilcox, Frissell and Henderson attacked the frowning black precipices of snow-capped Mount Lefroy; it repelled its first assailants. A tremendous boulder toppled from the rotten cliffs above, painfully grazing young Frissell and leaving him perfectly helpless far up on the mountain. His shaken companions managed to get him down to the glacier; Wilcox rushed for help to the chalet and sent for the doctor to come from Banff by hand-car on the railway. Happily, the young man soon recovered in the hospital although William Twin, an Indian helping to carry him back to the chalet, was touchingly concerned for his welfare. It was probably not too reassuring to the patient to hear his rescuer solicitously asking time and again, "You think you die? Me think so too!"

A few days later the rest of the party were again on the Lefroy Glacier struggling toward a notch east of the forbidding mountain, discovery bent this time. It was a "cloudy cheerless day" as they worked hard cutting steps up the steep icy slopes. Each wondered separately why on earth he'd come; it was "like trudging through some lonely polar land of desolate grandeur." Amid squalls of rain and snow they arrived at last on the summit of Mitre Pass where the curtain was raised: the last tatters of cloud rolled from the summits and the sun revealed in all its glory a beautiful green valley far below. They were so elated by the dramatic change from grey arctic gloom that they roped up and glissaded merrily down the fifteen hundred-foot slope to see the "sunlit fairyland" which they named Paradise Valley. Returning to Lake Louise, they ambitiously outfitted themselves with an ancient packhorse and set out to investigate their new-found valley.

What the youthful quartette didn't know about tracking through moun-

Jim Brewster, Walter Wilcox and Tom Wilson.
COURTESY WHYTE MUSEUM OF THE CANADIAN ROCKIES, BANFF (M517/43)

tain wilderness and about the ways of horses would, as Mr. Wilcox said, have filled volumes. One day, leading their "very stupid old horse" through forest and streams, over boulders and hidden potholes, they approached a tree inclined over the path. They couldn't go around; it was too low to go under and too high to jump—or so they thought. But their old nag thought otherwise and prepared "for the effort of its life." The man in the lead jumped aside and in his haste fell headlong into the bush; the horse made its tremendous leap, caught its hind leg on the tree and went sprawling onto its back with four legs pointing to the sky, its large packs rendering it as helpless "as a great overturned turtle." The man behind, getting the full backlash from the springing tree, was sent flying with a resounding smack in the face. The little party blundered blissfully on, but by the end of the season they were ready to travel with local guides.

To climax their explorations in Paradise Valley they climbed Mount Aberdeen and the imposing Mount Temple, where they "stood on the highest point then reached in Canada."

The year before, when Allen and Wilcox had been defeated on Mount Temple, Wilcox had turned a corner in a vain attempt to find another way up. From his vantage point he saw below "a narrow, secluded valley with a small lake enclosed by wild rugged precipices—a scene of awesome desolation." And Desolation Valley he named it six years later when exploring it. Climbing a ridge of enormous fallen rocks which ages ago had been hurled from the naked cliffs above, he saw before him "one of the most beautiful lakes that I have ever seen . . . No scene has ever given me an equal impression of inspiring solitude and rugged grandeur. I stood on a great stone of the moraine where, from a slight elevation, a magnificent view of the lake lay before me, and while studying the details of this unknown and unvisited spot, spent the happiest half hour of my life." He called it Moraine Lake.

Setting off on a separate expedition in 1894, Allen and Yule Carryer, a young Indian college student from Toronto who was working for the C.P.R. during the summer, made their way to that gem of mountain lakes, Lake O'Hara, which surveyor McArthur had visited in 1890. From there they explored Wenkchemna, Wastach, Opabin and Abbot Pass.

When the Yale Lake Louise Club left at the end of the summer of 1894 they had explored fifty square miles of country around Lake Louise. From their data they subsequently prepared the first detailed map of the area after Allen had consulted local Indians and Tom Wilson about Stoney words—hence the picturesque names for the Ten Peaks at Moraine Lake and some of the mountains and lakelets in the O'Hara region. An interesting exception to this commendable practice of choosing native names for outstanding natural features is that of O'Hara itself. Wilcox camped at the lake in 1895 with Tom Wilson and must have been considerably impressed by the distinguished sixty-year-old Colonel O'Hara, camped there with one of Wilson's guides, Jim Tabuteau. Wilcox remembered very vividly how the sedate Irish officer had taken an involuntary dip in the lake by falling from his raft and how, with the help of his stick (and the expenditure of some very colourful language), he made his way ashore.

Wilcox wrote the first major book about the Rockies, *Camping in the Canadian Rockies*. He carried cumbersome photographic equipment on his explorations and, with great artistic skill and infinite patience, returned again and again to some treasured scene until he got the desired result; his book and the articles he wrote for major publications were consequently enhanced by his own superb illustrations.

As the explorers were reluctantly preparing to leave Lake Louise that summer, Professor Fay arrived. Eagerly they took him for a sail on the lake and tried to persuade him to join them on another assault on Mount Victoria. To the professor's intense disappointment he couldn't stay a moment longer, but the next year he came with fellow Appalachians Philip S. Abbot and C. S. Thompson to attempt mighty Mount Lefroy. It remained unconquered. In 1896 the same party renewed the attack and this time, before the horror-stricken eyes of his companions, Mr. Abbot fell to his death onto the rocks below.

In his memory, exactly a year later a strong party of Appalachians led by Professor Fay and accompanied by professors Collie and Dixon of the British Alpine Club and the first Swiss guide in the Rockies, Peter Sarbach, conquered the proud summit. A few days later Fay, Collie, Professor Michael of Boston and the Swiss guide trod the thigh-deep snow along the ridgepole of the continent on Mount Victoria.

Treacherous glaciers, gaping crevasses, boulder-strewn precipices, crumbling crags, soaring peaks—irresistible challenges to a certain breed of man.

When the challenges had been met, when human art, skill, endurance and will had triumphed, the reward for those who stood on the windswept heights above Lake Louise was a peerless panorama of an untenanted and unknown land. Year after year those briefly glimpsed, faraway places drew them like a magnet. The mountaineers set out to open up the Rockies.

From the peaks rising above Lake Louise, in 1894 Wilcox and Allen had seen, enchantingly mysterious in the haze of distance, the giant of the south, Mount Assiniboine—the next year would see them secretly racing each other to that alluring snowy cone. And toward the north Walter Wilcox had looked longingly at the great retaining wall of the Continental Divide where gleaming snowfields spilled icy tongues to distant blue lakes.

Tom Wilson had told him of the upper Bow Valley and in August of 1895, with one of Wilson's guides, he started north from Laggan. During railway construction, fires had burned huge tracts of timber and for miles the ghost of a trail meandered through deadfall and muskeg. Not many had pushed up the valley since young Dr. Hector had passed that way and in his footsteps Wilcox and his companion rode for two days until they rounded the broad bastion of today's Bow Peak. They halted beside "the noblest lake so far discovered in the Rockies," Bow Lake. Camping in a grove of towering spruce, they looked out onto the glacier-hung cliffs, scoured and chiselled by the ages, dipping their brown fans of moraine into the turquoise water; from the skyline in the west Bow Glacier crept right to the lake's edge.

Next day they made the easy ascent to Bow Pass. On its marshy summit, the birthplace of the North and South Saskatchewan rivers, they crossed meadows bright with untrampled masses of alpine flowers and emerged onto a rocky spur where there opened before them the breathtaking view of the Mistaya River trench. At their feet, a thousand feet below, opaque, liquid jade, exquisitely sculptured out of the dark spruce forest, lay Peyto Lake.

Wilcox's guide was none other than the colourful and eccentric Bill Peyto. According to Wilcox this swarthy Englishman with restless "wicked blue eyes" and full moustache "assumed a wild and picturesque attire"; on the trail he wore a fringed buckskin coat, blue shirt set off by a jaunty white kerchief (which had apparently seen duty as a table napkin at some time), ranger's hat tilted at a rakish angle and (with "a distinct air of bravado"), a cartridge belt, hunting knife and six shooter. He usually started his trips

The legendary Bill Peyto, Banff's most colourful and eccentric guide.
COURTESY WHYTE MUSEUM OF THE CANADIAN ROCKIES, BANFF (M517/43)

wearing two pair of trousers, the more ancient ones on the outside. As the vicissitudes of the trail continued, each day he tore off a few tattered inches with a dramatic flourish, so that eventually he was wearing fringed shorts over undamaged trousers. Most of this, Wilcox says, was for effect—the tough westerner showing off to his dudes. Actually he was a conscientious, experienced and daring guide who in later years became a park warden.

Wilcox doesn't say that he named the lake himself for his guide but there is a local story of how it got its name. By the time Wilcox's book was published, a few parties were beginning to make their way north as far as Bow Lake: as the tiny handful of individuals set up camp there in the midst of the wilderness, Peyto (who was usually silent and withdrawn in the presence of strangers) would sometimes rise suddenly from his place beside the camp-fire, snatch up his blanket and with the abrupt announcement, "There's too darn many people around! I'm going where there's some peace and quiet," depart for Bow Pass to spend the night. Naturally the men called the lake below his lonely bivouac, Peyto's Lake.

It was too late in the season for any more extensive exploring when Wilcox visited Bow Pass, but his longing to go north became even more compelling. From the viewpoint above Peyto Lake the vista stretches to the forks of the North Saskatchewan: in that historic valley David Thompson had sought Howse Pass; there Hector had wandered; there another branch of the great river came in from unknown regions to the northwest. What lay in that fascinating maze of peaks and valleys? The maps showed blank spaces. And still farther north? There at Thompson's deserted Athabasca Pass lay the solution to a tantalizing mystery.

In 1896 Wilcox set out to investigate the riddle. He was not the first—nor the last—to go in search of two legendary mountains beside the Committee's Punch Bowl.

15

THE QUAINT BOTANIST AND
THE LEGENDARY MOUNTAINS

Since 1829 the vague and fragmentary maps of the North American mountain regions had given Canada the distinction of possessing the highest peaks between Alaska and Mexico. They were situated in the rugged hinterland of the northern Rockies at Athabasca Pass.

When a little redheaded Scottish botanist put them on the map he probably never gave a thought to the sensational interest that would be created by recording the altitudes of Mount Brown and Mount Hooker as between fifteen and seventeen thousand feet. If he had, David Douglas would have realized with satisfaction that just as surely as he roamed to remote corners of the earth in search of rare things, some day men would set out into unknown country looking for the "highest mountains yet known in the Northern Continent of America." That schoolboys would one day sit with open atlases, dreaming of visiting those soaring peaks wouldn't have surprised him, for as a boy, apprenticed to the head gardener at Scotland's Scone Palace, he had dreamed of expeditions to far-off lands where he would collect plants hitherto unknown.

His ambitions were realized when the Royal Horticultural Society, urged by the renowned botanist Sir William Hooker (who early recognized the ability and enthusiasm of his protegé), sent him to the Pacific Coast of North America in 1824. He intended to stay only one year; indeed after the first season of fruitful scrambling through the lush dripping forests of the American Pacific Northwest, he was plagued with rheumatism during the wet depress-

138

ing winter and gave up all hope of ever returning home again, fearing he "would shortly be consigned to the tomb." But when spring with its blossoms returned, he decided to stay two more years and then on the way home, tramp across the continent with the spring fur brigades.

In 1827, after a most successful one-man collecting expedition, the twenty-eight-year-old Douglas was travelling with the Hudson's Bay Company traders and voyageurs along the Columbia River route on the way to his momentous crossing of Athabasca Pass. He walked most of the way, still collecting, scrambling on to a snowfield to dig up a precious bulb of the lovely glacier lily and occasionally taking short rests in the canoes. He tried studying while the paddling voyageurs pulled hard against the current but "was molested out of my life by the men singing boat songs!" It is not at all unlikely that he told them so too.

On one occasion when he was guest of a Hudson's Bay man at a lonely post, he remarked that that venerable institution was "simply a mercenary corporation and there wasn't an officer in it with a soul above a beaver's skin." He may have been startled when his fellow countryman, a loyal company man, took violent umbrage and challenged him to a duel at dawn, but in the ensuing heated give-and-take he accepted. However when the summons came at his window, "Mister Douglas, are ye ready?" he'd made up his mind about it. He ignored the challenge. There were more important things to do than take potshots at one another at break of day.

The voyageurs ferrying him across the continent must have thought their passenger rather quaint in any event. Before he crawled into his blanket at night, he donned over his balding pate an elegant nightcap of mountain sheep's hair and wool which had been made to order by Indian women. But if his companions harboured any suspicion that he was a prissy fainthearted tenderfoot they were mistaken.

Once, in the United States, he had wandered far afield in search of the giant western sugar pine. Standing at last in a grove of the long-sought treasure, he was thrilled to see the precious purple cones dangling hundreds of feet above; some of them he needed for his seed collection so he carefully aimed his gun and bagged away at the twigs, with gratifying success. The shots, however, had been heard and as he began gathering up his treasures he was startled to find himself surrounded by eight very hostile-looking

Indians, armed to the teeth with bows, spears and knives. When his friendly overtures were ignored and the leader continued sharpening his knife ominously, the little botanist cocked his gun, stepped back six paces, drew his pistol and waited defiantly. Seeing that Two-Gun Douglas didn't intend to be intimidated the Indians relaxed, saying he could go if gifts of tobacco were forthcoming. But the wee Scot was annoyed and struck a more favourable bargain than that: they would get tobacco if they collected some more cones for him. Once they had scattered on their botanising expedition he prudently strode back to the safety of his camp.

As the long journey to Athabasca Pass continued Douglas looked expectantly for "the dividing ridge of the continent." When at last his party of traders and voyageurs approached the Rockies he found that "no matter how familiar one had become with high snowy mountains, all that we had seen before was forgotten before these high, indescribably sharp and rugged peaks, glaciers and snow."

On the ascent to the pass he proved he was the equal of his seasoned companions. Carrying his precious seeds and notes in a tin box, he cheerfully shouldered a forty-pound pack, forded the innumerable streams where "the feet cannot be lifted in safety above the pebbly bottom but must be slided along," and emerged from the icy water to trot briskly over the hoar frost as his wet clothing froze, noting that "withal no inconvenience whatever was sustained"! The snow on the "Big Hill" was so deep that the blazes marking the trail were hard to find and the abominable snowshoes, with wet laces slackening, hurled him into snowdrifts where he "lay feebly like a waggon horse entangled in its harness, weltering to rescue itself . . . Dreamed last night of being in Regent Street, London! Yet far distant."

They camped near the summit and Douglas' "ankles and feet pained so much from exertions that my sleep was short and interrupted." Rising at three A.M. he kindled the fire to warm himself and then started off alone for the Committee's Punch Bowl, where the most laborious part of the crossing would be behind them.

Next day, off alone again down the Whirlpool, he missed the path and late in the afternoon realized he was lost. "As the sun was edging on the mountains I descried, curling blue smoke issuing from trees, a sign which gave me great pleasure." Fortunately he'd stumbled onto the camp of Jacques

Cardinal who was bringing horses up to the pass for the brigade's trip to Jasper House. The genial Jacques offered to "share his hut and excellent supper. He observed that he had no spirit to give me, but turning round and pointing to the river he said 'This is my barrel and it is always running.' So having nothing to drink out of, I had to take my shoulder of mountain sheep and move to the brook to help myself when necessary."

This unscheduled picnic had caused Edward Ermatinger, the leader of the brigade, some "distress" but when the missing traveller was found they continued down the valley, Douglas preferring to walk so that he wouldn't miss any plant specimens in the new country east of the Divide. He had to make the most of every opportunity to add to his collection, for time was running out for the dedicated little botanist. His eyesight was failing, alarmingly and painfully. For him the beloved green earth with its tapestry of glowing beauty would soon be veiled in darkness.

His travels were already risky because of his growing handicap. Back on the Columbia, in pursuit of a deer he'd wounded, he had crashed blindly into a deep ravine where he lay in agonizing pain for five hours before Indians rescued him—a near tragedy which grimly foreshadowed his untimely death.

At Hudson's Bay he took the boat for England where he found himself something of a celebrity in the botanical world. After writing about his expedition, superintending the mapmaking and seeing his priceless collection of plants safely growing in the world-famous Kew Gardens, he returned to the Pacific coast. Completing his expedition, he sailed to Hawaii. He was now totally blind in one eye and the other gave only cloudy vision, even with the strongest spectacles.

But he could still climb mountains and in July of 1834, with a tiny black dog for company, he took to an upland trail. He had been warned to watch for the bullock pits which the natives dug and loosely covered with brush to trap wild cattle. He passed two empty pits. Hours later passersby found the little dog waiting forlornly beside the third pit. Below was a black bull, a battered botanical collecting case—and the mangled body of David Douglas.

That gruesome tragedy spared one of the world's most successful exploring botanists from years of interminable, perhaps intolerable darkness. His name is enshrined in western forests by the majestic Douglas fir. That noble tree, truly the King of the Conifers, is unique—it is neither a true spruce nor a true fir. Distinctive too is the place David Douglas holds in the history of the Canadian Rockies. From his vivid experience at the summit of Athabasca Pass he unwittingly created a legend.

Of the halt at the Committee's Punch Bowl he wrote: "Being well rested by one o'clock, I set out with the view of ascending what seemed to be the highest peak on the north. Its height does not appear to be less than 16,000 or 17,000 feet above the level of the sea . . .

"The labour of ascending the lower part, which is covered with pines, is great beyond description, sinking on many occasions to the middle. Half way up vegetation ceases entirely, not so much as a vestige of Moss or Lichen on the stones . . . One third from the summit it becomes a mountain of pure ice . . . The ascent took me five hours . . . I remained twenty minutes . . . The sensation I felt is beyond what I can give utterance to. Nothing as far as the eye could perceive, but Mountains such as I was on, . . . some rugged beyond description . . . The aerial tints of the snow, the heavenly azure of the solid glaciers, the rainbow-like hues of their thin broken fragments . . . the snow sliding from the steep southern rocks with amazing velocity, producing a crash and grumbling like the shock of an earthquake, the echo of which resounding in the valley for several minutes . . .

"This peak, the highest yet known in the Northern Continent of America, I felt a sincere pleasure in naming MOUNT BROWN, in honour of R. Brown, Esq., the Illustrious Botanist . . . A little to the South is one nearly of the same height rising more into a sharp point which I named MOUNT HOOKER, in honour of my early patron, the enlightened and learned Professor of Botany in the University of Glasgow, Dr. Hooker . . ."

Poring over those words in an ancient journal seventy years later, Professor Norman Collie found the answer to the mystery of fabulous Mount Hooker and Mount Brown—but by then the legend had done its work.

16

SEARCHING FOR THE MYSTERIOUS MOUNTAINS

Years before the engaging Walter Wilcox came to the Rockies, the two Titans of Athabasca Pass had fascinated a young Canadian professor. Whenever A. P. Coleman, professor of geology at the University of Toronto, looked at a map of Canada his "eyes turned irresistibly" to Mount Brown and Mount Hooker. Why, he wondered, hadn't that indefatigable artist, Paul Kane, sketched them? Surely two peaks towering thousands of feet above all the other mountains in the Rockies must have been tremendously impressive. How was it that none of Sandford Fleming's surveyors mentioned them? He made up his mind "to visit and if possible, climb them."

Coleman had climbed in the Alps and in Norway, and as soon as the railway made them accessible he visited the Rockies. Travelling from Winnipeg in 1884, the C.P.R. Transcontinental "was not in a hurry. It took its time at the stations so that you could pick spring flowers from the Prairie and eat a dinner of wild goose in a restaurant tent, or enjoy a supper of antelope in a shack beside a station . . . Twenty miles an hour meant a serious spurt . . ."

From the end of steel at Laggan he made a quick trip to Lake Louise. Then, with an old prospector and a strapping French Canadian lad, he continued on over the tote road—that "inexpressible" trail where trembling ponies had to be firmly grasped by halter and tail and edged around dizzy precipices. At Golden they rafted across the Columbia to the Selkirks where Coleman got his first taste of slashing trail through the rank British

Columbia forests. But "the overwhelming view from a mountain top" out-weighed all the trials with "the diabolical Devil's Club," and he decided to come again.

Returning to the mountains in 1885, Coleman saw the scar of the C.P.R. being gashed through the Selkirks as he sat on the flatcar of a construction train, swinging his legs over an abyss or jerking them out of the way of half-fallen trees. At Stony Creek, where the rails awaited completion of the high-est wooden bridge in the world, he started off alone over "the vilest road imaginable" up to the "clean-cup splendour of Rogers Pass" and on down to Revelstoke. In a dugout canoe with three prospectors he toiled up the Columbia to the worked-out goldfields on the Big Bend.

In the intervening three years before he came back to the mountains he thought again and again about Mount Brown and Mount Hooker. At the Big Bend, after all, he had approached the territory of the legendary giants—there the voyageurs used to strike out for Athabasca Pass. "All one had to do," he thought, "was to canoe seventy miles down the Columbia from Beavermouth on the railway and then follow the old portage trail to the foot of Mount Hooker."

In July of 1888 he and a young companion embarked on this expedition, launching their canoe in the surging Columbia. Frank Stover "had excellent reasons" for joining Coleman on his romantic trip west: "he had never pad-dled a canoe, nor climbed a mountain, nor shot a grizzly, and earnestly desired to do these things." Like Milton and Cheadle long before, their first few hours on the river were "ones of enchantment; a great river was taking us into the mysterious world of mountains."

The weeks to come, however, were "mournfully enlightening": hordes of venomous mosquitoes and blackflies, back-breaking hours of chopping through labyrinths of forest and fallen trees, searching for faint trails entan-gled in maddening underbrush and fighting treacherous "white water."

When they dragged themselves from the Columbia they felt heroic about having escaped from the icy, trampling cauldron of Surprise Rapids. Discovering that cutting a trail to portage past the rapids would take days, they had run them in a raft! They might then have poled merrily to Kinbasket Lake but Frank was ill and, understandably enough, had formed a decided dislike for rafting. They set out on foot to cover the fifty miles;

Professor A. P. Coleman,
who followed a legend
of two giant mountains
and opened the trail
from the Sunwapta
to Jasper.
COURTESY ALPINE
CLUB OF CANADA

Frank's condition deteriorated, however, and he lay feverish in the tiny tent for three days, miles from medical help. Fortunately, he recovered and, since "one hates to turn back before every effort has been made," they tramped on.

From a mountain they "looked with special eagerness away to the north, beyond the gleam of Lake Kinbasket, where a great pale mass, faint as a cloud, but with delicately exact outlines, lifted itself above the long valley. Could it be Mount Brown? Nearer and more to the east stood another giant that might be Mount Hooker. There stretched the promised land . . ." If they could just find the old fur trail they "might yet camp at the foot of Mount Brown within a week." They didn't find it although they doggedly pushed on to Kinbasket Lake, a scant twenty-five miles (as the crow flies) from Athabasca Pass, before the alarming state of their larder made them beat a heartbreaking retreat. Mount Brown and Mount Hooker, it appeared, were not to be reached by the old canoe route.

"The fiasco on the Columbia" only made Coleman "all the more eager to come to close quarters with the giants." He studied Palliser's map, decided after reading Milton and Cheadle's account that the Edmonton to Jasper trail had little to recommend it and in 1892, came back to undertake a much more ambitious search.

Accompanied by his brother L. Q. Coleman, who ranched at Morley (near Calgary), L. G. Stewart, professor of surveying at the University of Toronto, and two companions, the party started on horseback along the eastern foothills. They planned to enter at one of the gaps in the outlying range and climb from valley to valley until they found the historic Whirlpool, which would lead them to the goal. Because they were going into entirely unmapped country they took along two Stoney Indians from Morley. One famous and enterprising member of this tribe, Job Beaver, had been almost as far as their destination; however he was too busy to come along, and beyond Kootenay Plains their guides were of little help.

Crossing the Saskatchewan and the Cataract rivers with the water lapping at the saddles, they made their way along the Brazeau River to Brazeau Lake. There a crisis forced a halt for almost two weeks; L. Q. Coleman had to return to Morley with one of their companions who had become so seriously ill that he could scarcely sit on his horse. While they waited at the lake, Professor Coleman and Stewart climbed a mountain, as young Duncan

McGillivray had done nearly a hundred years before, and saw a pass leading to a large river which headed in a magnificent tangle of high snowy mountains. Might one of those soaring summits to the north be the longed-for Mount Hooker?

When Mr. Coleman returned from taking the invalid safely to Morley the reunited party started out again. With the ponies slithering over rock and scree during the descent of Poboktan (the Stoney name for the big owls that blinked at them from the trees) Pass, the explorers eventually emerged beside a fair-sized river running in a wide valley. The stream obviously had a glacial source but it was too small to be the Athabasca, so they retained the Stoney name, Sunwapta. Downstream, it joined another river. Could that be the Whirlpool at last?

Following the river they found Sunwapta Falls, where the two Colemans and Stewart shouldered forty-pound packs and set out on foot along the Athabasca until they came to a tributary, which they followed because "it came from more nearly the right direction" for the Whirlpool. Coming to an imposing fortress-like mountain, they climbed to see what lay ahead. As they rounded a buttress there suddenly "opened out below the most marvellous lake imaginable . . . perfectly reflecting the surrounding glaciers, mountains and forest in its turquoise waters . . . Our hearts fairly stood still at the sight, for surely this must be the Committee's Punch Bowl . . . and the tall snowy peak behind the glacier to the south must be Mount Hooker. It was one of the great moments of a lifetime! . . .

"By the campfire that evening, however, our triumph was a little dimmed, for we could not make the Punch Bowl of the map fit in size or shape the lake we had found." Still puzzled, for days they scrambled on peaks looking for Mount Brown; beside the lake they picked up "here and there a vague path which might be an Indian trail or that of the voyageurs." Northward from the summits they looked—but nowhere was there a prodigious peak between fifteen and seventeen thousand feet high.

"We were cross as we lit a fire and made supper." The lake couldn't be the celebrated Punch Bowl. As they had neither the time nor enough supplies for further exploration, they turned homeward. Leaving Fortress Lake (as they christened it) they retraced their footsteps along the Chaba River—Stoney word for beaver—to the Sunwapta and crossed the eastern range by another

Looking into Job Pass, named for the respected Stoney chief, Job Beaver, by the Coleman brothers on their unsuccessful 1892 expedition to find the Whirlpool.
COURTESY WHYTE MUSEUM OF THE CANADIAN ROCKIES, BANFF (M517/43)

pass which they named Job Pass to honour the respected and venturesome Stoney chief, Job Beaver; they never met him, but his "graceful, smiling son," Samson, accompanied them part of the way back to their starting point at Morley.

During their ten-day excursion up the Chaba they had ventured into unknown country, without trails, to Fortress Lake. At the end of their summer's travel they had covered five hundred miles of territory which Professor Stewart mapped for the first time; they had found and named rivers, lakes and passes—but the puzzle of the two giant peaks remained. "There was only one conclusion: we must go back next summer . . .

"How cool and clean and healthful everything is by contrast with the dusty city left behind in the east!" It was the summer of 1893 and Coleman was back to make his third try for Athabasca Pass. With his brother and Professor Stewart and a young Morley rancher, Frank Sibbald, they travelled for a time with Chief Jonas who obligingly drew on an old ham wrapper a map of a new pass through which they emerged eventually into the Sunwapta Valley, having passed on the way through the ranges a lake rivalling in beauty the magnificent Lake Louise. This gem of mountain lakes which nestles at the base of a mountain soon to be named for the Colemans they christened Pinto Lake, to immortalize their most cantankerous pony! Through fire-blackened forest where nature healed the scars with bright magenta fireweed, they plodded ahead to Sunwapta Falls; picking their way round the mammoth rock slide which ages ago had torn from the mountain side "a cubic mile of rock" (still a conspicuous sight on today's Banff-Jasper highway) and over ever-present windfalls, they made their way slowly along the Athabasca.

At Athabasca Falls they sat on "a projecting rock which trembled with the concussion of the fall . . . and for a while forgot about slimy muskegs, tormenting blackflies, burnt trees and stifling heat in the delightfully cool breath of the cauldron beneath." Just as modern travellers do, they watched the swallows swooping into the cavern to feed their young, but in 1893 the bridge across the raging falls was made of six small newly felled spruce trees.

With mounting excitement they continued their journey, realizing that the long-sought Whirlpool could not be far off. The valley widened and one night a coyote's howl encouraged the southern rancher, Sibbald, to remark that they must at last be getting into "civilized country." There were signs of travellers too but the impatient party pushed ahead without investigating— it wasn't until fourteen years later that they discovered just how close they had come to the home of the only other white man for miles around. For a few days they were so busy dashing after exasperating ponies and chopping through dense forest with axes now very dull from long usage that they missed the junction of the Whirlpool and the Athabasca on the opposite side of the river. Indeed they forged ahead so vigorously that they were two days' journey up the Miette River before they realized that they were in the wrong valley!

When they had retraced their steps, "the real Whirlpool fulfilled all our expectations: it was rapid, it was turbid with glacial mud and it came from between lofty mountains." At last Coleman was making his way up this famous pass.

But the Whirlpool didn't live up to expectations after all. Things began to go wrong before the second camp was struck in the valley; a fall from his horse wrenched Professor Coleman's knee so badly that it was years before he could return to the mountains. However, after five days of ascending the old trail they "expected to find camp in the evening at the foot of Mount Brown. The giants should loom up just round the bend . . ." Through red and yellow paintbrush and lilac asters they rode in anticipation, until they came to a small pond.

"We were on the ridge pole of North America . . . ! But we felt no enthusiasm. Instead we felt disillusioned . . . Where were the giant mountains Brown and Hooker? We looked in vain for the magnificent summits rising ten thousand feet above the historic pass. We saw instead commonplace mountains . . . undoubtedly lower than half a dozen we had climbed as incidents along the way." The alpine equipment for high climbing would not be needed; the canvas boat laboriously trundled hundreds of miles in order to sail in triumph round the Punch Bowl would stay in its pack—the pond was too small to accommodate it.

"We pitched tent beside the Punch Bowl silently. We had reached our point after six weeks of toil and anxiety, after three summers of effort, to find that Mount Brown and Mount Hooker were frauds." It was sixty-six years since Douglas had made his famous ascent; Mount Brown was climbed again, measured and dethroned to just over nine thousand feet! Weary and dejected, they started the long homeward trek, asking themselves, "What had gone wrong with these two mighty peaks that they should suddenly shrink seven thousand feet in altitude?"

On the way back the canvas boat was put to use after all when Professor Stewart decided to paddle down the North Saskatchewan to Edmonton. The Colemans were concerned for his safety on the long voyage but they learned later that the 250 miles had been successfully and uneventfully negotiated—the only disappointment being that the traveller's shot had missed a big grizzly watching from shore!

Professor Coleman in the years to come was destined to lead the way to the genuine Monarch of the Rockies, but in his determined search for Douglas's celebrated peaks his party had forced the trail from the Sunwapta to Jasper.

Reading Coleman's report on the apparently fraudulent mountains, other explorers in the Rockies found it hard to believe that anyone, least of all a scientist like Douglas, could have made such a colossal blunder. The matter, concluded Walter Wilcox, deserved further investigation.

17

TRIPLE QUEST

In 1896 it was almost impossible to get any information about the country north of Bow Pass. Palliser's map, which sketchily covered the area to Saskatchewan River Crossing, was hard to get; trails were apparently nonexistent and no one knew how the valleys ran. To Walter Wilcox unexplored terrain was irresistible and with the possibility of finding Mount Brown and Mount Hooker as added inducement—"they must be *somewhere*"—he and R. L. Barrett, another American, started for the north with Tom Wilson's men, Tom Lusk and Fred Stephens, acting as wrangler, cook and trailmakers. Mr. Barrett (who had made an exciting trip with Tom Wilson three years before) had been convinced that he couldn't afford to return to the Rockies that year; then he got Tom Wilson's photograph of the mountains. "It knocked me flat. I've got to go!" So, provisioned for sixty days, they left the last remnant of civilization at Laggan and rode on to Bow Pass.

In a few hours they were "surrounded by muskets, burnt timber and bad language." The horses sank, sometimes to their necks, in bottomless quagmires; half of the sugar was dissolved, tea and coffee soaked and baking powder ruined. Reaching Bow Pass, the eagerly awaited vista down the Mistaya was blotted out by dense smoke; for a time they wondered if they could proceed at all, but they managed to bypass the forest fire, riding over still-smouldering ground until they reached the North Saskatchewan.

Fording the river, they rode beneath the shadow of today's Mount Wilson for fourteen miles, crossing and recrossing streams, searching for a

152

trail. The Alexandra River flowed from a serenely beautiful valley opening to the west where Mount Saskatchewan's gentle, forested slopes rose to a gigantic amphitheatre of rock, shattered and weirdly pinnacled. Not knowing whether they should follow the Saskatchewan or the Alexandra in order to reach the Athabasca, Wilcox climbed one of Mount Saskatchewan's outlying spurs and found that the Alexandra Valley was apparently blocked by a glacier. The main valley of the Saskatchewan looked "exceedingly deep and canyon-like," the river hemmed narrowly between precipices. But it seemed the only route to the north.

They rode into the confining gorge, left the river eventually and turned right, beginning a very steep ascent. As they gained height, flashing streams leapt from perpendicular cliffs; the massive tongue of the Saskatchewan Glacier flowed sinuously beyond a ridge on their left and on all sides they were surrounded by "the tremendous grandeur of mountain scenery." As the picturesque train of horses cautiously picked a safe passage along the rocky pathway, "there loomed ahead a beautiful glacier-hung peak."

From their high camp they looked for a route to the Athabasca, Mr. Barrett setting out to climb the imposing peak they'd seen to the west. It was farther away than they thought and he returned without reaching what is today Mount Athabasca. From their reconnaissance they concluded that the only possible trail to the Athabasca must be made by following a high valley on their right. The valley where the Banff-Jasper road runs today was considered out of the question, for as far as they could determine it was blocked by a glacier; beyond that an impassable canyon barred the way. (Like most glaciers in the Rockies the Athabasca has been shrinking; seventy years ago it formed a formidable barrier.) Climbing to the summit of a pass named a few years later for Wilcox, they unknowingly passed the fringe of the great Columbia Icefields—their view to the west was blocked by the high ridge which rises east of today's Columbia Icefields Chalet. Scrambling down another precipitous rock-strewn ridge, they entered the Sunwapta Valley. The little party had made the first recorded crossing from the Saskatchewan to the Athabasca, along a route that subsequently would be used by travellers until the Banff-Jasper road was built.

Finding Coleman's blazed trail eventually, they rode to Fortress Lake, intrigued by the possibility that it might after all be the Committee's Punch

Bowl. Surely two of the surrounding mountains must be Mount Brown and Mount Hooker! To their great disappointment the weather worsened and they couldn't do any climbing; only once did the clouds part to reveal, ten miles to the southwest, "the most beautiful mountain" they had seen on their entire journey, "a splendid wedge-shaped peak." Could it be one of the Titans? Unfortunately they found that they had only enough food left for fourteen days—they had been out for forty-four days—and there was nothing to do but turn back, making a forced march of thirteen days on two meals a day until they met a party at Bow Lake. Nothing had been settled about the perplexing mountains but the trail had been forced from Saskatchewan Crossing to the Athabasca.

Norman Collie, the quiet, amiable Scottish professor of chemistry at London University also found it incredible that Douglas should have made such a whopping error about the mountains at Athabasca Pass; on the other hand it seemed equally unlikely that geologist Coleman had been wrong about the altitudes. Could it be that Coleman had found his way to the wrong pass?

The year after Wilcox's expedition, when Collie and Professor Fay with their associates at Lake Louise had climbed Mount Victoria (the first ascent of a mountain on the Divide since Douglas had done so seventy years before), Collie had four or five weeks to spare and decided to go north, hoping to shed some light on the fascinating Hooker-Brown question.

After their successes on Victoria and Lefroy the combined American-British party had climbed peaks on the way to Bow Lake. Returning over the glacier from Mount Gordon, Mr. Thompson had suddenly disappeared headlong into a crevasse. With lightning speed a stirrup was made in a rope and Collie, "being the lightest member—and withal unmarried"!—was told to put his feet into it and was pushed into the abyss to effect a rescue. Dangling sixty feet down, tightly wedged between the blue green jaws of ice, he managed to lasso his companion and both were hauled to safety. A brisk march to camp restored the two soaking, freezing climbers, but round the campfire Thompson emphatically insisted that "whatever scientific explorations or observations in future might be necessary on the summits of Rocky Mountains, investigations made alone, sixty feet below the surface of the ice, in an inverted position were extremely dangerous and even unworthy of record!" An opinion heartily endorsed by his rescuer, no doubt.

Parting from their American friends, Collie, G. P. Baker (another British climber), the Swiss guide Sarbach and Bill Peyto crossed Bow Pass and continued down the Mistaya, keeping a sharp lookout for Mount Murchison, referred to by Hector as "the highest mountain the Indians know of in the area." An imposing peak rising above the junction of the Mistaya and the North Saskatchewan, it was demoted by more than two thousand feet from Hector's estimated height of 13,500 feet. But after climbing and naming Mount Sarbach across the Mistaya, they followed along Hector's trail to Glacier Lake; there they saw that another mountain Hector had noted was indeed preeminent. Awesome precipices soaring to "a ramp of stainless snow whose knife-edged ridges culminate in a sharp pyramid that pierces the blue heavens like a javelin"—Mount Forbes was a peak to thrill the heart of any climber!

A valiant attempt to reach the proud summit was turned back. The mountain didn't defeat them—snow and rain cheated them of the prize and their diminished provisions didn't permit a longer stay to await good weather.

The untrodden summit of Mount Forbes presented the most exciting challenge Collie had encountered in the Rockies, but on his modest means, would a return trip be justified? The issue was settled for him when the party climbed on the great Freshfield Glacier. They could easily have captured Mount Freshfield but Collie, with customary good humour, agreed to forgo that satisfaction in the interests of science: Baker wanted to finish his survey for their map of the area and Collie casually tramped around a rock buttress while this was being done. From his vantage point he looked north. A soaring snowy cone rose high above the trailing mists in the distance. It could only be one of Douglas's mysterious mountains! Collie would indeed return!

Resuming the trail along Hector's historic route, Peyto led them over Howse Pass—"a holy terror" Collie called it—and with great difficulty they crossed a steep pass, which Collie named for Baker, to reach Field and the end of their explorations for 1897.

Today, mountains on their route to Field commemorate Collie and Baker. In the same area Collie named Mount Mummery for A. F. Mummery, the renowned British alpinist with whom he and Geoffrey Hastings had climbed two years before in the Himalayas. Among the earliest expeditions to the world's highest mountains, this tiny contingent had attempted to scale Nanga Parbat, one of the most fearsome peaks on earth. They failed, but their effort still stands as "the most exacting mountaineering that has ever been done in the Himalayas." Mummery died on a lone attempt to reach the summit.

At Field, Collie met Dr. Habel, a German climber-explorer who had just sought out the splendours of the Yoho Valley including the famous falls which Van Horne later named Takakkaw—the Stoney word for "It is wonderful!" (It is quite probable that Tom Wilson had urged Habel to visit the valley.)

What the German visitor heard from Collie about a great mountain glimpsed to the north sent the sixty-year-old professor scurrying over Wilcox Pass and on to Fortress Lake in 1901. During that expedition the trail was maddeningly hard to find and Habel was greatly exercised about locating Coleman and Wilcox's blazes, as fire had scarred the trees. However, he probed far toward the source of the Athabasca where he found and photographed a magnificent peak which he named Gamma. As was so often the case on those early expeditions, his food supply was inadequate and he had to hurry back to civilization before he could determine whether the mountain he had seen was indeed the one Professor Collie had glimpsed from the Freshfield region.

The tall, dignified German, with curt beard neatly parted down the middle, was highly esteemed in alpine circles but (like another famous climber) he was not always popular among the westerners who worked with him on his sojourns in the wilderness. The camp cook for the Fortress Lake trip was a former Michigan lumberjack, Fred Ballard, who had a decided distaste for all things German, largely because a husky Teuton had made off with his girlfriend. Habel, on his part, harboured old-world ideas about relations between the classes which the free-wheeling American found infuriating.

One day Herr Doctor, with Prussian brusqueness, handed his cook a soup tablet with the crisp order: "Ballard, eztablish me zom zoop!" When it was served, he tasted it gingerly and announced with a grimace, "It iss altogedder too zalt!" Ballard insisted he hadn't added any salt. "Vell den, it iss de pepper!" he grumbled.

With impish glee Ballard schemed to get even with his hard-to-please employer: he packed a lunch of mouldy hardtack for the professor when he strode off alone to the heights. At season's end, bidding farewell at the station, the professor astonished his men by insisting that Ballard accept as a parting gift the perfectly good overcoat Habel had been wearing. Ballard donned it happily and as the old gentleman climbed aboard the waiting train, Ballard stuffed his hands experimentally into the pockets—and found them filled with neat packets of mouldy hardtack! The smiling professor waved genially from the departing train.

The following winter Habel made meticulous plans for an extended expedition to Collie's big mountain, which he intended to reach by the old voyageurs' route on the Columbia. His letters to Tom Wilson protested that expenses must be drastically pared; for one thing, he wouldn't need as many packhorses as Tom proposed because "instruments of music, violin or so on MUST BE LEFT BEHIND!" He had obviously heard about Peyto's fellow packer breaking out a fiddle to welcome home the conquering heroes from another coveted peak that summer and he didn't intend to have any of that kind of western frivolity on his trip!

The doughty professor had done valuable work in the Rockies and his unbounded enthusiasm did a great deal to promote the new-found glories of the Yoho Valley. On the eve of his proposed trip to the Columbia, Tom Wilson received a wire announcing Habel's sudden death. The men who had been with him the year before found it hard to believe that the stout-hearted man who had scrambled so vigorously in the unexplored wilderness wouldn't be back. The unrepentant Ballard muttered philosophically, "Well, anyway, now he'll be able to see the blazes!"

Habel had insisted on the strictest secrecy about his ambitious expedition to the beautiful mountain at the source of the Athabasca, for at the same time Norman Collie was making his own careful plans to reach the beckoning peak. He had discovered it on a momentous journey in 1898.

18

SOLUTION AND EXCITING DISCOVERY

The last load was adjusted, the hitch secured; the last complaining cayuse was tightly cinched and, with the surrounding peaks diamond sharp against an azure sky, the long packtrain wound up the valley and was swallowed in the depths of the forest beyond the little station at Laggan. The colourful Bill Peyto led the way on his trusty black mare. Following the swaying packs, three men in comfortably battered hats, gaiters and sturdy tweeds rode in happy anticipation, five thousand miles away from stuffy London lecture rooms, labs and executive offices.

"For weeks it was good-bye to civilization with its featherbeds, tall hats, frock coats and stick-up collars—we could be as disreputable as we pleased." Drawn irresistibly by the lonely grandeur of the Rockies, Norman Collie was back, bringing with him the wryly humourous Hugh Stutfield and the imperturbably goodnatured publisher-climber Herman Woolley. Collie had convinced them that "Canada should not surrender without a struggle its claim to the highest mountains on the continent" and they were anxious to help him "rehabilitate the outraged majesty of Mount Brown and Mount Hooker, if the facts allowed."

To reach the Saskatchewan, Peyto took them by way of Pipestone Pass where Southesk and Hector had travelled. Soon they were threading the maze of burnt-over forests where the merest breeze set the charred skeletons rubbing against each other with weird creaking and groaning; fireweed and golden sunbursts of arnica contrasted strikingly with the black satin of the gaunt, still-standing trees. Indians no longer kept the trails open and Peyto's axe rang industriously while his charges sat meditatively scratching mosquito bites or scrambling over mounds of deadfall, where one of them found a tattered copy of *Hamlet,* a memento of Southesk's literary browsing by the campfire in the lonely valley.

Round their own cheering fire at nightfall the British climbers listened to tales of the Klondike, of hunting and trapping and "other topics of an entertaining and improving character," including such hair-raising accounts of Indians and grizzlies that Stutfield elected to sleep right at Woolley's feet. Unfortunately that husky chap had once been a football player of considerable prowess who still "practiced place-kicks in his sleep," rudely disturbing his hapless bedfellow.

They reached Saskatchewan Crossing where the lusty green Mistaya rushed over its rocky bed, and they contemplated the risky crossing with some apprehension. Peyto put them all at ease: "We'll probably make it. If someone falls in, he'll likely manage to struggle ashore somehow—unless he knocks his head on one of the big stones on the bottom. In that case one would die easy"!

Happily, all escaped such a blissful end and they camped by the great bastions of the Saskatchewan (one of which Collie named for Tom Wilson), admiring "what would surely one day be an ideal mountain playground when once the remote peaks and valleys of this beautiful region have been made accessible to the outside world." As the party followed Wilcox's trail north, flooded rivers almost forced abandonment of the whole expedition; the dogged and resourceful Peyto persisted, even though for a time they advanced only three or four miles a day. One of the party ventured some distance up the lovely Alexandra Valley; a few years later C. S. Thompson was to ascend the valley to its head (finding that it was not after all blocked by a glacier as Wilcox had thought), and discover the pass later named for him— a pass which would soon provide the key to a great alpine conquest.

In the evenings, weary after back-breaking hours of slogging, the climbers relaxed beside the campfire in the quiet valley. Not unmoved by their surroundings, the talk turned one evening to the subject of Creation. Byers, their cook ("a most amusing talker and theologian of somewhat unorthodox views"), delivered "a glowing eulogy upon the scheme of

Peter Sarbach, the first Swiss guide in the Canadian Rockies, G. P. Baker and
Professor Norman Collie on the steps of the Banff Springs Hotel in 1897.
COURTESY GLENBOW ARCHIVES, CALGARY (NA-673-14)

Creation, which in a passage of singular eloquence he described as 'a mighty fine outfit.'" Some rash person, attempting to qualify his interpretation of certain passages in Genesis "was promptly overwhelmed with a torrent of backwoods satire and invective; and the would-be objector crushed in argument, took refuge in an outburst of somewhat pointless profanity. Then the tobacco was passed round and the discussion ended—as such discussions usually do end—in smoke."

With difficulty they made their way up the narrow valley of the Saskatchewan. One night Stutfield and Collie were awakened by a great commotion: the rest of their party was returning by lantern light, armed to the teeth with every available axe and gun. Apparently a grizzly had been heard thrashing about menacingly and a massive assault was mounted. It turned out to be poor devoted Woolley, stumbling about in the thicket, vainly looking for a place out of the moonlight where he could change his precious photographic plates!

They had been on the trail for nearly three weeks when they climbed up from the cleft of the Saskatchewan toward Wilcox Pass to camp. "Opposite there stood a noble snow-crowned peak, with splendid rock precipices and hanging glaciers. Our hearts soared at the thought of climbing it on the morrow!" And no wonder! They had walked for 150 miles and "never in the experience of the three of us who had scaled heights in the Alps, the Caucasus and the Himalayas, had travelling for nineteen days to get to a sought-after mountain been part of the program." However, as the long march had made heavy inroads into their food supply, meat was desperately needed. Stutfield magnanimously elected to go for bighorn while Woolley and Collie headed for an exhilarating climb. A brisk scramble took them all day, but at five they stood on the summit of Mount Athabasca, as they named it, the highest mountain climbed in the Rockies up to that time.

"The view that lay beneath us in the evening light was one that does not often fall to the lot of modern mountaineers. A new world was spread at our feet; to the westward stretched a vast icefield, probably never before seen by human eye, and surrounded by entirely unknown, unnamed and unclimbed peaks. From its vast expanse of snows the Saskatchewan Glacier takes its rise and it also supplies the headwaters of the Athabasca; while far away to the west, bending over in those unknown valleys glowing in the evening light, the level snows stretched, to finally melt and flow down more than one channel into the Columbia River, and thence to the Pacific Ocean." They had found the Columbia Icefields.

Directly west of the peak they were on "rose probably the highest summit in this region of the Rocky Mountains; chisel-shaped at the head, covered with glaciers and snow, it stood alone . . ." Collie "at once recognized the great peak I was in search of; moreover, a short distance to the north-east of this mountain, another, almost as high, also flat-topped but ringed round with sheer precipices . . ." The two lost mountains, Brown and Hooker!

Quickly they measured and surveyed and then in gathering darkness made their way back down, reaching camp at eleven o'clock where they found Stutfield trying to reassure the anxious men about the climbers' safety. Listening to Collie and Woolley relate their momentous discovery, the members of the expedition decided to cross the icefield, climb the great mountain and look for Athabasca Pass.

Stutfield, Peyto and young Nigel Vavasour (for whom Collie named Nigel Peak across from Athabasca Glacier) had saved the expedition by replenishing the larder with meat. The next afternoon Stutfield, Woolley and Collie ascended the Athabasca Glacier; by bivouacking as far as possible up the glacier they hoped to reach the great mountain, ascend it and return in one day. After a lonely night on their bed of rock and ice where the glaciers creaked and groaned and thunder rattled from crag to crag, they were off at 1:30 A.M. by lantern light, zigzagging slowly between the maze of crevasses and ice pinnacles. It took them five hours to reach the crest of the icefall (which from today's vantage point on the highway looks so near) and Stutfield saw for the first time "the immense icefield, bigger than any in Switzerland . . . which stretched mile upon mile before us like a rolling snow-covered prairie . . ."

They started toward the distant snowy peak. The weather was sultry, threatening; ominous thunder growled. Thigh-deep, through seemingly endless snow they trudged, sadly realizing that the distance to the mountain was much greater than it had seemed. After a nine-hour trek they accepted defeat.

On their weary way back to camp they easily climbed an unusual snowy summit which they named the Snow Dome; christening a striking black mountain and its white neighbour, the Twins, with a last longing look at "the great peaks rising solemnly like lonely sea-stacks from an ocean of ice and snow," they descended the Athabasca Glacier. As on Mount Forbes, only the weather and the distance had prevented Collie from making a successful ascent of the mountain he'd made such a determined effort to reach.

As an added disappointment, on reflection it appeared unlikely from what they'd seen that the tremendous peaks were Mount Brown and Mount Hooker after all—no lake or pass had been revealed. So, still hoping to untangle the question of Douglas's mountains, they descended to the Sunwapta Valley by way of Wilcox Pass and camped beyond Sunwapta Canyon. Towering starkly above them the giant guardians of the icefield huddled enormous shoulders together to support their burden of ice—surely from one of those summits they would be able to see Athabasca Pass.

Collie named two massive glacier-crowned mountains for his companions and the trio decided to attempt the ascent of Mount Woolley. The storms which were to plague them for the rest of their stay in the valley now broke in earnest and early in their climb they had to take shelter briefly under a rocky ledge. Just as they roped up to continue, tons of ice hurtled over their intended route. The short halt had saved their lives. Mount Woolley was left strictly alone and Diadem Peak was climbed instead; from the diadem of snow, a hundred feet thick on the summit, a magnificent panorama stretched to the northern horizon. But nowhere could they see a pass flanked by two sixteen thousand-foot peaks.

An anxious counsel was held when they returned to camp: should they strike out for Athabasca Pass? It shouldn't take more than two or three days to find it (they found later that it would have taken two or three weeks). But the weather became even worse and stock-taking confirmed that they had only enough food for a few days. A forced march back to civilization was imperative—by the time they reached Bow Lake they were down to bread and porridge.

Back in England the following winter, still pondering over the unsolved riddle of Mount Brown and Mount Hooker, Collie diligently read everything he could find about Athabasca Pass. On a dusty library shelf he unearthed a faded copy of the *Companion to the Botanical Magazine* which contained David Douglas's account of his famous ascent of Mount Brown. Poring over every word, he read: "Being well rested by one o'clock I set out with the view of ascending what seemed to be the highest peak on the north . . . its height does not appear to be less than 16,000 or 17,000 feet above the level of the sea . . . The ascent took five hours . . ."

There was the answer! "Had this document ever been studied thoughtfully, the absurdity must have been at once apparent"—an unskilled climber (or any climber) ascending a sixteen to seventeen thousand-foot peak alone in five hours, over a "route by far the most difficult"? Collie, the mountaineer, knew that this was manifestly impossible. What Douglas had done, of course, was to climb the 9,156-foot Mount Brown that the Colemans had found. Professor Coleman was vindicated and later investigation appears to vindicate poor David Douglas too: he may not have been entirely responsible for the gross exaggeration. The altitude of Athabasca Pass is only just over 5700 feet, so Douglas actually climbed about 3500 feet—a considerable ascent for an inexperienced climber. He apparently calculated the height of his giant peaks from a previous computation which gave the pass an altitude of between ten and eleven thousand feet. Exactly who made the original error remains unclear.

But what a fruitful error it had proven to be! Thousands of square miles of mountain terrain had been mapped; valleys, lakes, rivers, passes—secrets locked for eons in the mountain fastness had been patiently uncovered *and* the trails had been blazed from Lake Louise to Jasper.

Collie, "with regret, chanted the requiem" of the intriguing legend of two exalted peaks; in their place the true monarch of the Alberta Rockies, his Mount Columbia, became the object of compelling fascination.

19

CONQUERING HEROES

In 1900 Collie and Stutfield had made a valiant attempt to reach Mount Columbia from the west, forcing a trail up the valley of the Bush River. After weeks of almost continuous rain, as they cut their way through the heavy forests on the Pacific slope they were again forced to retreat short of the goal. It was a heartbreaking disappointment. While Collie made plans for a third expedition, Walter Wilcox made his fourth assault on a coveted peak far to the south.

By 1901 Mount Assiniboine, the highest mountain south of Banff, was known as the Matterhorn of the Rockies, partly because of its striking resemblance to that supremely beautiful peak and partly because it had gained a similar reputation of awesome inaccessibility, having repulsed more attacks than any other Canadian summit.

The magnificent rock pyramid, horizontally banded with dark cliffs and glistening snow, soars fifteen hundred feet above the surrounding peaks. It was seen from afar and named by surveyor Dr. Dawson in 1885, but the first white visitors were Tom Wilson and R. L. Barrett, who camped at its feet in 1893. Years later, when Mr. Barrett was spending some time among the giants of the Himalayas, he wrote to Tom about his impression of the second highest peak in the world: "K2 at 28,000 feet didn't look as high and imposing and terrible as Assiniboine when you and I finally won through to where we could get a look at him."

When young Wilcox and Allen saw it during their climbs at Lake Louise

Mount Assiniboine, "the Matterhorn of the Rockies."
PHOTO BY LIA KATHLEEN FRASER, VICTORIA

they each vowed secretly to take up its challenge; in fact Allen, accompanied by Yule Carryer, dashed off for a quick visit to its base at the end of the season's climbing at Lake Louise in 1894. But Wilcox was determined to do more. The next year, with Peyto, Mr. Barrett and Mr. Porter, he started out, making an arduous trek over snowy Simpson Pass. Although Assiniboine is only about twenty miles by direct route from Banff it took them six days to fight a circuitous, obstructed way to its base. With Peyto's keen ability to find trails through untrodden wilds (a skill acquired by the best pioneer local guides, and of invaluable, if sometimes unsung assistance to all the mountaineer-explorers) and Wilcox and Barrett's zest for exploration, they accomplished the first circuit of the mighty obelisk.

For forty-eight gruelling hours they tramped through lake and glacier-adorned valleys, clambered over fallen trees stacked ten or twelve feet high in forests devastated by fire and toiled up precipitous ridges, to arrive in "torn garments and black as coal-heavers" at a lovely lake near their starting point where, to their mutual surprise, they came upon the camp of friendly rival Samuel Allen, who was also making a preliminary reconnaissance of the mountain.

Wilcox became Assiniboine's "first biographer," its attractions crystallized in his perfect photographs, and he intended to be the first man to stand on its summit. Poor Mr. Allen wasn't destined to resume his try for the peak—tragically, he never returned to the Rockies he loved. In a few years he was confined to a mental hospital where he died after forty long years.

Armed with details of Assiniboine's defences, Wilcox returned in 1899 accompanied by Mr. Steele, an Englishman, and H. G. Bryant, a well-known American Arctic explorer. Tom Wilson had suggested a shorter route to the mountain and they arrived at the base ready for a determined assault. Bryant and Steele reached ten thousand feet before a storm spelled defeat; during the descent they narrowly escaped a fatal six hundred-foot plunge to the glacier below. The next year two relatively inexperienced American climbers brought three Swiss guides to the attack—but Assiniboine remained inviolate.

To Wilcox exploring was as attractive as climbing and in 1901 he was on his way to the almost unknown Kananaskis region. But he was convinced that, with one more determined effort, Assiniboine could be won. Setting out with Mr. Bryant and Swiss guides Feuz and Michel, their high hopes were dampened at the start when Michel fell from his horse and was seriously disabled by a painfully dislocated shoulder—a handicap of considerable magnitude, for heavy snow and rain as they approached the mountain indicated that they would encounter formidable obstacles, requiring all the stamina and skill the party could muster.

Reaching their destination, for eight hours they inched cautiously up the forbidding mountain face. Every few minutes the heavy mantle of fresh snow avalanched in crashing fusillades; with each advancing step the hot sun increased that peril. Only one thousand feet below the summit they had to turn back. They had gone higher than any previous party, and the peak "that Wilcox so richly deserved" was successfully scaled by their route just five weeks later by a newcomer to the Rockies—one whose towering figure had already been silhouetted on many a commanding peak.

Wilcox continued the work which places him in the top rank of explorers in the Rockies; during the long winters he wrote for well-known publications, presented illustrated lectures about the Rockies and eagerly awaited the earliest possible return to the Canadian mountains.

As Wilcox had retreated from the Matterhorn of the Rockies to make his way into the Kananaskis Valley, the great conqueror of the real Matterhorn was climbing in the Yoho Valley.

1901 was a banner year for the C.P.R.: they were shepherding across the continent their first royal train, carrying the future King George V and Queen Mary and, of even greater interest to mountain enthusiasts, they had brought to the mountains "the Prince of Mountaineers," Sir Edward Whymper.

The resorts in the Rockies buzzed with excitement, the anticipation heightened by the fact that, as usual, the great man was tight-lipped about his plans. But he was bringing his own quartette of crack Swiss guides—obviously big things were afoot! No effort was spared to give the world's most renowned mountaineer a clear field—even the topographical survey planned for the mountains that summer was postponed in case it might interfere with the momentous alpine feats about to be accomplished. Surely Whymper would seek as his first conquest the unscaled heights of Assiniboine!

But the proud, arrogant, celebrated veteran had no intention of risking his reputation on a climb which at sixty-two might spell defeat. He stalked impressively off to less challenging but equally invigorating surroundings where he was joined by an admiring younger man, in many respects strikingly like him.

James Outram, eldest son of a British baronet, had been a vicar in the Church of England for ten years when a nervous breakdown forced retirement from his profession. He had done considerable climbing in the Alps, and to regain his health he came to the Rockies in 1900. Exhilarated by the splendour and extent of the Canadian Alps, he sharpened his already keen thirst for first ascents, the abiding passion of the great Whymper, whose competence among the crags and audacious drive to surmount their difficulties was shared to a considerable degree by the younger man. Both were tall, imposing men but Outram lacked the bold, sharply sculptured, aggressive features of his famous companion.

In some strange way the news of Wilcox's latest failure on Assiniboine filtered through to their remote camp in the Yoho. Outram too had coveted the challenging peak from afar but he hadn't the means for making the extended trip to its base. There was lively discussion around the campfire about Wilcox's defeat on the invincible mountain; listening silently was their outfitter, Bill Peyto, who six years before had taken Wilcox to Assiniboine. With startling vehemence Peyto suddenly declared that for an experienced and skillful party there was absolutely nothing to prevent a conquest; if Outram would elect to go and scale the heights, he would get him there in two days and bring him back in less, although the journey had never been made in less than three!

It was the last day of August and they were faced with the possibility that the weather might break any day. But it was "now or never," for undoubtedly Wilcox would renew his attack the next year. With the greatest despatch and secrecy Peyto organized the expedition and at breakneck speed led Outram and two of Whymper's Swiss guides along Healy Creek, through tangled and desolate valleys under increasingly threatening skies, to bring them safely to the foot of their lofty goal. He then indicated the best approach for the ascent, helped them carry supplies up to bivouac at ten thousand feet and departed to prospect nearby for minerals!

Sir James Outram, conqueror of Mount Assiniboine.
PHOTO BY SIDNEY R. VALLANCE. COURTESY WHYTE MUSEUM OF THE CANADIAN ROCKIES, BANFF (M517/44)

The first day Outram and the guides, Hasler and Bohren, were driven back by lowering clouds. Next morning dawned brilliantly and their superb peak was sharply etched against a cloudless sky. In six hours they "stood as conquerors on the loftiest spot in Canada on which a human foot had then been planted . . .

"One at a time—the other two securely anchored—we crawled with the utmost caution to the actual highest point and peeped over the edge of the huge overhanging crest, down the sheer wall to a great shining glacier 6,000 feet or more below . . . The main ridge northward, after a sharp descent of fifty feet, falls gently for a hundred yards and then makes a wild pitch down to the mountain's base. When we arrived at this point (only through my most strenuous insistence, for the guides were anxious to return at once by the way we came) . . . the scheme that had been simmering in my brain . . . at last found utterance: could we not manage to get down this way?"—and crown their victory by a traverse of the mountain after conquering its reputedly inaccessible ramparts! In seven hours it was done and Peyto's fellow packer broke out his fiddle to welcome them back with the strains of "Home the Conquering Heroes Come." It was, according to Outram, "perhaps the most sensational mountaineering feat then achieved in North America." His triumph was as heady as wine.

Lady Luck had smiled on him, of course—a favour not granted to Wilcox. The next morning everything was deep in snow and Assiniboine was shrouded in clouds. Their climb had been made on the very last possible day of good weather that season.

What impression the spectacular victory had on Outram's host in the Yoho camp is uncertain. There are reports that Whymper had asked Outram to climb for him but this, in view of Whymper's character, is extremely unlikely. What is certain is that the old warrior was content to scramble to the modest heights of Mount Collie and nearby peaks with Outram who, even before his dramatic dash to Assiniboine, was casting a longing eye toward the giants standing guard over the Columbia Icefields.

The lanky parson was to earn a formidable reputation in the Rockies—Whymper a more dubious one although he returned many times, rambling hundreds of miles and making valuable scientific observations. The Alpine Club of Canada was graced by his august presence where hushed members had the privilege of hearing his eloquent speeches; on his last visit in 1909, two years before his death, he dramatically presented his alpine equipment to be auctioned, the handsome proceeds to be donated to the building of a clubhouse.

But for the local population his aura soon seemed slightly tarnished. A character of unusual complexity—brilliant, but frustrated and bitter as a youth, he early assumed "a ruthless aggressiveness toward much of mankind," which in old age made him appear as unbending as the crags he conquered. His destiny had been strangely bound up with and scarred by the terrible tragedy that marred his supreme moment—the day the rope broke and four of his companions hurtled into hideous oblivion onto the glaciers of the mighty Matterhorn. His long stubborn silence about that accident which had so shocked the world, the "hints of dark deeds unrevealed," his almost unbelievable and paranoic suspicions of the two surviving Swiss guides—all these were part of his life and the stuff of the Whymper legend.

But many at Banff saw only that there was trouble from the start. His curt servant-master attitudes were offensive; trail guides grumbled about meals which featured concentrates and tablets instead of the usual steaming coffee, sizzling bacon and pancakes. It was observed that he dined in magnificent aloofness, enjoying—according to rumour—prodigious potations of the finest wines. Although the effects weren't apparent, reports circulated too that on his long walks he consumed a quart of the best whisky and half a dozen pints of ale each day—all imported and trundled along in heavy crates. Someone couldn't resist gathering the material evidence and photographing it for posterity—an act Whymper considered an outrage.

On the other hand, he kept up a cordial correspondence with Tom Wilson, offering to carry advertisements for his outfitting business in his own famous alpine guidebook and giving homely advice about "drawing more custom" by planting flowers around his home and place of business in Banff. Incredible as it seems today, he also asked Tom to find for him "a young Stony lad, heathen preferred," whom he "wished to buy"!

In 1903 his visit was marked by tragicomedy. With Tom Wilson and two Swiss guides he was going to try for unclimbed Crowsnest Mountain, which he "had been given to understand was impossible of ascent." A few days later a most indignant article appeared in the Banff newspaper: "Mr. Whymper who had promised himself the addition of another laurel to his crown of fame, reported that 'the only thing in climbing a difficult mountain is the credit of being the first to accomplish the feat . . .'" The men had been sent ahead to locate the best route of ascent and for some reason were a long time returning. "Owing to a breach of faith," the article continued, "or perhaps over-enthusiasm on the part of his assistants, Mr. Whymper did not enjoy the distinction of leading the ascent . . . 'I feel much chagrined, the more so as it was my own men who got there ahead of me'"! An explanation was bound to be widely circulated—the Prince of Mountaineers had in fact been in his cups and his men couldn't resist committing the unforgivable act of beating their master to the summit, as a prank.

Tom was apparently forgiven for this bit of treachery for Whymper kept up the correspondence and five years later Mrs. Wilson received a birth announcement: "Mother well—infant cries"! A bachelor until he was sixty-six, he had married a buxom girl forty-five years his junior and two years later had the much-desired heir.

Visiting the Alps in 1911 he remarked: "I am seventy-two and I'm finished. Every night I see my comrades of the Matterhorn disaster slipping on their backs, their arms outstretched . . ." A few days later he became ill, locked himself in his room, refused all aid and died. His contributions to the alpine world are commemorated in the Rockies—above Vermilion Valley, Mount Whymper honours the Lion of the Matterhorn.

Mount Outram, the memorial to the conqueror of the Canadian Matterhorn, rises above the Howse River west of Saskatchewan River Crossing. Just beyond it, Mount Forbes "rears its splendid forehead far into the skies . . ." Outram and Professor Collie set out to climb it in 1902.

TRIUMPHS, DISAPPOINTMENT AND FAILURE

Norman Collie's real objective was Mount Columbia. He did everything he could to assure success on his third attempt to reach the fascinating and elusive mountain: he started two weeks earlier than usual, doubled the provisions and, as it was to be a serious climbing expedition, augmented his strong party to Stutfield and Woolley with the Swiss guide, Hans Kaufman.

Previous arrangements had been made for Outram to join the party for the assault on Mount Forbes. The eager parson, however, managed to get away a fortnight before Collie, leaving word that he would meet him at Saskatchewan River Crossing. His was to have been a strong contingent too; at the last minute his two companions couldn't come, but it would have taken a great deal to keep Outram away from the beckoning regions of the north. He decided to continue accompanied only by Christian Kaufman, one of Whymper's guides of the year before (and brother of Collie's guide) whose services the C.P.R. had placed at his disposal for the entire season. After the dramatic dash to Assiniboine the previous year, "Of course, my outfitter was Peyto"!

Peyto had been away at the Boer War in 1900 and Collie's outfitter and guide for the Bush River trip had been Fred Stephens who, like Peyto after his return from the war, had gone into business for himself. Stephens became Collie's lifelong "friend, guide and philosopher"—"there was a man!" Collie recalled years later. On the way to the Saskatchewan, Stephens overtook the Outram packtrain and hurried ahead to cache supplies for his employer who was maddeningly delayed at Laggan waiting for missing luggage.

Beyond Bow Lake the country was new to Outram; he tramped happily under "Italian blue skies" with fleecy clouds drifting lazily over the lovely peaks beside Waterfowl Lakes, and continued serenely and reverently through the great silent forests ("the most fitting and inspiring place of worship") until his party arrived at the Saskatchewan.

This was as far as Peyto could go; his thriving business necessitated a return to Banff, and Outram's packtrain was left in the charge of young Jim Simpson and Habel's former cook, Fred Ballard. Before he left, however, Peyto superintended the fording of the broad Saskatchewan. Simpson led the way followed by a long string of horses; as the water rose and they had to swim, the animals balked and turned back, Peyto's mount "ducking him artistically in mid-stream." Jim had to return and take them across in detachments.

Ballard had apparently become a culinary master since his trying experiences with Habel, for now he prepared "the most delicious mustard" and with Jim's able assistance whipped up "sumptuous meals." The country they were travelling through was familiar to young Ballard and Simpson; they had spent the winter trapping there, making their headquarters at a lonely cabin by the Mistaya—"the first human habitation in a spot which future generations will probably see transformed into a populous mountain resort," Stutfield observed when he saw it.

Jim Simpson had come west from England and found in the Rockies the object of his long wandering: "Here, there was room to hunt—and explore!" Spending all available time alone in the mountain wilderness, with his intelligent horse "sniffing out old Indian trails," he was acquiring the knowledge which would make him one of the best hunting guides in the region.

Collie's party meanwhile was on its way at last, finding the trail much improved and the packtrain more disciplined than on their previous trips, "the ponies showing less disposition to bathe and soak the supplies, and only occasionally careening off into the bush, scattering pots and pans"—and Stutfield's precious mattress! Because of that luxury he was subjected to some barbed and witty criticism from his companions; it made a most awkward and cumbersome load, but he insisted on trundling it along and at the end of the trip he "penned an ode" to his pride and joy.

When they reached Simpson and Ballard's cabin where they were to meet Outram, they found only a note saying that he had been up the Alexandra Valley and was now at Glacier Lake. They set out to meet him, anxious for their climbing to begin. That night Outram rode triumphantly into their camp on Freshfield Creek and announced that he had made a phenomenal dash and climbed Mount Lyell—and Mount Columbia!

Reaping the rewards of the careful exploring, mapping and reporting of Wilcox, Collie and Thompson, he had vigourously approached the Columbia Icefields by way of Thompson Pass. As he climbed the outlying ramparts, the last shrouds of mist rolled away. "The great dome appeared in all the golden radiance of the evening glow, dazzlingly bright under an azure sky"—Mount Columbia, the supreme summit he had quietly planned to capture as the first ascent of the season, and the first since his triumph on Assiniboine!

Starting the wearying trek over the vast field of snow and ice at one A.M., eleven hours later Outram and his guide "planted the Union Jack upon the broad white platform which crowns the summit of the highest point so far occupied in Canada." Twenty-two hours after leaving camp, they stumbled back into their tent.

On two more occasions Outram and the indefatigable Kaufman fought dense and fallen timber at midnight after twenty-hour outings to coveted peaks. After a successful climb to the knife-edged triple summit atop the black precipices of Mount Bryce they descended seventy feet of fearsome cliff at night, "helplessly groping in the depths for something to rest a foot upon . . . searching for a knob or tiny crack where numbed fingers might find a hold . . ." Pushing himself and his men hard (sending young Jim to hunt up the horses at midnight for an early start, in the manner of Sir George Simpson), he climbed peak after peak—by the end of the season in 1902 he had proudly recorded first ascents of eight mountains over ten thousand feet.

Mount Forbes was captured by the combined party after their rendezvous; characteristically, Collie graciously volunteered to abandon the ascent part way rather than increase the risk to his companions by having a fourth man on the rope. Outram, however, recognizing that Collie, "more than all the rest, deserved the gratification and honour of being the first to conquer Mount Forbes," sent back the two guides to accompany Collie up to the party awaiting the final dash to victory.

It was Outram's greatest year and at season's end, on the top of Mount Wilson, "the panorama furnished a complete resumé of our entire trip. What memories those peaks, passes, streams and valleys conjured up! Toils and fatigues, dangers and difficulties . . . but oh! what crowning joys and satisfying conquests! From those proud crests, secrets of nature, hidden for centuries had been revealed; and the vast sea of mountains, in all their majesty and might, the valleys filled with treasures of perfect beauty, glacier and forest depth, sparkling streams and flower-decked glades, have graven with imperishable strokes upon my memory a record that will be a never-ceasing joy through life."

There can be little doubt that the enchantment of the Rockies formed the basis of his decision to make his home within their reach. "In the lonely woods or on the solitary mountain tops of Canada" he found "the long-sought sanctuary of the storm-tossed soul. There, burdens that seemed too heavy to be borne are rolled away." A strangely troubled man, it is to be hoped that the solace he found "among the hills" compensated for the difficulties which accompanied his determination to carve a career for himself in Canada.

A devout man, he none the less never returned to his profession in the church, and on inheriting the baronetcy in 1912 he entered the business world. It is an intriguing mystery why this reserved aristocrat formed an association with the flamboyant Count de Topor, a polished and wily real estate speculator of obscure European origin. Probably, after hearing Outram's glowing accounts of unlimited possibilities in the great empty dominion of Canada, de Topor seized a golden opportunity and enlisted Outram in a grandiose land development company, astutely realizing the advantage of having the charming (but inexperienced) nobleman as a "front man."

Outram's baronetcy did not make him a wealthy man, but he invested substantially in the company and with the collaboration of two Englishmen and prominent Canadian businessmen, branches were set up in Canada. In the rich farming country at Vermilion, Alberta, they established headquarters, sold plots, built modest houses and a fine business block, and prepared to bring in hundreds of settlers.

Sir James fitted easily into the life of the tiny community; he worked vigorously for its development, serving on the village council and, of course, lecturing on the beauties of the Rockies and donating the proceeds of the evenings to the local church. The tall, handsome baronet cut a dashing figure, shepherding the town's ladies about in his stunning black automobile. The mysterious de Topor, however, appeared only infrequently and was early recognized as a lady's man of a different stamp: it was whispered that many a wealthy widow across the country had been persuaded by his charms to invest in the Northern and Vermilion Development Company.

Two years after the company was established in Vermilion the First World War broke out. The bottom fell out of the real estate market; immigration stopped and high taxes spelled ruin. All this was common enough at the time. The two English partners saw the cloud on the horizon and pulled out early while Outram (at fifty years of age) served with the militia in Vermilion and Calgary. De Topor prudently disappeared.

After the war Outram faced it out, making his home in Calgary where he was within sight of his beloved mountains. The Northern and Vermilion Development Company never recovered from the financial blow; Outram did what he could to salvage matters, but he was not really a businessman. He must have been troubled by the knowledge that humble people had suffered financial hardship because of the business failure. But he stayed on rather than return to England, living very modestly, almost in genteel poverty. De Topor turned up years later in Costa Rica, safely out of reach, where he died an extremely wealthy man. He remains an enigma—only recently it was discovered that "Count" was just one of the many aliases he adopted as he made his way from Europe to Canada and South America.

Outram returned every year to wander in the mountains where he was a familiar figure at Alpine Club camps. Late in life, much to everyone's surprise, he quietly married an Englishwoman he'd known for many years; four years later, in 1925, he died while visiting friends in Victoria.

It must have been one of the great disappointments of Collie's life when he heard that Outram had beaten him to Mount Columbia. After climbing

Mount Freshfield and Howse Peak, he returned home without going on to the great mountain he'd come so far to climb. Eight years later he would come back to "the great lone land awaiting the first footsteps"—a land irresistibly fascinating to a little Quaker woman from Philadelphia.

FROM DRAWING ROOM TO CHABA IMNE

Two young women sat beside the railway at Laggan, quietly and wistfully watching. Once again, strapping outfitter-guides stowed great mounds of supplies into packs, expertly heaved and secured unwieldy loads onto the backs of restless ponies, tightened cinches and, with their employers safely mounted, led another packtrain "north to adventure."

Had they been anything but cultivated, gentle Quaker ladies, Mary Schäffer and Mary Adams would have stamped dainty feet in frustration. Instead they "gazed with longing eyes" as the adventurers rode into "the vast, glorious unexplored country beyond"—and envied the superior endurance of men. Wilcox, Habel, Coleman, Collie, Thompson, Outram—*they* were tasting the delights of discovery "amid the hills we so longed to see, the hills which had lured and beckoned us for years before this long list of men ever set foot in the country!"

Three years after the railroad was built, sheltered, dark-haired, eighteen-year-old Mary Sharples had come to the Rockies on an extended tour with her mother. She met an eminent American botanist, Dr. Charles S. Schäffer, and the next year she returned as his bride. With Quaker friends, including the wealthy and influential Vaux family of Philadelphia, they came back every year. Having "learned to value at its true worth the great unlonely silence of the wilderness," she found solace there when her husband died in 1903. With the American botanist, Stewardson Brown, she compiled from her husband's work a book on the alpine flora of the Rockies for which she did the watercolour and photographic illustrations. And every spring "as soon as the warm breezes blew," she and her friends answered "the call, 'Come back, come back to the blue hills of the Rockies!'"

As the tourists began to come in hordes, the little band of pioneers saw their "secret haunts laid bare to all." To recover the enchantment of the early exquisite loneliness, they pushed on to newly discovered Moraine Lake, the Yoho Valley and Lake O'Hara. By the early 1900s these too were being invaded and they "yearned for the wider views and new, untrammelled ways."

In 1906, once again left sitting "with folded hands" beside the station at Laggan as another expedition set out on the trail north, the young widow suddenly turned to her companion: "Why not? We can starve as well as they; the muskeg will be no softer for us than for them; the ground will be no harder to sleep upon; the waters no deeper to swim, nor the bath colder if we fall in!"

Outfitter Billy Warren ("Chief," as Mrs. Schäffer called him) had for three years been initiating the two young women into the ways of camping, teaching them how to ride a horse astride and jump it over logs. They hurried to outline their audacious proposal to him. He was aghast. Take two feminine "tenderfeet" hundreds of miles away from civilization into country where only a handful of men had ventured? Nothing doing! Quietly they persisted. He told tales of coming to grief crossing icy torrents and facing starvation. To no avail. In the face of their determination to go whether he accompanied them or not, he at last agreed to take them on a trial run. Fording the Saskatchewan might banish their rosy dreams of a northern adventure.

Arriving at its banks, they watched the swollen torrent sweep relentlessly along while Warren gave final orders. "Remember. If your horse rolls over, get out of your saddle, cling to his mane or tail . . . don't let go of him *altogether*! He may get out—you *never* will, alone." Sid Unwin, their other guide, rode into the water, found a ford, and the others followed. The horses bent their whole bodies to the force of the stream; the icy water rose frighteningly higher—to the ponies' shoulders; the current threatened to force the riders' feet from the stirrups. Mrs. Schäffer's powerful bay quivered, paused, and carefully inched forward; at midstream her only thought was for "self-

Mary Adams, left, and Mary Schäffer with "Chief,"
Billy Warren. (The figure on the right is unidentified.)
COURTESY WHYTE MUSEUM OF THE CANADIAN ROCKIES, BANFF (V439/PS-1)

preservation . . . and one longed for the courage to turn back." At last the ponies scrambled up onto the steep banks. Warren's determined charges had passed the test.

They visited Glacier Lake and pushed on to snowy Wilcox Pass. How they longed to follow the Athabasca! But Warren turned back, taking them to Coleman's Pinto Lake and over to historic Kootenay Plains. They were tenderfeet no more; their plans for the next year were already made. They were going on a four-month expedition!

In the face of protests from horrified relatives and friends in the drawing rooms of Philadelphia the two women made preparations, and waited with mounting impatience for spring. On June 20th, 1907, curious bystanders at Laggan saw a packtrain heading north. Proudly in the vanguard rode two ladies, wearing buckskin jackets over long black gowns.

Starting out under leaden skies, Unwin and Warren led the two Marys through the fire-devastated timber and familiar muskegs along the Bow and up to Bow Pass, where at last the sun broke through. Past crystal pools seeping down to join the rivers, beside glacier lilies thrusting golden heads through snowdrifts, riding over clumps of pale spring beauties and yellow vetches, they descended into the forests of the Mistaya Valley. The treacherous Saskatchewan was forded again and they rode north, following the river banks along a ragged trail clinging to the cliffs of the narrowing gorge.

Time and again the horses plunged into the water, bobbing about like corks and thoroughly soaking the flour; eventually it was rendered impervious to further wetting by its own gluey casing. The ugly, deceptively stupid-looking Pinky ducked their sleeping bags as he revelled in a cool bathe; delighted by the agreeable lightening of his burden he ignored their frantic yells and emerged in his own good time, strolling nonchalantly into camp where he craftily stood beside a tree, hoping it would be assumed that he had been tied there with his more obedient companions long ago.

The little party made the stiff ascent to Wilcox Pass; along the way, they were stealthily followed by one of the beautiful tawny cats for whom they named Panther Falls. They celebrated "the Glorious Fourth of July" in a blinding snowstorm on the summit where their feast of bacon and boiled beans resembled "lumps of candle grease." Slithering down what they named Tangle Ridge to the wide shingle flats of the Sunwapta, they rode for days along Coleman and Habel's trail beside the strikingly coloured Endless Chain Ridge (as they christened it) and west to Fortress Lake, "a long, pale blue-green ribbon tossed among the fir-clad hills."

Hoping to find Habel's trail to the source of the Athabasca, the men scouted ahead one day, leaving the ladies with strict instructions: "Don't meddle in the kitchen department and don't waste the laundry soap!" As soon as their "guardians" were out of sight—naturally—they "flew to the collapsible rubber hand basin" and with generous applications of the precious soap indulged in a laundering orgy! Then, carefully looking out for possible trees to climb in case the feared grizzly should appear, they wandered toward Habel's path, finding his blaze on a felled tree and the old camp where "the boughs of his bed curled wanly and the fireplace was overgrown by moss." Returning to camp, thoughtfully reflecting on the transience of human life, they cheered themselves (and the hungry scouts, they hoped) by creating a magnificent pudding. Unhappily, it resembled in every way "a cannon ball" and was left behind where all were certain it would endure long after every trace of their camp had disintegrated!

From the low valley of the Athabasca they saw, as Habel had, the snow-clad, glacier-draped pyramid of Mount Columbia—"a beautiful example of exquisite symmetry." On the way back to Wilcox Pass, under Diadem Peak, they passed through great beds of luscious strawberries and for days enjoyed delicious strawberry shortcake. (Apparently the men had reestablished their rights in the culinary department!) Once more they camped on Wilcox Pass in the snow.

As it was still snowing in the morning, the women snuggled back into their sleeping bags, drowsily listening to male voices in the distance. Suddenly they were startled by a discreet cough; at the door of their tent stood a bespectacled, bearded stranger, immaculate in a neat black raincoat. Bowing and doffing his hat, he said he hoped he hadn't intruded, but were there men in the camp? Sitting up and, "as gracefully as sleeping bags allowed," returning his bow, they pointed out the men's tent. After his departure they marvelled at the man's remarkable poise; "Surely two women camped at Wilcox Pass must have been the last thing he expected to see, but not by so much as a quiver in his voice did he indicate his surprise."

No one had thought to ask the stranger's identity; he and his party were

camping two miles down the valley and Warren remarked that their caller
had said he'd been to Fortress Lake in 1893. Fortress Lake? In 1893? The visitor must have been Coleman! Courtesy of the trail or not, Mrs. Schäffer
intended to find out, and when they encountered him a few hours later she
inquired. To her delight she found herself talking to L.Q. Coleman who, with
his brother, was on his way north on a momentous expedition. "Here we
were," she said, "falling over the man whose maps and notes we had been
unable to obtain before leaving home and whose trails and camps were all
we had read on the long days on the Athabasca!"

Happily, they found occasion to visit the Colemans' camp as they
returned a pony which had attached itself to their packtrain; of that "act of
good neighborliness" Coleman wrote: "It was a delightful surprise to have a
charming woman ride out of the snow in the midst of the Rockies to share
our lunch of bannock, bacon and tea." Around their campfire mutually helpful information was exchanged; undoubtedly it resulted in the Quaker ladies
embarking on a very long side trip the next year.

Mrs. Schäffer's party returned to a former camp near the junction of the
Alexandra and the North Saskatchewan rivers. Since their provisions were
now seriously depleted, Warren and Unwin hurried eighteen miles south to
one of Jim Simpson's winter cabins where they had cached extra supplies. As
the two women watched their "preservers disappearing in the distance, leaving us with only our two saddle ponies, the wide shingle flats and the frowning hills as protectors," they experienced "an uncanny sensation of loneliness
. . . Except for our two departed friends, not another human being within a
hundred miles of us."

Suddenly their horses whinnied and out of the distance came a packtrain led by their good friend Jim Simpson—and his companion appeared
to be a woman! Mounting quickly, Mrs. Schäffer rode out to meet them and
there in the wilderness, "a woman from the civilization of London . . . every
inch a lady" in spite of weatherbeaten black gown, storm-swept Panama hat
and scarred hobnail boots, graciously greeted one from the drawing rooms
of Philadelphia. Jim's companion was an aristocratic little sixty-year-old
Welsh grandmother, daughter of a British chancellor of the exchequer who,
after raising six children, roamed the globe catching butterflies for her own
famous collection and those of Baron Rothschild and the British Museum.

It was probably around their shared campfire that evening that Jim, hearing of their delight in visiting almost unknown country, told them of a lake the Stonies called Chaba Imne. As the beaver for which it was named had long since been trapped out or shot, the Indians no longer went there. But they had told their friend Jim about it and he passed the information along for what it was worth.

Jim no doubt thoroughly approved of their planned excursion up the Alexandra River Valley; he still maintains that this is one of the most beautiful valleys in the Rockies. When the men returned, the adventurous foursome started out along the Alexandra, which they called Nashanesen, Stoney for "wolverine-go-quick," the Indians' name for Jim whose speed on snowshoes had earned him this appelation. Mrs. Schäffer thought Jim deserved to have a valley and river named for him as he "had done so much to make the old trails passable." Unfortunately Mr. Outram's earlier nomenclature had been officially adopted.

The little party camped beneath Watchman Peak; "the exquisite lake" at its base was bordered by a "ready-made garden" where "columbines nodded their yellow heads from stalks three feet tall, while deep blue larkspurs, snowy valerian, flaming castilleia and golden arnicas hailed our coming . . ." From camp, Mrs. Schäffer and the men climbed to the summit of Thompson Pass and made a short ascent on Mount Bryce. Before them lay "the frozen, snow-packed, silent sea" of the Columbia Icefields.

At their camp beneath Watchman Peak "no ripple of worry from the outside world could touch us . . . It was hard to go from that beautiful place, to leave the little lake to the butterflies, the gophers, the ducks, the bears and the flowers . . ." But leave they must, for they had decided to make yet another journey before season's end.

The two Marys had followed in the footsteps of Wilcox, Collie, Habel, the Colemans, Thompson and Outram to become the first white women to see many of the outstanding attractions in today's Banff and Jasper parks. Now they had their hearts set on going where even those intrepid explorers had not yet penetrated. They were going to find Chaba Imne.

Returning to the valley of the Saskatchewan, they journeyed north toward Wilcox Pass and crossed Nigel Pass (east of today's Icefields Chalet). "Though it was September the 8th and the best part of the summer gone, we started again for valleys new to us." On September 9th they reached Brazeau Lake where they set up camp in brilliant sunshine. After a violent thunderstorm, they awoke next morning to find their tents sagging under a burden of snow. For two days they waited "impatiently in camp watching that persistent and aggravating snow . . ."

Still hoping to reach their goal, they pressed on in the teeth of icy winds and swirling snow, straining to catch a glimpse of a warm, inviting, lake-gemmed valley. Valleys they saw, but each was more dreary and dismal than the last.

Travelling back toward Nigel Pass, they clambered over Coleman's high Jonas Pass and in a scene of bone-chilling desolation, camped where hurricane winds shrieked among the peaks and threatened to blow them back up the mountain. Over the "snow-laden heights" of Cataract Pass they made an arduous trek. To Mary Schäffer it was "a hideous nightmare." Painfully snow-blind, she rode with bandaged eyes, buffetted by every thrusting tree branch. It was late September; they were in urgent need of more supplies. The search for the secluded lake had to be abandoned. Continuing south and west, they set out for Tom Wilson's ranch on the Kootenay Plains. When at last they descended to the historic plains, they rode into a beautiful Indian summer. Mary Schäffer had visited the Stoney Indians camped on the plains the year before and there was great excitement when Yahe Weha ("the Mountain Woman") passed among the teepees. In one she was especially welcome. There, lovely mother Leah Beaver and her winsomely beautiful little girl remembered the doll Yahe Weha had fashioned for her "forest baby" out of a table napkin stuffed with newspapers; there, in the evening, they renewed old friendships.

Suddenly there was a gentle pat of moccasined feet. The teepee flap swung back and out of the darkness came a handsome young chief. As he stepped to the fire, its glow flashed on the brass earrings and black glossy braids of Samson Beaver, "the graceful, smiling boy" who had ridden with the Colemans in 1892, son of the famous hunter Job Beaver, grown to manhood now and head of the family.

When the two Marys walked back to their tent that evening, Mrs. Schäffer clutched a precious scrap of paper. Beside the fire she quickly labelled it; a year from now it might be difficult to remember that "a very

Mary Schäffer's own photograph of the "graceful, smiling boy,"
Samson Beaver, her "forest baby" and Leah Beaver.

PHOTO BY MARY SCHÄFFER. COURTESY WHYTE MUSEUM OF THE
CANADIAN ROCKIES, BANFF (V527/NG-124)

scribbly spot" signified an important pass, and that "something that looked like a squashed spider" identified a prominent peak. Samson Beaver had visited Chaba Imne with his father nearly twenty years before as a boy of fourteen, and from memory had drawn her a map.

Wistfully they realized that their wonderful adventure was nearly over for the year, but as they struggled down over Howse Pass and up the fearfully steep precipices of Baker Pass (where the horses, "constantly springing to reach a higher level," arrived at the summit dripping from the heaving effort and descended "by clutching the icy mud with their toes"), the two women consoled themselves by planning next year's search for the hidden lake.

Just before reaching Field, and civilization, the party undertook a most vigourous "special toilet"—clothes were patched, brushed and washed. Then, smiling in "sincere admiration as we beheld the scrubbed elegance of our appearance," they set out on their last morning's ride. Approaching the road, a handsome carriage flashed by and whatever vanity a Quaker lady might possess was shattered in one awful fleeting glimpse. In the shining equipage sat a gentleman and his lady—"her gown was blue, her hat was graced by a white wing" and she wore *gloves*. "Oh! the tragedy of the comparison!"

Soon, however, like Mrs. Rudyard Kipling whose elegance had contrasted so sharply with their shabby appearance, the two Marys were appropriately gowned for cosmopolitan eastern society—and longing for the wild, free life in their beloved Rockies!

In June 1908 they rode out from Laggan and proceeded to Bow Pass during a solid week of rain—but they were blissfully happy to be gazing again "on all that vastness which was ours." Again they rode to Brazeau Lake; when they crossed Poboktan Pass, they experienced the excitement of venturing into new regions. Hitherto they had followed trails blazed by others; now they had to rely on Samson's map, which indicated that they should turn up the third creek coming in from the right. They had already passed several valleys and not one of them could they follow because there wasn't enough feed in them for their twenty-two horses.

Another Fourth of July camp was made in the snow; buffetted by howling winds, the men scouted a pass where they could see for miles. No lake gleamed below. For days they looked for the right pass; camping at last in a beautiful green valley where flowers formed an unbroken carpet, they climbed a hill to look for the lake. In vain. Were they lost? Was Samson's map any good?

After lunch, Sid Unwin announced abruptly: "I'm going off to climb something that's high enough to see if that lake's within twenty miles of here and I'm not coming back till I know!"

Slowly the hours crept by; night came and the anxious "little household" lit a huge bonfire to serve as a beacon for their wandering companion. At 10:30 he staggered in and grinned, "I've found the lake!"

Hurrying along in high spirits next morning, in just two hours they reached the shore of Samson's Chaba Imne. Since leaving Poboktan Creek they hadn't seen "one sign of a civilized hand," and as they stood in the secluded valley they wondered if they were the first white people ever to see that gem of the Canadian Rockies—Maligne Lake.

Determined to explore its blue expanse, the men spent all of the next day building a raft. Early the following morning the ladies were escorted to H.M.S. *Chaba* for its maiden voyage. Equipped for a three-day journey (which they thought would take them to the head of the lake where they intended to look for the high mountain Professor Coleman had climbed in 1903), the men hustled the feminine contingent unceremoniously up onto a mound of blankets, air mattresses, tents, flour and slabs of bacon. They carefully avoided looking down at the icy green depths shining between the logs of their heavily laden raft. Leisurely, under a gloriously blue sky, the little party drifted "past exquisite bays and inlets as the mountains closed in" around them. At night they camped on the shore in a garden of fragrant crimson vetch across from Mount Unwin, which they promptly christened when Sid identified it as the one from which he'd seen the lake.

As the head of the lake seemed only a mile away they set out next morning on the final lap, puzzling about Samson's map. So far it had been very accurate and yet it seemed seriously at fault now; he had clearly indicated narrows about two-thirds of the way up the lake.

Rounding the point where they intended to disembark at the end of their expedition on the lake, "there burst upon us that which, all in our little company agreed, was the finest view any of us had ever beheld in the Rockies"—that most photographed spot in the Rockies—Maligne Lake from the Narrows. "There it lay, for the time being all ours—those miles and miles of lake, the unnamed peaks rising above us . . . each more beautiful than the last."

A "magnificent double-headed pile of rock" of massive and "simple dignity" they named Mount Warren, "in honour of Chief through whose grit and determination we were able to behold this splendour"; for Mrs. Schäffer's absent friend they named Mount Mary Vaux, and as a memorial to the Stoney Indian who'd made the map, Samson Narrows, Samson Peak, and Mount Leah for his wife.

They spent nearly two weeks in their Eden and during that time they searched for some sign that others had been there. There wasn't so much as a "teepee pole, a charred stick," a blazed tree or even a game trail—"just masses of flowers, the lap-lap of the waters on the shore, the occasional reverberating roar of an avalanche and our own voices stilled by a nameless Presence."

Theirs was the first recorded exploration of the lake and it is fairly certain that they were the first white people to approach it from the south, although it had been visited by one of the railway surveyors, Henry McLeod, who reached it from the Athabasca in the 1870s and named it Sorefoot Lake.

No matter how idyllic the surroundings, there came the day when they had to leave, for they wanted to visit the historic Jasper Valley which they hoped to reach by crossing and following Maligne River. But when Unwin rode into its "innocent-looking, crystal green waters" the savage undertow instantly swept his horse off its feet and for a sickening moment it appeared as if horse and rider were doomed. Clearly the river had been well named and fording it was out of the question. Unwin and Warren then discovered why McLeod had named their beautiful lake Sorefoot: for six days they stubbornly worked to cut a trail to Medicine Lake, only to return exhausted and defeated—it would take weeks of back-breaking work. To get to their destination, they retraced their steps all the way back south and west to the Sunwapta Valley and followed Coleman's trail along the Athabasca.

Reaching the wide valley near today's Jasper townsite, they took their horses over a "rock wall" (probably today's Old Fort Point), rode through the quiet pines beside Lac Beauvert where Jasper Park Lodge now stands, and made their way up to the great gash of Maligne Canyon where, in a last leap of white fury, the river from Chaba Imne flings itself down to the Athabasca.

Returning to the Jasper Valley, they saw across the Athabasca three or four log dwellings. At a signal from Sid's rifle the only white inhabitant of that lovely valley launched his boat and came to ferry them across. "Women in your party?" he said to Sid. "Well, well, whatever brought them here, prospecting or timber cruising? I've been in this valley thirteen years and they're the first white women I've seen around these parts!"

After a few days the Schäffer party left on the last side trip of the season. When they had met the Colemans on Wilcox Pass the year before, those pioneer climbers were on their way to "the Monarch of the Rockies," Mount Robson. And where the Colemans had been the two Quaker ladies and their escorts were determined to follow. After six gruelling days over frightful trails along the Yellowhead route, their goal was revealed: "Cold, icy, clean-cut, in a sky unclouded and of intensest blue . . . Mount Robson, a noble, massive vision to the pilgrims who had come so far to see her."

Each year Mary Schäffer continued her pilgrimage to the Rockies and in 1912, the cultivated and moderately wealthy widow decided to make her home among them. To her lovely cottage in Banff she brought her beautiful 18th century heirlooms. And there, in 1915, she married Chief.

Gentlemanly, college-trained Boer War hero, Sid Unwin stayed in Banff too, the Prince of Guides for later expeditions—until he fell on the battlefields of the First World War.

In 1939 Mary Schäffer-Warren died. Beside Chief she lies in the little cemetery below Tunnel Mountain, their names engraved on slabs of beautiful Mount Rundle stone. But the blithe pioneer woman's true memorial is lovely Maligne Lake with which her name will always be romantically identified.

22

DRAMA AT MOUNT ROBSON

Five years after Coleman's crushing disappointment at Athabasca Pass in 1893, government surveyor James McEvoy, working west of Yellowhead Pass, saw a snowy monolith which he calculated to be 13,700 feet high—Mount Robson, the highest mountain in the Canadian Rockies. The origin of its name remains a fascinating mystery; there has been speculation that Milton and Cheadle named it, but the most reliable evidence indicates that it was already locally known by that name when they passed by. Coleman, however, wasn't greatly impressed by "rumours of its unrivalled height and splendour"—he didn't intend to make a long and difficult journey only to find that once again a Canadian peak had been grossly overestimated!

Then, in the winter of 1906, the human dynamo of the Rockies pointed out precisely why the Colemans should go to the mountain and, if possible, climb it: for nearly half a century explorers and surveyors had wandered past Canada's highest known peak and yet no one had ever actually visited it— the "finest virgin peak in America awaited conquest!" And now was the time for Canadians to storm its heights, for what could possibly be a more fitting and dramatic way to launch the Alpine Club of Canada? Presenting his imaginative plan with characteristic gusto, A. O. Wheeler won hands down. The Colemans would go.

The proposal was made at the founding meeting of the Alpine Club of Canada. With the inauguration of that organization, Wheeler saw the fulfillment of a cherished dream, just as twenty-nine years before he'd realized a boyhood ambition to spend a summer on Canada's Great Lakes in a birch-bark canoe. Educated in a private school, he had come to Canada with his parents as a boy of sixteen, trained as a surveyor, and at eighteen was travelling the broad reaches of the empty prairies in a Red River cart, surveying for pioneer settlements. In 1900 he worked in the Crowsnest Pass mining area and the next year journeyed to the Selkirks, where he was to make the first extensive use of the newly developed photo-topographical surveying technique.

This meant packing cumbersome equipment to mountain tops, so with great zest he set out to master the art of climbing under the tutelage of the Swiss guides at Glacier House. That was the beginning of a lifelong passion for his Great Hills; for nearly forty-five years this sturdy, able and fantastically energetic Irishman strode through the Selkirks and the Rockies, amassing an unequalled store of knowledge about them and vigourously spreading "the gospel of the mountains."

At Glacier House he met Professor Fay who encouraged him to proceed with plans for forming a Canadian alpine club. Wheeler knew that just a few miles away, twenty-three years before, such a club had been in existence for a few playful moments. On the summit of the pass through the Selkirks, when Rogers had triumphantly demonstrated to Sandford Fleming that the long-sought railway route had been found—on that occasion, as the celebrants rested from their famous game of leapfrog they "viewed the landscape" and, still exhilarated, decided that "some memorial should be preserved of our visit here." So they organized a Canadian Alpine Club, elected Fleming president and drank a toast to its success from "one of the springs rippling down to the Illecillewaet . . . and conceived the bold idea of climbing Mount Sir Donald as a fitting virgin attempt" of the club. But the idea was "not put into execution," and the major wasn't able to carry out his intention of planting the Union Jack on the highest pinnacle of that peak the day that the first train roared through his pass. When the club became a reality, however, Sir Sandford became honorary president (a post he proudly held until his death in 1915) and faraway, untrodden Mount Robson replaced the much-climbed Mount Sir Donald as the "fitting virgin attempt."

The Colemans carefully considered the best way to approach their goal.

The shortest route was from Beavermouth on the C.P.R., but that would mean following the old voyageur trail on the Columbia and the professor remembered that twenty years before he and young Frank Stover had "had no love" for *that* particular piece of country. The trail from Edmonton was reported to be poor, so they decided to proceed from Laggan—they had never travelled from the Bow to the Saskatchewan by that route, but as a handful of packtrains had begun using the trail they expected it would be in tolerable condition; as they had themselves blazed the trail from the Sunwapta to the Miette, they hoped to make good time.

They started north on August 1st, 1907, accompanied by a third experienced and enthusiastic young Canadian climber, the Reverend George B. Kinney. Although it gave the Colemans great pleasure to see the fine mountain Collie had named for them in the valley of the Saskatchewan, their journey was still impeded by the familiar trials of the trail. It took them forty-one days to reach their destination, weeks longer than they had anticipated. But they saw at last "the imperial mountain of our aspiration; one vast, lone, snow-clad, cloud-capped peak wrapped in the solitude of centuries."

It became even more snow clad and cloud capped. Robson, a notorious gathering place for storms, kept its austere summit hidden for the rest of their stay. Doggedly awaiting just a day or two of good weather, they explored the valleys and climbed to timberline where camp was made in a foot of snow. But they had arrived too late in the season; their food was almost gone, their horses hungry, lame and sick. Defeated, the first climbing expedition to Mount Robson started on the long trek back to civilization.

As a young man on the Columbia, Coleman had said: "Still, one hates to turn back before every effort has been made"; at fifty-five, retreating from Mount Robson, he made new plans to reach his goal—and that of Wheeler and the Alpine Club of Canada—next year.

In August of 1908 the Colemans and Mr. Kinney made their way from Edmonton to Robson in a little more than three weeks, which was ten days longer than they had hoped to be on the trail. As they approached the foot of the mountain it began to snow. Two days later it cleared—but it was Sunday, and "in deference to the Minister" they didn't climb. They had to wait for five days before climbing weather returned and then they ascended to over ten thousand feet before rain and approaching nightfall drove them down. Next day the tantalizing summit "gleamed like burnished silver," but it was Sunday again. The Colemans must have secretly seethed with impatience at the parson's unshakeable no-climbing-on-the-Sabbath rule!

For three snow-plagued weeks they camped at the base of the mountain: they toiled up the Robson Glacier, and a snowstorm turned them back; they bivouacked up high, but a blizzard threatened to bury them and they descended. The condition of their larder made retreat imperative but Kinney insisted on one more try—alone.

On the cold rocks at the seven thousand-foot level, he wrapped himself in his blanket and shivered without a fire until dawn when he assaulted the heights; "for thousands of feet the great rock towered overhead, fringed and fretted with dripping icicles that hung in masses from the overhanging cliffs, sometimes as much as 50 feet in length." Knee-deep in fresh-fallen snow he inched over narrow dwindling ledges to 10,500 feet. A screaming gale sent him back—three times he was literally blown off his feet. He was lucky to return alive. On the other hand, if Kinney hadn't promised his companions that he would be out only one night, he could have found shelter in "some nook" and tried again the next morning. If he had, in all probability the peak would have been his.

For days the party had been living on tough dried goat meat. They intended to leave as soon as Kinney returned, but when the next day dawned the finest yet, they couldn't resist one more attempt. Carrying camp high up onto the Robson Glacier, the following day everything pointed to success; they fought their way to within twelve hundred feet of the summit. But it was four in the afternoon and a great impassable cavern yawned between the glacier and the rock wall above. They seriously considered making the necessary detour, but it would have entailed another night on the mountain at a bivouac much higher than Kinney's; that meant every possibility of frostbitten limbs—and they were hundreds of miles from civilization. "The game was up"—till next year!

Before parting from their packer, John Yates of Lac Ste. Anne, they arranged to start from Edmonton again the next August.

But in May Kinney heard the disturbing rumour that "a party of foreigners" was coming to assault Mount Robson that summer. He was galvanized into action, sending a frantic wire to Yates and hurrying from his home in Victoria, B.C., to Edmonton. Awaiting him was a letter from Yates, explaining that it would be madness to start for the mountains so early in the year, especially since spring had been very late and the snowfall exceptionally heavy. Kinney, however, would not be deterred. "On Friday, June 11th, with only $2.85 in my pocket, but with three good horses packed with three months' provisions, I started off alone for Mount Robson, hoping to pick up someone on the trail who would share fortune with me."

Except for an oldtimer who travelled with him for a few days from the McLeod River, he made the trek alone. The Rocky River was in flood and he and his horses "had to swim for our lives"; a mighty cloudburst "flooded the entire Athabasca Valley," leaving him stranded for days on a little island with his horses on another, until at last he "waded waist-deep through raging waters to a place of safety."

Then into his camp rode a young man "wearing on his Stetson the silver badge of the Guides' Association of Ontario"—the "someone who would share fortune" with him. Twenty-five-year-old Donald ("Curly") Phillips was looking over the country for future guiding purposes, and had similarly spent six anxious days on an island in the flooded river. He was to become one of the most respected guides in Jasper: "fearless, resourceful, even-tempered," A. O. Wheeler said of him, adding that when it came to travelling through untracked bush country (where Wheeler considered himself to be "no slouch"), "he was a superman." Phillips had never climbed a mountain in his life. In short order, however, Kinney had persuaded him to tackle Mount Robson!

As they plodded up the Miette Valley they carried few provisions, having agreed to rely on fish and the game they would shoot with Kinney's gun. From a chance encounter with travellers Phillips learned that his companion was "a preacher," which meant that forthwith he "had to lay aside any superfluous language that comes in so handy to a fellow driving pack horses and doing other ornery chores . . ." He was sorely tempted, though, when he discovered that their only gun was so badly bent as to be almost useless and he had to continue watching the big goats sauntering by, wagging saucy whiskers at him. Birds and marmot stew became the mainstay of their diet.

On July 24th they camped at the base of the same north side of Robson upon which Kinney had made his valiant attempt the year before. Phillips

Cornice near the summit of Mount Robson. It was through just such a cornice that Reverend Kinney struck a hole and found himself "looking down a sheer wall of precipice that reached to the glacier at the foot of Berg Lake, thousands of feet below."

PHOTO BY ED COOPER, SAN FRANCISCO

had no climbing equipment but with a bit of ordinary rope strung tenuously between them, and with Phillips using a stick instead of an ice axe, in three days they hacked their way up to eleven thousand feet as Robson's artillery of avalanches swished menacingly by. They retreated, brought up more supplies and camped at ten thousand feet. Kinney cut steps up the ice slopes to twelve thousand feet—but it was late in the day and falling rock and ice sent them hurrying for their lives. During that harrowing descent, when "the now-melting snow-masses that covered every ledge threatened to slide from under our weight and drag us over the cliffs," Kinney noticed that "Phillips was fast becoming an expert in climbing"!

They waited out eight days of storm and snow, set out again when it cleared, and were driven back when the storm began anew. When the weather improved on August 12th they quickly packed back up to the 10,500-foot level. Climbing to the west shoulder they dug down two feet of snow on a narrow ledge, built a little wall of stones to keep themselves from rolling off into the depths below and spent a bitter night awaiting the dawn—they knew it had to be their very last attempt. On the morning of Friday the thirteenth the weather was fine; then it began to snow. They continued to move up; their whole world was confined to the wall before and above them. Heavy clouds and sleet closed in around them, "a blessing in a way for they shut out the view of the fearful depths below." Slowly they climbed the ridge amid enormous, precariously perched snow cornices—up to the final steep icecap of the summit crest.

Kinney "struck the edge of the snow with the staff of my ice axe and it cut into my very feet, and through the little gap that I had made in the cornice, I was looking down a sheer wall of precipice that reached to the glacier at the foot of Berg Lake, thousands of feet below. I was on a needle peak that rose so abruptly that even cornices cannot build out very far on it. Baring my head I said: 'In the name of Almighty God, by Whose strength I have climbed here, I capture this peak Mt. Robson, for my own country, and for the Alpine Club of Canada.'"

As he and Phillips were leaving Jasper on their way home they met the "foreigners" who were bent on capturing his mountain. What a perfectly satisfying moment it must have been for the triumphant clergyman when he announced his victory . . . or was it?

They congratulated him warmly. "Surely no mountaineering success was ever more richly deserved, or won by a finer exhibition of courage, skill and indomitable perseverance," one of them wrote later. A well-deserved tribute. What then could have marred Kinney's moment of triumph?

He was widely acclaimed in alpine circles for what had truly been an epic achievement. But in the Alpine Club of Canada, where he remained an honoured member, there gradually arose a tiny suspicion that he'd been turned back within a few feet of the top.

A. O. Wheeler didn't intend to leave any doubt as to whether or not his Alpine Club deserved the honour of having made the first ascent of the highest mountain in the Canadian Rockies. Setting up the club's camp at the base of Mount Robson in 1913, he picked a crack team for the first attempt. Ably and courageously led by Conrad Kain, that "Prince of Canadian Alpine Guides," Albert MacCarthy and William Foster took to the mountain all their skill, strength and endurance. Leaving their rocky bivouac in the cold light of dawn they struggled upward, sinking hip-deep in the snow; Kain cut steps "as though inspired" as they inched up the walls of rock and ice. After eight hours, they saw above "great masses of ice and rock, dome upon dome, swept clear by raging storms to reveal clear green ice scintillating in the sun"—beyond was the spire of the summit.

There was not much room to stand on the summit. With all of the great bastion's defences overcome, the unique satisfaction of the successful climber was theirs. For a few brief moments they experienced the sense of having transcended themselves and some of Nature's mightiest obstacles. From one of earth's high quiet places, looking out upon her vast and majestic beauty, they felt detached from life's petty concerns—and a little nearer to an "Unfathomable Presence."

It was an experience that the Reverend Mr. Kinney must have known on many a peak. But not on Mount Robson. Curly Phillips had confided to Conrad Kain that in 1909 he and Kinney had "reached on our ascent (in mist and storm) an ice-dome 50 or 60 feet high, which we took for the peak. The danger was too great to ascend the dome."

As Kain made the fearful descent with MacCarthy and Foster, he noted Kinney's and Phillips's route and pronounced it "quite the most dangerous way that could be chosen up the peak." Later he wrote: "They deserve more credit than we . . . for in 1909 they had many more obstacles to overcome than we; for at that time the railway . . . was no less than 200 miles from their goal and their way had to be made over rocks and brush, and we must not forget the dangerous river crossings."

The achievement of Kinney and Phillips was in no way diminished by acknowledgment of the truth. Perhaps the great clergyman-climber was a much happier man when he finally conceded nearly fifty years later that he had probably been "mistaken" and that he had been a few feet short of the summit.

In 1909, when he'd encountered the "foreigners" who'd driven him to such a desperate last attempt to reach the summit, he had claimed total victory. He may have harboured a faint hope that they would turn back. For these were indeed most formidable rivals!

23

Extending the Domain

The "foreigners" had come directly from A. O. Wheeler's Alpine Club camp at Lake O'Hara. His fledgling organization had prospered since the first annual camp, when eager novices had trooped in with men suitably dressed for a golf course, derby hatted or in summer straws (some even carrying umbrellas); the lady hopefuls were no less elegant in trailing skirts and flower-decked hats. But he "soon licked them into shape."

A bearded, amiable bear of a man, he ruled his camps with the hand of a "benevolent despot." Every year climbing classes were conducted and no one left to climb without permission and the company of a competent guide; Wheeler himself roused the tardy in the mornings and after breakfast, "planted on as sturdy a pair of legs as ever trod a mountain side," he had them file past on their way to the heights while he issued last minute advice, terse instructions and warm encouragement.

The camp of 1909 had been especially memorable. Present were the great Whymper and three more of the most illustrious figures in the alpine world—British Alpine Club members Arnold Mumm, Geoffrey Hastings and climber-statesman Leopold S. Amery. All had twenty thousand-foot peaks in their records and their presence was a real feather in Wheeler's cap. Delivering a rousing speech about the glories of the Rockies to the Canadian Club in Winnipeg, he had discovered that outstanding climbers, scientists and statesmen were coming to another meeting of the British Association for the Advancement of Science. Immediately, he had fired off salvos of invitations to have them visit the mountains—with most gratifying results.

However, he must have watched Mumm, Hastings and Amery leaving for Mount Robson with some misgivings; after all *his* club was still making its bid to realize his pet project there. When Amery announced that they intended to make the trip from Edmonton to Robson in two weeks, Wheeler gravely shook his head and muttered something about it taking more like six. They were not long out of Edmonton before wealthy lawyer-publisher Mumm decided Wheeler had been only too right!

Travelling in horse-drawn buggies through the timbered country west of Edmonton proved to be "one of the most remarkable in some respects of all my Canadian experiences." Mumm further gave it as his considered opinion that he'd "just lived through the longest week I've ever known" when they arrived at Wolf Creek, and heartily wished himself back with Mr. Wheeler at Lake O'Hara. By the time they got to Jasper Lake, after being on the trail for sixteen days, he had begun to feel as if "the rest of our lives would be spent in struggling through those woods." When, after all this, they met Mr. Kinney, they had of course not the slightest intention of turning back!

Almost two weeks later they finally reached the mountain; Mumm found the view superb and his personal Swiss guide, Moritz Inderbinen (who travelled all over the world with his patron), calmly remarked that they'd climb Robson in nine hours.

At once the renowned quartette set out to break a record—unintentionally. Undertaking a reconnaissance, they got off to an early start at 12:45 A.M. by lantern light and after tramping most of the day, were indeed rewarded with "a remarkably fine viewpoint" of their splendid goal. Serenely they admired it, considering the problems and exhilarating challenges ahead. Mumm had for some time been quietly "exercising my mind with the question of how we were to get back" to camp and at last "the others developed a tardy interest in it also." They managed to get down to the forest by nightfall and, as they had been scrambling for twenty hours with almost nothing to eat, they decided to halt for dinner. Camp was only a few hours away now and it wasn't "very material" if they got back at one or two A.M. They "consumed luxuriously and leisurely" the rest of their provisions and opted to

A. O. Wheeler, "Grand Old Man of the Mountains" and architect of the Alpine Club of Canada.

COURTESY THE HARRY POLLARD COLLECTION, PROVINCIAL ARCHIVES OF ALBERTA, EDMONTON (P5018)

JOYCE ON 4TH IRISH PUB
506 24TH AVENUE S.W.
CALGARY, AB

Term ID: 05073493

Purchase

xxxxxxxxxxxx1260

MASTERCARD   Entry Method: C

Clerk ID: 1186

Amount:$ 9.71

Tip: $ 0.02
                         ================
Total: $ 9.73

2013/06/09   09:34:21

Seq #:   0010015560

Appr Code: 11342B

Resp Code: 01/027

MasterCard
A0000000041010
A1 EF EC 6A 7D 87 96 C8
00 00 00 80 00
E8 00
E3 5A 70 3A 29 C2 97 E6

APPROVED
Thank You

Customer Copy

- IMPORTANT -
retain this copy for your records

Purchase

xxxxxxxxxxxx2250
MASTERCARD
Clerk ID: 1136   Entry Method: C?

Amount: $ 9.71
Tip: $ 0.02
Total: $ 9.73

01/30/06   05:32:41
Seq #:   001001550
Appr Code: 113428
Resp Code: 00.02?

APPROVED
Thanks You

"repose until 11" so they could enjoy a beautiful moonlit view of Robson as they strolled to camp.

But it became apparent that in a Canadian forest things are not quite so easy. Soon after they began their "stroll" Mumm discovered that the floor of the forest dropped away alarmingly and below yawned an "enormous gap" about one hundred feet wide, from which rose an immense slab of smooth slippery rock about one thousand feet high. As they tackled this, Mumm noted wryly that a walk "would have been delightful, but of walking there was practically none, only clambering, crawling, balancing and attending ceaselessly to where one was putting one's feet . . .!" After the second such "horrible detour" they were all "too subdued to use bad language . . . Dodging through the unending complexities of almost continuous wind-falls," they slogged ahead for seemingly interminable hours. When they came to a raging torrent, bridged only by a tree trunk, each struggled silently over—even the unfailingly solicitous Inderbinen went stolidly on without so much as a backward glance or the usual helping hand for his master. They got back to camp at six A.M. after being out for twenty-nine hours. *That* was a record for Mumm and one which he "sincerely hoped would remain so!"

At 1:15 A.M. on September 7th they started for Robson's summit; the day became beautifully warm and Inderbinen was "extraordinarily sanguine" about doing the climb in record time. Working masterfully, he led his skill-ful "herren" upward, tantalizingly nearer to the roof of the Rockies. At one very "nasty" section of the wall they paused while the guide cut steps again. Mumm was tremendously impressed by the length and steepness of the bar-rier which confronted them; the melting snow dripped on him frigidly; the sun disappeared and a chilly breeze bit through his wet clothing. He looked at his watch. It was two o'clock. A few minutes of calculation and, so far as he was concerned, their situation "became alarmingly obvious": they "had not the faintest chance" of getting up the wall they faced, on to the summit and back down from the steep pitch before dark. If they continued they would have to spend a night either on the ridge above or on the face of the wall. The fifty-year-old Mumm was "appalled" and promptly announced "apologetically, but firmly, that nothing would induce me to face either prospect . . . Amery's gentle accents floated up to me, 'You only want a rest, Mumm. We'll be on the ridge in half an hour and we can stop a bit and have

something to eat and you'll be all right.' This remark was meant to be sooth-
ing and like most remarks made with that amiable object, it produced
exactly the opposite effect. I replied rather tartly that I was as prepared for a
long grind as anyone and quite ready to go on for another six hours, but
spend the night on the ridge or face I *would* NOT!"

His companions reluctantly agreed and the party started back down.
Seconds later, from their intended line of ascent came a savage volley of ice
and rock. "Very little was said; indeed there was little to say," Mumm recalled.
Had they continued upward "We should all have been kilt!" Inderbinen
observed thoughtfully.

The season was late; Robson's cloud and storm descended and although
Mumm and his party had been very nearly to the summit, they rode down
the Miette with "a rankling sense of defeat."

However the challenge remained; in spite of the vicissitudes of travel in
Canadian forests, Mumm returned the next year and had no difficulty in
persuading Norman Collie to come back to the Rockies with him. For weeks
they waited for the clinging clouds to clear from storm-bound Mount
Robson. It remained shrouded in snow, frigidly aloof. So they rode north
and west with Collie's good friend Fred Stephens and fellow packer John
Yates, ascended beautiful Mount Bess on the Divide and then found their
way through miles of unmapped wilderness, south and east back to Brûlé
Lake. Again Collie had glimpsed "a new world" of wild and untouched splendour.

Like MacCarthy, Foster and Kain when they had stood on Robson's summit, Mumm and Collie had seen on their climbs "eight to nine thousand
square miles of wonderful alpine terrain" and like Robson's conquerors, they
must have been "awed by the realization that this was but a tithe of this
country's vast scenic heritage . . ."

To A. O. Wheeler, reports like this represented an opportunity not to be
missed. His Alpine Club had not been formed merely to turn out climbers;
its objectives included "the scientific study and exploration of Canadian
alpine regions, the education of Canadians to an appreciation of their
mountain heritage and the opening of new regions as national mountain
playgrounds." With his usual competence and zest he enlisted widespread
official cooperation, recruited a team of scientists and in 1911 set off on

a three-month expedition to Mount Robson, Jasper and Maligne Lake—areas which the Colemans, Kinney, Mumm, Amery, Collie and Mrs. Schäffer (all Alpine Club members) had done so much "to bring into prominence."

At Mount Robson, where Curly Phillips had cut trails for the British Columbia government the winter before, scientists from the Smithsonian Institute in Washington fanned out to make the first reports on the flora, fauna and geology of the region. One of the local guides working with them was a young member of the Brewster family, Fred; also from Banff came the expedition's official photographer, Byron Harmon, who had arrived in the mountains wondering if he could make a living developing visitors' films and was now building up his own collection of soon-to-be-famous photographs. The mountaineering guide Wheeler had brought along to direct and assist the climbs to be undertaken by the topographical surveyors was one-time Austrian goatherd, the incomparable Conrad Kain.

One rainy day Conrad was "overcome by ennui" and wandered off. In the evening he wasn't back and the rain was coming down in slashing torrents. His anxious companions shouted, fired guns and lit a huge fire to serve as a beacon. At bedtime there was still no sign of him. At daybreak he crept back into the tent he shared with Mr. Kinney: when questioned next day, he casually announced that he'd climbed 11,130-foot Mount Whitehorn!

Thirty peaks were climbed; one hundred miles of terrain were mapped and Wheeler marked the boundary at Yellowhead Pass, the beginning of a monumental fourteen-year task during which he and fellow members of the Interprovincial Boundary Commission were to scramble over six hundred miles of the high mountains forming the Continental Divide. Ecstatic about "the vast possibilities of this new alpine paradise"—a combination of "snow-crowned mountains, ice-encircled amphitheatres, tumbling glaciers, turquoise lakes and flashing waterfalls"—Wheeler urged the government of British Columbia to establish a provincial park at Mount Robson.

From his climbs he had seen the wild and awesomely beautiful Tonquin Valley and as he rode through the valley of the Athabasca on the way to Maligne Lake, his mind was busy with recommendations for developing this "future playground," abounding in "lovely lakes, gleaming glaciers, tantalizing peaks, pyramids, crags and precipices of every shade and form . . ." Three years before, the dominion government had been equally impressed with the

Jasper region and had established a national park there. They had been one of the sponsors of Wheeler's expedition. Another organization had "cooperated handsomely"—the Grand Trunk Pacific Railway. As it had been in the days of the fur trade, Jasper was once again to be on a transcontinental route.

24

SEVERING THE LAST LINKS WITH THE PAST

For nearly half a century the white man had made only sporadic incursions into the Jasper Valley; the only links with the fur trade era were Jasper House and a scattered remnant of native people. Descendants of the Iroquois brought west by the Nor'westers, these tall, fine-featured people had mastered the ways of snowshoe and packhorse and when the fur traders left, they made their home in the shadow of the mountains.

Then in 1872 the white man had threatened to disrupt their way of life by building a railway through the valley. Walter Moberly wintered there with his surveyors when Sandford Fleming decided on the Yellowhead Pass route for the transcontinental railway. It was late autumn by the time the whole party reached Boat Encampment from Howse Pass; the men wanted to stay there for the winter, but Moberly had them move headquarters. Getting 250 packhorses over Athabasca Pass must have been almost as difficult as the harassing crossing Paul Kane had made with the Indians in 1847. As on that earlier occasion, game was scarce around Jasper House; at Christmas time the men "were bewailing the loss of dinner," so Moberly invited them "to partake of the luxuries of my camp . . . I had several courses prepared, the first being pemmican raw, the second pemmican boiled and in due season the dessert, which was pemmican fried . . ."!

The Iroquois and Métis ("quiet, extremely civil, fine handsome athletic fellows") helped Moberly when he was working near Fiddle River ferrying supplies by dogsled. Louis had recruited his daughters to assist him with

Henry J. Moberly, the fur trader who rebuilt Jasper House in the 1850s.
COURTESY HUDSON'S BAY COMPANY ARCHIVES, WINNIPEG (N13616)

these chores and, coming to a ridge blown bare of snow, one of them, "a tall and very powerful young woman, took an enormous load without difficulty" across and down to a large pond. There was water to a considerable depth on top of the ice and detouring would have meant a long trek. Moberly sat down to enjoy a pipe before tackling the icy crossing. "The Amazon" returned from taking her load over and announced that her father had ordered her to carry Moberly across. He protested vigorously but she persisted, saying he was much lighter than the load she'd just packed over and if she didn't take him her father would be very angry. So, "I resigned myself and was ignominiously packed over." Louis was immensely proud of his strapping daughter, and that evening over a leisurely pipe went on at some length about the "great advantages of having such a powerful girl . . ." If Moberly could bear to part with a fine horse Louis much admired, he could acquire this handy helpmate as his bride. The offer was courteously declined—Moberly was not prepared to enter into any marital arrangements.

His younger brother Henry, the fur trader who had rebuilt Jasper House twenty years before, had been much more amenable, distributing his favours generously during his stay in the valley—his progeny formed a conspicuous part of the local population.

When the railway survey was called off the white man departed beyond the peaks until, in the 1890s, the Moberlys and their neighbours welcomed a lone American. Thirty-eight-year-old Lewis J. Swift only intended to stop overnight in their charming oasis of prairie amid the Rockies. He stayed for the rest of his life. Starting west from Buffalo, New York, young Swift had driven a stagecoach in North Dakota; succumbing to gold fever, he eventually arrived in British Columbia. It is quite possible that he had come across the international border with some haste—as many others did—looking back across this shoulder for possible pursuers. He made a modest stake, bought a pack outfit and worked his way to Kamloops and Tête Jaune Cache, where the Indians told him he could easily cross Yellowhead Pass and proceed to Edmonton.

He did go to Edmonton but only to bring back trade goods and livestock—and in 1897, a wife. On her honeymoon trip, Suzette, a fair-skinned Métis girl from St. Albert, was accompanied by a load of squealing pigs and cackling hens. She arrived to set up housekeeping temporarily in their first home at old Jasper House.

Swift had not given up his hope of making a fortune, however, and picked the site for a homestead with care. Beneath the wall of the Palisades, against the magnificent backdrop of Pyramid Mountain and facing the slate grey Colin Range, he resourcefully built up a fine farm on the 160 acres to which he was granted homestead rights. Over the years he and Suzette could look with pride at their comfortable house, sturdy buildings, fenced fields of grain, neat gardens and even a waterwheel which Swift ingeniously fashioned to grind his own flour.

Shortly after he had established himself, the Colemans, during their frantic bushwacking search for the Whirlpool mouth in 1893, had been startled to hear the unexpected sound of a cowbell along the Athabasca and had wondered about fresh blazes and recent tracks. In their haste they didn't stop to investigate. Fourteen years later when the Colemans were on their way to Robson, they were "enchanted to see pasturing horses in peaceful meadows" beside the Athabasca and welcomed the civilization offered by Swift's hospitable roofs. In the intervening years, non-native visitors must have been rather rare. Soon they became almost commonplace.

In 1908 it was Swift who had ferried Mary Schäffer's outfit across the Athabasca and sent his children to their camp with fresh milk, eggs and vegetables. The two Marys had called on Suzette Swift, admiring her spotless cabin furnished with handcrafted furniture; Suzette, warmed by their friendship, shyly displayed her exquisitely embroidered bridal finery and they bought some of her wonderfully made buckskin gloves, moccasins and coats.

Shortly after these visitors departed, the Colemans and Kinney called on one of Swift's neighbours, John Moberly, to inquire about the possibility of hiring his nephew, Dolphus, as trail guide and hunter. That "legendary native" was out hunting, but they admired Mrs. Moberly's embroidered, otter-trimmed buckskin suits which she offered to sell for sixty dollars. They were considered "much too grand" for the everyday use of hard-travelling mountaineers, dressed in garments tattered and torn. But when they met young Dolphus, "proudly erect on his sleek black pony" leading his entourage of relatives back from a successful hunt, he was "resplendent" in

Old Jasper House, last link with the fur trade era, before it was torn down by surveyors and the timber used to build a raft.
COURTESY JASPER-YELLOWHEAD MUSEUM AND ARCHIVES, JASPER (78/1)

one of the admired suits! As he accompanied them to Mount Robson, the Colemans learned the greatest respect for the twenty-one-year-old grandson of Henry Moberly: "a striking figure with a powerful physique, a mighty hunter and born leader" equal to all the challenges of wilderness life. However, one evening as Coleman was struggling to put up their teepee, he asked Dolphus to show him how. Their guide smiled contemptuously: "Don't know how." That was *woman's* work!

On their way home, John Moberly dealt fairly with them when they stopped to replenish their supplies at his store. At the well-built house of Dolphus's father, Ewan, they glimpsed a sewing machine—and a battered phonograph belting out "a ragtime tune in a very brazen voice." The white man's ways were creeping inexorably into what Coleman considered "an ancient, well-ordered civilization."

As they continued their journey to Edmonton, the Colemans and Kinney saw virgin timber being slashed by labouring men and beasts; quivering bogs were being made passable by creeping bands of steel and a soaring network of wooden trestles was beginning to span the deep ravines. Returning from Mount Robson, Mumm and his companions had finished their journey from Entwistle to Edmonton by train—"the first pleasure party to use the line." And west beyond the end of steel the tote road wound; up on to Disaster Point the heaving horses scrambled to slither down into the wide valley where rivers meandered over gravel benches and broadened into lakes. That deeply grooved trail underlined the passing of an era—to Swift it meant the possibility of realizing his long-awaited fortune.

When the park was established the handful of native families in the valley accepted the government's offer of a cash settlement for their property and left their homeland to live among the mountains outside the park boundaries. Swift, however, self-sufficient and content, refused to sell. He had deliberately chosen his homestead with admirable foresight; finding Walter Moberly's survey stakes he had shrewdly reckoned that the rumoured second transcontinental railway would pass there some day and it would be the logical place for a terminal.

In 1911 the train brought Wheeler's expedition as far as Brûlé Lake; after Swift had sent them "off rejoicing" along the tote road on the way to Yellowhead Pass, they travelled beside the railway builders' loaded wagons, mules and packtrains. Summit City (one of the railroad's construction camps) consisted of three or four makeshift log and canvas stores but boasted its share of "billiard and soft drink saloons"; social life was quite lively in the camp, especially when a wild-west shooting broke out as Wheeler's party camped nearby. No one was hurt. Just west of the British Columbia boundary, at Moose Lake, the night life was even more "spirited." Wheeler and his companions were awakened one midnight by a frightful clamour; iron triangles and tin cans were being beaten and guns fired off to herald the arrival of "a new brand of soft drink." During the ensuing celebration in the workers' camp, Conrad's clothes were stolen when his back was turned, considerable food disappeared and one of the expedition's iron stoves was carted off forcibly to appear later as a stake in a poker game!

When the labouring army left the mountains, not one, but two railways ran through Yellowhead Pass. Both had passed Swift by. His vision of riches was revived, however, when one of the railway barons formed an ambitiously promoted development company; as part of the plan Swift's property was to be the site of a luxurious resort and townsite. But during the First World War the folly of running two lines cheek by jowl through the mountains came home to roost; financial ruin threatened the railways; the government's Canadian National Railway took over and surplus lines were torn up to provide scrap steel for the war. Swift's last castle in the air burst like a bubble when the promoter of Swiftholme was tragically lost in the sinking of the *Titanic*. But Swift only sold his land—and then to a private buyer—in 1935 when he was ready to retire and live in the village of Jasper.

In 1910 he had been appointed game guardian (the forerunner of today's park warden); on one inspection trip he found the Grand Trunk's railway surveyors working at the site of his old home, Jasper House. With zealous attention to his official duty he reported to the government what may have seemed a trivial incident. (It is believed by some that he may thereby have forfeited his chances for the long-awaited fortune for, in retribution, the surveyors neatly bypassed his property). He reported that historic Jasper House had been torn down and its timber used to build a raft.

Tottering, weatherbeaten—in its heyday it had sheltered a host of weary travellers; its destruction severed the last link with the days "when fur was king."

THE WONDER TRAIL

At the 1913 Alpine Club camp when Wheeler finally realized his ambition to have his members make the first complete ascent of Mount Robson, pioneers Fay, C. S. Thompson, Coleman, Kinney and Mumm were on hand to congratulate the victorious team. Another notable British climber, Geoffrey Howard, had also come to see the new alpine paradise.

On his 1910 trip, Mumm had seen from his climbs in the Robson area the black, ravaged, "fiercely steep" precipices of Mount Geikie towering among the ramparts flanking the Tonquin Valley. Three years later he decided it must be climbed. Writing to packer John Yates, he outlined a plan to go from Robson to Mount Geikie and then find a way directly from the Tonquin Valley to romantic Athabasca Pass. But Yates suggested that they go to the pass by the old Whirlpool route and then make their way to the mountain, as little was known about approaching Athabasca Pass from the Tonquin Valley and they might spend a great deal of time searching without ever seeing the famous pass.

Geoffrey Howard had also arranged to do some exploring in the Jasper area with Fred Stephens and the two parties combined forces. It was raining dismally when they arrived in Jasper; among "the huddle of log shacks and bales of hay" that comprised the town they sought shelter in the "Pool Saloon where picturesque persons in high boots politely regaled us with tall stories and soft drinks." (Probably the local inhabitants regarded the visitors as being a bit picturesque too!) Very helpfully their hosts provided an abundance of information about Athabasca Pass and Mount Geikie. So little was definitely known about the area that even Mr. Wheeler wasn't positive whether today's Mount Edith Cavell was the Mount Geikie reported by surveyor McEvoy. Mumm accepted the local assumption that Cavell was in fact the mountain he sought.

Fortunately, it seemed that many people had made a circuit of the mountain—it just happened that none of them were present to enlighten the climbers! To add to the confusion, some insisted that the trail was impossible and others, with equal conviction, pronounced it "a dandy boulevard all the way"! Even more puzzling, "that prince of pioneers, Old Swift" kept telling them about colossal Mount Hooker and Mount Brown. At the end of two days the visiting mountaineers were "bewildered": surely Coleman had settled the Brown and Hooker mystery and all the accounts about the trail round Mount Geikie could not have come "from people perennially intoxicated"! They must go and see for themselves.

"A kind friend" conducted them across the Miette bridge, pointed out the trail along the Athabasca and, with a cheery farewell, assured them they'd have no problems. In just three minutes Stephens called back to Yates, "John, just bring up the big axe, will you?" They resigned themselves to "that familiar and heartbreaking sound of the steady whang of the axe and the crash of fallen trees. The dandy boulevard was a sad fraud."

With "the huge bulk of Geikie" beckoning, they worked their way along the Athabasca and on the second day Mumm, Howard and Inderbinen decided to climb a high ridge for a better view of their objective. Once again Mumm found himself enmeshed in the exasperating trials of Canadian mountain trails: "what looked like a pleasant two-hour" scramble would "take SIX OR SEVEN"! With many "strenuous gymnastics" negotiating windfalls, they descended, to rejoin their guides along the Athabasca.

A flooded creek barred the way ahead; the three climbers found that Yates and Stephens had made what they considered to be a substantial bridge of "two thin and sensationally wobbly saplings." Howard watched with subdued amusement as Mumm and the faithful Inderbinen "with imperturbable dignity" slowly pulled themselves across with their hands; he, in his turn, "was so absorbed in the frightful peril" to his "only serviceable nether garments" as he crossed on the seat of his pants, that he didn't notice the suppressed merriment of his companions.

Travelling up the famous pass, occasionally they found the old trail and between the clouds caught "exciting glimpses" of glaciers and peaks ahead. Climbing above timberline they saw "many glorious summits never seen by Coleman," who had kept to the Whirlpool River. At the Punch Bowl Mumm and Inderbinen climbed Mount Brown. Though it didn't deserve its former fame, from its summit they looked out onto the "wonderful panorama" David Douglas had seen. The huge glacier which had awed earlier travellers was "of exceptional grandeur and impressiveness"; Mumm named it and surrounding peaks for members of the Scott expedition to the South Pole.

Returning down the Whirlpool, Mumm made a determined attempt to climb Mount Edith Cavell, but a snowstorm drove him back just short of the summit. As he rode toward Jasper the weather changed and "Mount Geikie's snowy summit, gleaming placidly in a quiet sky, looked down on us with solemn derision."

Howard had been forced to return before they reached the summit of Athabasca Pass—a bitter disappointment, for he longed to see the Committee's Punch Bowl—but his time was up. However, he was happy to have travelled along the historic valley for as he rode down the Whirlpool he saw in imagination the riding path of the future, followed in due course by a road and then, inevitably, a "luxury hotel with ladies promenading . . ."

The hotel was built—but not in that lonely valley.

When the Interprovincial Boundary Commission was working at the pass in 1921, R. W. Cautley's men found near the summit a few corroded musket balls that David Thompson had left behind on his first crossing 109 years before. Of the old trail there were "curiously few traces . . . a few completely grown-over blazes, and that faint indentation of the surface in which vegetation betrays the slight difference which always manifests itself in horse-trodden paths . . . a few old cut logs, covered with lichen, that crumble to the touch . . ."

After the First World War the Canadian National Railway pressed forward with its promotion and development in Jasper. An imaginative advertising campaign had brought visitors returning from the 1915 World Fair in San Francisco and to accommodate them, the railway suggested that Major

Fred Brewster and his brother Jack erect tents on the shore of Lac Beauvert. By 1921, Brewster's Tent City was no longer adequate for the increasing number of guests and the C.N.R. took it over. Retaining the idea suggested by the tents, eight rustic log cabins were built surrounding a central lodge. On the shores of the lovely little green lake where the daring, pipe-smoking "Company servant, Miette" had made his humble home, Jasper Park Lodge nestled among the pines. Soon the privileged few came to the exclusive new mountain retreat; royalty strolled in the gardens, film stars played on the world-famous golf course and Guggenheims, Curtises, Colgates, renowned writers, artists and sportsmen, with local guides, tasted the delights of quiet days on secluded trails at Maligne Lake and in the Tonquin Valley.

Farther south, quiet trails were becoming roadways. Van Horne's Banff Springs Hotel grew to baronial proportions and where a tiny log cabin had been headquarters for the Yale Lake Louise Club, a spacious chateau arose. Increasing numbers of visitors wanted to wander farther afield; for their convenience the C.P.R. established bungalow camps at Lake Wapta, O'Hara, Moraine, Storm Mountain, Radium, Lake Windermere and the Yoho Valley, and John Murray Gibbon, who ably took over Van Horne's promotion of the Rockies, initiated the Skyline Trail Riders.

Those of some means still hired their own outfitter-guides; at least one party of professors, scientists, their wives and friends came year after year to roam far from beaten paths with Fred Stephens, and many a desk-weary captain of industry relaxed over a campfire and for a few weeks lived (as one of them said) "with men who know how to live." A wealthy jewel expert from Tiffany's could afford to bring a professional photographer and publish a limited edition of a beautiful book to present to his men as a memento of his trip—he also recorded his surprise that Jim Simpson, his "typical mountain man," should live in "a wonderfully beautiful home" in Banff showing evidence of a cultivated interest in music, painting, sculpture and books.

The men with climbing rope and ice axe continued to play their part in fulfilling a prophecy A. O. Wheeler made on his first visit to Jasper: from Banff to Jasper over a pony trail blazed "through dense primeval forests, muskeg, burnt and fallen timber and along rough and steeply sloping hillsides, a constant flow of travel will demand a broad well-ballasted motor road . . . This wonder trail will be world renowned."

Major Fred Brewster, "the Gentleman of the Mountains," who carried on his colourful family's long tradition, making the Rockies accessible to generations of visitors.

PHOTO BY RAY O'NEILL, JASPER. COURTESY JASPER-YELLOWHEAD MUSEUM AND ARCHIVES, JASPER (990-20-04)

The constant flow began as a tiny trickle. Some members of Wheeler's 1911 expedition had come directly from Banff to Mount Robson with Fred Brewster. When Wheeler left Kain, Phillips, Kinney and Harmon at Maligne Lake, they returned "from steel to steel" by packtrain. In the high country it snowed "as if it were two months behind time and wanted to make up," as Curly put it; they were impeded by the big rock slide on the Sunwapta and over Wilcox Pass the blazed trail was hard to find. But they made the trip in thirteen days.

In 1923 and 1924 Dr. Thorington's American party climbed Mount Saskatchewan and another of the Columbia Icefields giants, the North Twin, for the first time. On the second ascent of Mount Columbia, they were delighted to help Jim Simpson fulfill an ambition that had been frustrated twenty-one years before when he'd taken Outram within sight of the mountain—tied with the climbers behind Conrad Kain, he ascended Alberta's highest mountain. In subsequent years Thorington went north to Athabasca Pass, the Tonquin Valley and Maligne Lake. Outram travelled to Maligne and Robson the year before his death, and Byron Harmon realized his ambition to photograph the country along "the wonder trail" when he and writer Lewis Freeman made the trip in 1924.

For twenty years the Right Honourable Leopold S. Amery had often found his mind wandering from business in the British House of Commons to the trip from Edmonton to Mount Robson, when "Roche Miette and the Athabasca gap below it grew day by day from the tiniest notches in the sky-line to a stupendous cliff . . ." In 1929 he came back to the Rockies. He wanted to see and climb the mountain at the junction of the Alexandra and Saskatchewan rivers which had been named for him. To his delight, old friend Wheeler accompanied him but "begged to be excused from serious climbing"; he'd just broken a few ribs falling down a crevasse, yet "at sixty-nine he was the life and soul, as well as the handy man of the team"!

On a beautiful morning, from the forks of the Saskatchewan Amery saw the "mighty snow-crowned buttresses" of his mountain. With Swiss guide Edward Feuz he met "the challenge to prove myself as a mountaineer." A blizzard marred his enjoyment of the summit but a few days later he enjoyed the view he'd missed—he climbed Mount Saskatchewan. He too continued on to the Columbia Icefields, Maligne Lake and Jasper.

Byron Harmon. His photographs of the Rockies, as eloquent as Van Horne's advertisements, helped to make the Canadian Alps world-famous.

COURTESY WHYTE MUSEUM OF THE CANADIAN ROCKIES, BANFF (V263 NA71-2400)

Norman Collie, as president of the British Alpine Club, was during those years sending out the early expeditions to Mount Everest. In his letters to Tom Wilson he wrote nostalgically about coming just once more to "the most beautiful mountain country I know of." Soon it would be seen by thousands.

When Wheeler's "connecting roadway of the future" came to be seriously considered, some of the packers who'd been over the trail shook their heads: "It can't be done!" But the Depression came and constructing such a road would provide work for the legion of the unemployed. Young professional men, university graduates, students and every other breed of man worked gratefully for twenty cents a day plus lodging and meals. With human brawn, horse-drawn loaders and scrapers and a few primitive thirty to forty horse-power tractors, they dug, graded, drilled and blasted; mile by slow mile they slashed through muskeg and timber where climber-explorers and guides had blazed the trail. Season after season, from both Banff and Jasper the road was pushed toward the one crucial stretch—the culmination of Wheeler's "wonder-trail" at Athabasca Glacier.

The old trail had detoured round Sunwapta Canyon by going over Wilcox Pass; that route was impossible for a road because of the steep sliding rock on Tangle Ridge. Long spiral cuttings carved out of the rocky walls took the road steeply over the canyon and at the same time brought the highway within sight of one of the most impressive alpine scenes on the continent. South of the icefields, a hair-raising, twisting grade was blasted out of the mountains to descend into the spectacular Saskatchewan gorge—the gentle grades of today's rebuilt roadway give travellers no idea of the magnitude of the task.

In 1939 it was done. The opening of the road was scarcely noticed; war broke out, gasoline was rationed and there were few tourists. In 1940 Walter Wilcox came back to Wilcox Pass. The trail he'd blazed forty-four years before had been transformed. But for a time the narrow gravel ribbon would wind through a solitude almost as unbroken as that savoured by the pioneers.

In his eighties Professor Coleman visited the Alpine Club camp at Mount Fryatt. At the foot of its forested slopes the mighty Athabasca flowed—there his little company had sought the trail to the legendary mountains.

Norman Collie had retired to the hills of Scotland to climb and fish. A letter from Fred Stephens arrived: ". . . I know of some valleys hidden away

Jim Simpson, one of the last of the adventuring pioneers who helped blaze the trails into Canada's alpine wilderness. The Stonies respectfully called him Nashan-esen ("wolverine-go-quick"), in admiration of his speed on snowshoes.

COURTESY WHYTE MUSEUM OF THE CANADIAN ROCKIES, BANFF (M517/44)

where the beaver still build lodges, where there are fish in the streams, where caribou roam and wild raspberries grow. Say, Friend Norman, come, and let the whole damn world race for the dollars!" But Collie's modest pension wouldn't stretch to meet expenses for the longed-for reunion. When Tom Wilson was unsuccessful in getting a railway pass for his old friend, Collie wrote: "We had the cream of the wandering . . . Those were the great days when one wandered free through hundreds of miles of virgin land . . . One remembers the camps beneath the solemn pines with resinous odours; the great open spaces at the summits of passes with the flowers all ablaze in the sunshine; the marmots and merry little chipmunks, the unearthly wail of the loon . . ."

At a little inn amid Scotland's mountains three airmen on leave sat down to dinner. "Pressed close at a window table alone with his wine and memories sat an old man who had returned there to die. His hair was white, but his face and bearing were still those of a mountaineer . . . we thought him rather fine." With youthful eagerness they related the day's exciting climbs to the landlord. He grunted in indifference, but from his window table, Norman Collie turned to the new generation of adventurers and smiled—sharing, approving, and remembering.

A. O. Wheeler, at sixty-two, had known the thrill of surveying from a fragile aircraft which dipped precariously in and out of the swirling cloud and mist clinging to the peaks north of Mount Robson. Retiring from his profession when the work of the Interprovincial Boundary Commission was finished, he remained an eager and beloved guest at the Alpine Club's camps, a dashing figure in colourful Tyrolean costume complete with gold watch chain and flowing cape. The Grand Old Man of the Mountains lived to see the completion of his "wonder trail," but when the flood of people began travelling the roadway running among the Great Hills to which he had devoted his long life, he had been laid to rest beside other pioneers in the little cemetery at Banff.

Jim Simpson witnessed the coming of the new age of the automobile. In the 1920s, beside Bow Lake where the packtrains of long ago had rested in "the silent sea of pines," he and his beautiful and talented Scottish wife, Billie, built Num-ti-Jah Lodge. In his ninetieth year Jim still strode briskly along the paths there, the once-powerful shoulders only slightly bent, the

A. O. Wheeler's "wonder trail" today: the Banff-Jasper highway.
PHOTO BY HARRY ROWED. COURTESY SCOTT ROWED, BANFF

flaming red hair now a shock of white, but the stetson still set at a jaunty angle and the intense blue eyes twinkling mischievously—or dimming in the faraway gaze of remembrance. And at Jasper, vigorous and keen in his eighties, chatting knowledgeably about the history of the Rockies, that "Gentleman of the Mountains," soft-spoken, modest Fred Brewster, lived to see the long-delayed second transcontinental highway being built through Yellowhead Pass. Two of the last surviving members of the band of pioneers who helped blaze the trails which left accessible to millions one of the most extensive and beautiful alpine regions in the world.

Epilogue

Entering the Rockies on the Trans-Canada highway, at Exshaw a high ridge on the right rises above the Bow—there in 1800 Duncan McGillivray and David Thompson gazed westward into a sea of rocky peaks, looking in vain for a pass to the Columbia. At the Gap, on Grotto Mountain, Hector and Bourgeau scrambled eagerly; past the Three Sisters they rode, where Father De Smet had come from the west on his mission of peace. Here in the valley, the earnest missionary, the Reverend Mr. Rundle rode, ecstatically happy to be "at last in the midst of the mountains." Beneath silvery grey Cascade Mountain the Little Emperor travelled strenuously after his enforced delay at Lake Minnewanka . . .

Beside the blue Bow, the black ribbon of highway flows, with the turrets of Hector's Castle Mountain towering over the green valley. Here he turned west to cross his first pass; on past the Paint Pots and Marble Canyon, the Banff-Windermere highway follows his route.

Turning north at Radium, where the Little Emperor's "horrid gorge" yawns, the road runs beside the great historic Columbia—here fur-laden voyageurs toiled. At Golden the awesomely impressive Kicking Horse trench comes into view—there the injured Hector and his men made their desperate trek eastward across Kicking Horse Pass . . .

North of Golden, beside the Van Horne Range, the Trans-Canada passes the little station at Moberly—here that veteran surveyor supervised the examination of Howse Pass; here Hector and, before him, David Thompson emerged into the Columbia Valley after descending the Blaeberry . . .

Still the mighty Columbia thrusts its loop northward around the Selkirks—there Coleman and young Frank Stover slogged stubbornly to Kinbasket Lake before turning back in weary defeat from the trail to Athabasca Pass . . .

At Donald the Trans-Canada leaves the Columbia, climbs west, and dips to breathtaking Rogers Pass: Mount Macdonald and Mount Sir Donald— titanic monuments to a prime minister with a dream of a nation stretching from sea to sea and to a fur trader-railroad tycoon; Mount Rogers and Fleming Peak, granite memorials of the first Alpine Club of Canada . . .

Beyond the Continental Divide, from Eisenhower Junction the travellers stream north on Wheeler's "wonder trail." The glistening purity of Mount Temple's helmet of snow marks the knot of peaks embracing Lake Louise: there Tom Wilson stood in awe; there clergymen Green and Swanzy scrambled to stand on its shore and Wilcox and the Yale Lake Louise Club explored with youthful exuberance . . .

Where the station stands today at Lake Louise, Southesk entered the valley of the Bow, homeward bound with his trophies and tattered copies of Shakespeare; from there Wilcox, Collie, Habel, Outram and the two Quaker Marys rode north to lands unexplored . . .

On over Bow Pass and down the Mistaya to historic Saskatchewan Crossing: from the east comes the David Thompson highway; along that trail he travelled with his young wife and family, past Kootenay Plains and on to cross the Divide by the pass those friendly nomadic people helped him find . . .

Beyond Mount Wilson and Mount Coleman, the wide valley closes in: among the maze of peaks ahead lies the high saddle of Wilcox Pass; the highway climbs smoothly above the cleft of the Saskatchewan to the summit of Sunwapta Pass.

Rounding Mount Athabasca—an immense, beautifully sculptured sea shell of brown rock filled to the brim with wind-driven snow—there is an awesome glimpse into eons past. When Collie, Stutfield and Woolley climbed there and gazed on "a new world," they saw also a very ancient one: the Columbia Icefields are a stark reminder of how these glacier-locked valleys looked during the Ice Ages.

Over the rocky gash of Sunwapta Canyon the roadway climbs and dips to follow Coleman's Sunwapta trail, past Mary Schäffer's Endless Chain Ridge and on to the mighty Athabasca. Round Mount Kerkeslin and along the flank of Mount Hardisty—from a ridge here, on a wintery day Hector looked down at the gateway to romantic Athabasca Pass. No road ascends that quiet valley; there is only the solitude of the ages where Mount Brown, Mount Hooker and Mount Kane stand guard . . .

From Jasper, Canada's second transcontinental highway runs west beside the Miette to Yellowhead Pass, past Mount Fitzwilliam—Lord Milton's family name—and on to Kamloops along the route of that dauntless "party of pleasure." On the way, Mount Robson, sublime in repose, reigns majestically over Kinney Lake, Coleman Glacier, Mount Kain and Mount Phillips . . .

Back at Jasper, the tourists drive north beneath the shadow of the Palisades—there Swift's homestead huddled in seclusion; along the valley the fur brigades trudged with their distinguished companions to Jasper House on their way to Roche Miette, and left the mountains . . .

Looking west, from a high point on the highway to Edmonton there is a last glimpse of crest after crest marching in blue haze along the rim of the horizon—the same vista that was revealed to the Reverend George Grant when he travelled the Yellowhead with Sandford Fleming in 1872.

> The line was defined, and the scarp as clear, as if they had been hewn and chiseled for a fortification . . . Everything was imposing. And these too were ours, an inheritance as precious . . . as the vast rich plains they guarded.

Just so, far to the south, they rose sharply from the prairies when young Anthony Henday first saw the Shining Mountains. So, still they stand—a heritage enhanced. For in the quiet valleys amid the peaks the ghosts of the past linger.

APPENDIX

Data pertaining to some of the major peaks in the Banff-Jasper region whose first ascents are discussed in the text. [Unless otherwise designated, nomenclature was chosen by the Canadian Geographic Board.]

MOUNTAIN	ALTITUDE	NAMED BY	NAMED FOR	FIRST ASCENT
ABERDEEN	10,350			S. E. S. Allen, L. F. Frissell, W. D. Wilcox. 1894.
ASSINIBOINE	11,870	Sir George Dawson	Assiniboine Indians	J. Outram, C. Bohren, C. Hasler. 1901.
ATHABASCA	11,452	J. N. Collie		J. N. Collie, H. Woolley. 1898.
COLUMBIA	12,294			J. Outram, C. Kaufmann. 1902.
DIADEM PEAK	11,060	J. N. Collie		J. N. Collie, H. E. M. Stutfield, H. Woolley. 1898.
FORBES	11,902	James Hector	noted British geologist	J. N. Collie, J. Outram, H. E. M. Stutfield, G. M. Weed, H. Woolley, C. Kaufmann, H. Kaufmann. 1902.
FRESHFIELD	10,945	J. N. Collie	noted British climber	J. N. Collie, J. Outram, H. E. M. Stutfield, G. M. Weed, H. Woolley, C. Kaufmann, H. Kaufmann. 1902.

MOUNTAIN	ALTITUDE	NAMED BY	NAMED FOR	FIRST ASCENT
HOWSE PEAK	10,800	J. N. Collie		J. N. Collie, H. E. M. Stutfield, H. Woolley, G. M. Weed, H. Kaufmann. 1902.
LEFROY	11,230	James Hector	noted astronomer	J. N. Collie, H. B. Dixon, C. E. Fay, A. Michael, C. L. Noyes, H. C. Parker, C. S. Thompson, J. R. Vanderlip, P. Sarbach. 1897.
LYELL	11,495	James Hector	noted geologist	J. Outram, C. Kaufmann. 1902.
MURCHISON	10,659	James Hector	noted geologist	J. N. Collie, H. E. M. Stutfield, G. M. Weed, H. Kaufmann. 1902.
NORTH TWIN	12,085	J. N. Collie		Dr. J. Monroe Thorington. 1923.
ROBSON	12,972	unknown	unknown	Albert MacCarthy, Wm. Foster, Conrad Kain. 1913.
SARBACH	10,260	J. N. Collie	first Swiss guide in the Rockies	J. N. Collie, G. P. Baker. 1897.
SASKATCHEWAN	10,964	J. N. Collie		J. Monroe Thorington. 1923.
SNOW DOME	11,340	J. N. Collie		J. N. Collie, H. E. M. Stutfield, H. Woolley. 1898.
TEMPLE	11,636			S. E. S. Allen, L. F. Frissell, W. D. Wilcox. 1894.
VICTORIA	11,365	J. J. McArthur, pioneer surveyor		J. N. Collie, C. E. Fay, A. Michael, P. Sarbach. 1897.
WILSON	10,631	J. N. Collie	Tom Wilson	J. Outram, C. Kaufmann. 1902.

A SELECTED BIBLIOGRAPHY

CHAPTER 1

Chalmers, John W. *Fur Trade Governor.* Edmonton: Institute of Applied Arts, 1960
Hudson's Bay Record Society. *Hudson's Bay Company, 1670-1890.* Edited by E. E. Rich. Toronto, 1960.
Lent, D. Geneva. *West of the Mountains.* Seattle: University of Washington Press, 1963.
MacGregor, James G. *Behold the Shining Mountains.* Edmonton: Institute of Applied Arts, 1954.
Simpson, Sir George, *Narrative of a Journey around the World.* London, 1847.
    Quotations are taken from Simpson's *Narrative.*

CHAPTERS 2 AND 3

Campbell, Marjorie Wilkins. *Lord of the North West.* Toronto: Clarke Irwin, 1962.
Champlain Society. *David Thompson's Narrative, 1784-1812.* Edited by Richard Glover. Toronto, 1962.
———. *David Thompson's Narrative of his Explorations in Western America 1784-1812.* Edited by J. B Tyrrell. Toronto, 1916.
Coues, Elliott. *New Light on the Early History of the Greater Northwest: The Manuscript Journals of Alexander Henry and of David Thompson.* Minneapolis, 1897.
"David Thompson Under Scrutiny." *Alberta Historical Review,* Winter 1964.
Fraser, Simon. *Letters and Journals.* Edited by W. Kaye Lamb. Toronto: Macmillan, 1960.
Henry, Alexander. *Travels and Adventures in Canada and the Indian Territories between the Years 1760 and 1776.* 1809. Reprint. Edmonton: M. G. Hurtig, 1969.
Howay, F. W. "David Thompson's Account of His First Attempt to Cross the Rockies." *Queen's Quarterly,* 1933.
Innis, Harold A. *The Fur Trade in Canada.* Toronto: University of Toronto Press, 1962.
Lavender, David. *Fist in the Wilderness.* New York: Doubleday, 1964.
Morton, A. S. "The North West Company's Columbian Enterprise and David Thompson." *Canadian Historical Review,* 1936.
"Thompson's Journey to the Bow River." *Alberta Historical Review,* Spring 1965.
"Thompson's Journey to the Red Deer River." *Alberta Historical Review,* Winter 1965.
Thorington, J. Monroe. *The Glittering Mountains of Canada.* Philadelphia, 1925.
Tyrrell, J. B. "David Thompson and the Columbia River." *Canadian Historical Review,* 1937.
———. "David Thompson and the Rocky Mountains." *Canadian Historical Review,* 1934.
———. "Did Duncan McGillivray and David Thompson Cross the Rockies in 1801?" *Canadian Historical Review,* 1937.
———. "Duncan McGillivray's Movements in 1801." *Canadian Historical Review,* 1939.
Wallace, J. Stewart, *The Pedlars from Quebec.* Toronto: Ryerson, 1954.

Quotation in Chapter 2 on David Thompson's crossing of Howse Pass is taken from Thorington's *The Glittering Mountains of Canada*; his source is the *Quarterly of the Oregon Historical Society* (March 1929) in which is published a copy of David Thompson's "Narrative of the Expedition to the Kootenae and Flat Bow Indian Countries on the Sources of the Columbia River, Pacific Ocean." The quotation in Chapter 3 on David Thompson's crossing of Athabasca Pass is taken from Tyrrell's edition of *David Thompson's Narrative*; the description of Thompson is from Dr. J. J. Bigsby's *The Shoe and Canoe* (London, 1919).

Historians have disagreed about Thompson's and McGillivray's journeys in 1800-01. The microfilm of volume 6 of Thompson's journals was kindly loaned to the author by the Ontario Archives; examination of the courses given therein indicates that McGillivray made at least one long journey toward the Pembina River as well as one to the Brazeau and those on which Thompson accompanied him. The urgency of Thompson's "mission" to the mouth of the Columbia in 1810-11 has also been a controversial subject. The explanation offered by David Lavender seems the most plausible one. In *First in the Wilderness*, p. 443, Lavender cites as evidence for his interpretation of this event: the "critical letters" exchanged by Thompson and the Astorians, published in the *Yale University Library Gazette*, vol. 24 (October 1949), pp. 52-55; a letter from Alexander Henry in the collections of the State Historical Society of Wisconsin, vol. 19, pp. 336-7; a letter of the wintering partners of the North West Company to William McGillivray reproduced by Dorothy Bridgewater, editor of "John Jacob Astor Relative to his Settlement on the Columbia River," published in the *Yale University Library Gazette*, vol. 24 (October 1949).

CHAPTER 4
Cox, Ross. *Adventures on the Columbia River.* New York, 1832.
Franchère, Gabriel. *Narrative of a Voyage to the North-West Coast of America.* New York, 1854.
Lavender, David. *Fist in the Wilderness.* New York: Doubleday, 1964.
"Where Was Henry House?" *Alberta Historical Review*, Autumn 1960.
   Quotations are taken from Franchère's *Narrative* and Cox's *Adventures.*

CHAPTER 5
Champlain Society. *Simpson's 1828 Journey to the Columbia.* Edited by E. E. Rich. Toronto, 1940.
Hudson's Bay Record Society. *Hudson's Bay Company, 1670-1870.* Edited by E. E. Rich. Toronto, 1960.
Merk, Frederick, ed. *Fur Trade and Empire.* Cambridge, Mass.: Harvard University Press, 1931.
Ross, Alexander. *Fur Hunters of the Far West.* London, 1855.
   Quotations are taken from Merk's *Fur Trade and Empire*, Ross's *Fur Hunters* and *Simpson's 1828 Journey.*

CHAPTER 6
Carter Alfred. "Robert Terrill Rundle." Thesis, Boston University Graduate School, 1952. Copy in Provincial Government Archives, Edmonton.

De Smet, Pierre-Jean. *Oregon Missions and Travel over the Rocky Mountains in 1845-46.* New York, 1847.

Edmonton. Provincial Government Archives. Extracts from the journal of the Reverend Robert Terrill Rundle.

Kane, Paul. *Wanderings of an Artist among the Indians of North America from Canada to Vancouver's Island and Oregon through the Hudson's Bay Company's Territory and Back Again.* 1859. Reprint. Edmonton: M. G. Hurtig, 1968.

Schafer, Joseph. "Documents Relating to Warre and Vavasour's Military Reconnaissance in Oregon 1845-6." *Quarterly of the Oregon Historical Society* 10, no. 1.

Thorington, J. Monroe. "White Man's God Comes to the Rockies." *Canadian Alpine Journal* 27, no. 2.

Wheeler, A. O. *The Selkirk Range.* Ottawa, 1905.

Quotations are taken from Kane's *Wanderings*, De Smet's *Oregon Missions* and the extracts from Rundle's journal.

CHAPTER 7

Kane, Paul. *Wanderings of an Artist among the Indians of North America from Canada to Vancouver's Island and Oregon through the Hudson's Bay Company's Territory and Back Again.* 1859. Reprint. Edmonton: M. G. Hurtig, 1968.

Wallace, Paul. *Baptiste Larocque: Legends of French Canada.* Toronto, 1923.

CHAPTER 8

Edmonton. Cameron Library, University of Alberta. J. N. Wallace collection.

Innis, Mary Quayle. *Travellers West.* Toronto: Clarke Irwin, 1956.

Southesk, James Carnegie, Earl. *Saskatchewan and the Rocky Mountains: A Diary and Narrative of Travel, Sport, and Adventure, during a Journey through the Hudson's Bay Company's Territories, in 1859 and 1860.* 1875. Reprint. Edmonton: M. G. Hurtig, 1969.

Quotations are taken from Southesk's *Saskatchewan and the Rocky Mountains.*

CHAPTER 9

Calgary. Glenbow-Alberta Institute. Autobiography of Peter Erasmus.

Edmonton. Cameron Library, University of Alberta. J. N. Wallace collection.

Palliser, John. *The Journals, Detailed Reports and Observations Relative to the Explorations by Captain Palliser.* London, 1863.

———. *Solitary Rambles and Adventures of a Hunter in the Prairies.* 1853. Reprint. Edmonton: M. G. Hurtig, 1969.

Report of the Commission Appointed to Delimit the Boundary between the Provinces of Alberta and British Columbia. Ottawa, 1917.

Spry, Irene. *The Palliser Expedition.* Toronto: Macmillan, 1963.

Thompson, Henry T. *Buffalo Days and Nights: Reminiscences of Peter Erasmus as told to Henry T. Thompson.* 1920.

Wheeler, A. O. *The Selkirk Range.* Ottawa, 1905.

Quotations are taken from Palliser's *Journals* and Erasmus's autobiography.

CHAPTER 10

Cheadle, Walter B. *Journal of a Trip across Canada 1862-63.* 1931. Reprint. Edmonton: M. G. Hurtig.

Hutchison, Bruce. *The Fraser.* Toronto: Clarke Irwin, 1950.

Innis, Mary Quayle. *Travellers West.* Toronto: Clarke Irwin, 1956.

McDougall, John. *Saddle, Sled and Snowshoe.* Toronto, 1896.

McMicking, Thomas. "The Overlanders in Alberta, 1862." *Alberta Historical Review,* Summer 1966.

Milton, William Fitzwilliam, Viscount and Cheadle, W. B. *The North-West Passage by Land.* London, 1867.

Wade, M. S. *The Overlanders of '62.* Victoria, B.C., 1931.

Quotations are taken from Cheadle's *Journal,* Milton and Cheadle's *North-West Passage by Land,* McDougall's *Saddle, Sled and Snowshoe* and McMicking's "Overlanders."

CHAPTER 11

Cheadle, Walter B. *Journal of a Trip across Canada 1862-63.* 1931. Reprint. Edmonton: M. G. Hurtig.

Milton, William Fitzwilliam, Viscount and Cheadle, W. B. *The North-West Passage by Land.* London, 1867.

White, James. "Cheadle's Journal Across the Mountains." *Canadian Alpine Journal* 14.

Quotations are taken from Cheadle's *Journal* and Milton and Cheadle's *North-West Passage by Land.*

CHAPTER 12

Bone, P. Turner. *When the Steel Went Through.* Toronto: Macmillan, 1947.

Fleming, Sir Sandford. *Canadian Pacific Railway: Report of Progress on the Explorations and Surveys up to January 1874.*

——. *England and Canada: A Summer Tour between Old and New Westminster.* Montreal, 1884.

Gibbon, John Murray. *Steel of Empire.* Toronto: McClelland and Stewart, 1935.

Gilbert, H. *Awakening Continent: The Life of Lord Mount Stephen.* Vol. 1. Aberdeen: Aberdeen University Press, 1965.

Grant, George. *Ocean to Ocean: Sandford Fleming's Expedition through Canada in 1872.* 1873. Reprint. Edmonton: M. G. Hurtig, 1967.

Hardy, W. G. *From Sea unto Sea.* New York: Doubleday, 1959.

Hudson's Bay Record Society. *Hudson's Bay Company, 1670-1870.* Edited by E. E. Rich. Toronto, 1960.

Moberly, Walter. *The Rocks and Rivers of British Columbia.* London, 1885.

Robinson, Noel. *Blazing the Trail Through the Rockies.* Vancouver News Advertiser.

Secretan, J. H. E. *Canada's Great Highway.* London, 1924.

Vaughan, Walter. *The Life and Work of Sir William Van Horne.* New York: Century, 1920.

Wheeler, A. O. *The Selkirk Range.* Ottawa, 1905.

Quotations are taken from Fleming's *England and Canada,* Hardy's *From Sea unto Sea* and A. L. Rogers's "Major A. B. Rogers's First Expedition up the Illecillewaet Valley, in 1881, Accompanied by his Nephew, A. L. Rogers" in Wheeler's *The Selkirk Range,* Appendix E.

CHAPTER 13

Bone, P. Turner. *When the Steel Went Through.* Toronto: Macmillan, 1947.

Edmonton. Mrs. Esther Fraser. Papers presented to the author by T. E. Wilson.

Fay, Chas. E. "Old Times in the Canadian Alps." *Canadian Alpine Journal* 12.

Fleming, Sir Sandford. "Memories of the Mountains." *Canadian Alpine Journal* 1, no. 2.

Green, William S. *Among the Selkirk Glaciers.* London and New York, 1890.

Parker, Elizabeth. "The Alpine Club of Canada." *Canadian Alpine Journal* 1, no. 1.

Pearce, William, "Establishment of National Parks in the Rockies." *Alberta Historical Review,* Summer 1962.

Vaughan, Walter. *The Life and Work of Sir William Van Horne.* New York: Century, 1920.

Wheeler, A. O. *The Selkirk Range.* Ottawa, 1905.

CHAPTER 14

Calgary. Glenbow-Alberta Institute. The Tom Wilson correspondence.

Fay, Chas. E. "Old Times in the Canadian Alps." *Canadian Alpine Journal* 12.

Green, Williams S. *Among the Selkirk Glaciers.* London and New York, 1890.

Henderson, Yandell. "The Summer of 1894 Around Lake Louise." *Canadian Alpine Journal* 12.

Longstaff, Major F. V. "Looking Back Along the Trail." *Skyline Trail,* Summer 1956.

Outram, James. *In the Heart of the Canadian Rockies.* London and New York: Macmillan, 1906.

Wilcox, Walter Dwight. *Camping in the Canadian Rockies.* New York and London, 1897.

CHAPTER 15

Douglas, David. *Journal Kept by David Douglas during his Travels in North America 1823-1827.* London: Royal Horticultural Society, 1914.

Eiffert, Virginia. *Tall Trees and Far Horizons.* New York: Dodd Mead, 1965.

Hudson's Bay Record Society. *Black's Rocky Mountain Journal 1824.* Edited by E. E. Rich. Toronto, 1955.

Thorington, J. Monroe. *The Glittering Mountains of Canada.* Philadelphia, 1925.

The Douglas *Journal* consists of a longer and a shorter journal; quotations are taken from both sources and from Thorington who refers as well to an article appearing in the *Companion to the Botanical Magazine* (1836).

CHAPTER 16

Coleman, A. P. *The Canadian Rockies: New and Old Trails.* London, 1911.

CHAPTER 17

Calgary. Glenbow-Alberta Institute. The Tom Wilson correspondence.

Edwards, Ralph. *Trail to the Charmed Land.* Saskatoon: H. R. Larson, 1950.

Herrligkoffer, Karl M. *Nanga Parbat.* London: Elek Books, 1954.

Outram, James. *In the Heart of the Canadian Rockies.* London and New York: Macmillan, 1906.

Stutfield, Hugh and Collie, J. Norman. *Climbs and Explorations in the Canadian Rockies.* London, New York and Bombay, 1903.

Thorington, J. Monroe. "Jean Habel in the Canadian Rockies." *Canadian Alpine Journal* 30.

Wilcox, Walter Dwight. *Camping in the Canadian Rockies.* New York and London, 1897.

CHAPTER 18
Stutfield, Hugh and Collie, J. Norman. *Climbs and Explorations in the Canadian Rockies.* London, New York and Bombay, 1903.

CHAPTER 19
Banff. Files of the *Banff Crag and Canyon.*
Calgary. Glenbow-Alberta Institute. The Tom Wilson correspondence.
Clark, Ronald William. *The Day the Rope Broke.* London: Secker and Warburg, 1965.
"In Memoriam: Edward Whymper." *Canadian Alpine Journal* 4.
"In Memoriam: Samuel E. S. Allen." *Canadian Alpine Journal* 29, no. 1.
"Official Report of 1909 Camp." *Canadian Alpine Journal* 2, no. 2.
Outram, James. *In the Heart of the Canadian Rockies.* London and New York: Macmillan, 1906.
Wilcox, Walter Dwight. "An Early Attempt to Climb Mount Assiniboine." *Canadian Alpine Journal* 2, no. 1.
——. *Camping in the Canadian Rockies.* New York and London, 1897.
Quotations are taken from Outram's *In the Heart of the Canadian Rockies.*

CHAPTER 20
Calgary. Glenbow-Alberta Institute. The Tom Wilson correspondence.
Outram, James. *In the Heart of the Canadian Rockies.* London and New York: Macmillan, 1906.
Stutfield, Hugh and Collie, J. Norman. *Climbs and Explorations in the Canadian Rockies.* London, New York and Bombay, 1903.

CHAPTER 21
Gowan, Elsie Park. "A Quaker in Buckskin." *Alberta Historical Review,* Summer 1957.
"In Memoriam: Mary Warren." *Canadian Alpine Journal* 27, no. 1.
Schäffer, Mary T. S. *Old Indian Trails.* New York, 1911.
——. "Untrodden Ways." *Canadian Alpine Journal* 2, no. 1.
Quotations are taken from Mary Schäffer's *Old Indian Trails.*

CHAPTER 22
Canadian Alpine Journal 27, no. 2 and 29, no. 1. (biographical material on A. O. Wheeler)
Coleman, A. P. *The Canadian Rockies: New and Old Trails.* London, 1911.
Foster, W. W. "Mount Robson (1913)." *Canadian Alpine Journal* 6.
Kain, Conrad. "The First Ascent of Mount Robson 1913." *Canadian Alpine Journal* 6.
——. *Where the Clouds Can Go.* Edited by J. Monroe Thorington. Boston: Charles T. Branford, 1954.
Kinney, Reverend G. B. "Mount Robson." *Canadian Alpine Journal* 2, no. 1.
Kinney, G. B. and Phillips, Donald. "To the Top of Mount Robson." *Canadian Alpine Journal* 2, no. 2.
Mumm, A. L. "An Expedition to Mount Robson." *Canadian Alpine Journal* 2, no. 2.
"Official Report of 1909 Camp." *Canadian Alpine Journal* 2, no. 2.
Robinson, Reverend J. J. "Vermilion Pass Camp 1912." *Canadian Alpine Journal* 5.
Sherman, Patrick. *The Cloud Walkers.* Toronto: Macmillan, 1965.

Chapter 23

Mumm, A. L. "An Expedition to Mount Robson." *Canadian Alpine Journal* 2, no. 2.

Mumm, A. L. and Collie, J. Norman. "Mountains of Northern Alberta." *Canadian Alpine Journal* 4.

Wheeler, A. O. "The Alpine Club of Canada's Expedition to Jasper Park, Yellowhead Pass and the Mount Robson Region 1911." *Canadian Alpine Journal* 4.

——. "Report of the Director." *Canadian Alpine Journal* 3.

Chapter 24

Coleman, A. P. *The Canadian Rockies: New and Old Trails.* London, 1911.

Jasper. Records of the Jasper-Yellowhead Historical Society.

Moberly, Walter. *The Rocks and Rivers of British Columbia.* London, 1885.

Schäffer, Mary T. S. *Old Indian Trails.* New York, 1911.

Washburn, Stanley. *Trails, Trappers and Tenderfeet in the New Empire of Western Canada.* 1912.

Wheeler, A. O. "The Alpine Club of Canada's Expedition to Jasper Park, Yellowhead Pass and the Mount Robson Region 1911." *Canadian Alpine Journal* 4.

Chapter 25

Amery, Leopold S. *In the Rain and the Sun.* London and New York: Hutchinson, 1946.

——. "A Month Between Lake Louise and Jasper." *Canadian Alpine Journal* 18.

Calgary. Glenbow-Alberta Institute. The Tom Wilson correspondence.

Cautley, R. W. "Character of Passes in the Canadian Rockies." *Canadian Alpine Journal* 12.

Collie, J. Norman. "The Canadian Rocky Mountains a Quarter of a Century Ago." *Canadian Alpine Journal* 14.

Howard, Geoffrey E. and Mumm, A. L. "The Whirlpool." *Canadian Alpine Journal* 6.

"In Memoriam: J. Norman Collie." *Canadian Alpine Journal* 28, no. 2.

Phillips, Donald. "Fitzhugh to Laggan." *Canadian Alpine Journal* 4.

Thorington, J. Monroe. *The Glittering Mountains of Canada.* Philadelphia, 1925.

Wheeler, A. O. "The Alpine Club of Canada's Expedition to Jasper Park, Yellowhead Pass and the Mount Robson Region 1911." *Canadian Alpine Journal* 4.

Williams, Mabel. *Banff-Jasper Highway.* Saskatoon: H. R. Lawson, 1948.

Epilogue

Grant, George. *Ocean to Ocean: Sandford Fleming's Expedition through Canada in 1872.* 1873. Reprint. Edmonton: M. G. Hurtig, 1967.

LIST OF FURTHER READINGS

Since the publication of *The Canadian Rockies: Early Travels and Explorations* in 1969, a number of books have been published about the major explorers and early travellers who passed through this mountain range. Most of these books focus on individuals highlighted in Esther Fraser's history and provide insight into their lives and adventures, both in the Rockies and beyond. Some of these titles are currently out-of-print (*), but readers can often find copies through libraries or purchase them through rare book dealers and out-of-print book services.

Beck, Janice Sanford. *No Ordinary Woman: The Story of Mary Schäffer*. (Calgary: Rocky Mountain Books, 2001). Biography of lady explorer Mary Schäffer, who rediscovered Maligne Lake in 1908.

Fraser, Esther. *Wheeler*. (Banff: Summerthought, 1978). A biography of A. O. Wheeler, the surveyor of the Great Divide, founder of the Alpine Club of Canada, and leader of expeditions to Mount Robson in 1911 and 1913.

*Galbraith, John S. *The Little Emperor: Governor Simpson of the Hudson's Bay Company*. (Toronto: Macmillan, 1976). A biography of Hudson Bay Company governor George Simpson, who oversaw and participated in exploration and travel in the Rockies from 1824 until 1860.

Hart, E. J. *A Hunter of Peace*. (Banff: Whyte Museum, 1983). Contains the original text of Mary Schäffer's *Old Indian Trails* and an account of her return journey to Maligne Lake in 1911. Includes a biography by the editor.

Hart, E. J. *Jimmy Simpson: Legend of the Rockies*. (Banff: Altitude, 1991). A biography of guide and outfitter Jimmy Simpson, who accompanied several early exploratory trips through the Rockies.

Hart, E. J. *The Place of Bows: Exploring the Heritage of the Banff-Bow Valley*. (Banff: EJH Literary Enterprises, 1999). A history covering the exploration, settlement, and development of the Canadian Rockies' Bow Valley to 1930.

Hart, E. J. *Diamond Hitch: The Pioneer Guides and Outfitters of Banff and Jasper*. (Banff: EJH Literary Enterprises, 2001). This reprint of the original 1979 history covers the early guides who outfitted tourist explorers to the last undiscovered regions of the Rockies.

Leduc, Joanne, ed. *Overland from Canada to British Columbia*. (Vancouver: University of British Columbia Press, 1981) The journal of gold-seeker Thomas McMicking, who travelled across the Rockies with the Overlanders in 1862.

*MacGregor, J.G. *Overland by the Yellowhead.* (Saskatoon: Western Producer, 1974). A history of the Yellowhead Pass region, including the Athabasca Valley and Mount Robson.

Nisbet, Jack. *Sources of the River: Tracking David Thompson Across Western North America.* (Seattle: Sasquatch Books, 1994). The author follows the routes of the fur trade-explorer through the Rocky Mountains and the ranges of the Pacific Northwest.

Patton, Brian, ed. *Tales from the Canadian Rockies.* (Toronto: McClelland and Stewart, 1993). A selection of writings by early fur traders, travellers and explorers as well as later settlers, tourist adventurers, journalists, novelists, and poets.

Spry, Irene M. *The Palliser Expedition.* (Calgary: Fifth House, 1999). Reprint of the excellent history of the British expedition that explored the Rockies in 1858-59.

*Taylor, William C. T*he Snows of Yesteryear: J. Norman Collie, Mountaineer.* (Toronto: Holt, Rinehart and Winston, 1973). A biography of the British mountaineer who discovered the Columbia Icefield.

Wright, Richard Thomas. *Overlanders.* (Williams Lake, B.C.: Winter Quarters, 2000). An account of the parties that crossed the Rockies to the gold fields of British Columbia 1858-1862.

INDEX

Note: Italic page numbers refer to photographs.